Lay Buddhism in
Contemporary Japan

Lay Buddhism
In Contemporary Japan:
Reiyūkai Kyōdan

Helen Hardacre

Princeton University Press
Princeton, New Jersey

Library of Congress Cataloging in Publication Data will be
found on the last printed page of this book

ISBN 0-691-07284-1

Publication of this book has been aided by
The Whitney Darrow Fund of Princeton University Press

This book has been composed in Monophoto Times Roman
by Asco Trade Typesetting Ltd., Hong Kong

Clothbound editions of Princeton University Press books
are printed on acid-free paper, and binding materials
are chosen for strength and durability

Printed in the United States of America
by Princeton University Press
Princeton, New Jersey

To my parents,
Gracia and Paul Hardacre

Contents

List of Illustrations

List of Figures

List of Tables

Note on Romanization

Japanese terms have been romanized according to the Hepburn system. After the first mention of a term, macrons and italics have been omitted, except in case of terms easily confused with English words, e.g., the English preposition "on" and the Japanese term for debt or obligation, *on* 恩. In the case of Japanese words commonly used in English or frequently herein, such as the place name Tokyo or Reiyukai, I have omitted macrons in first reference and when the term occurs in combination, e.g., the publishing house Tokyodō, or the publication *Reiyukaihō*.

Preface

The debts incurred in writing a book dealing with the deepest beliefs of the nearly three million people who belong to Reiyūkai Kyōdan, "The Society of Friends of the Spirits," are numerous and weighty. I owe to the members of Reiyukai for their aid, patience, and efforts to instruct me more than words can convey. Reiyukai believers strove over a period of four years to help me reach a full understanding of their religion. We became friends in the profound sense, and I believe we have understood each other. In their company I came to admire greatly their strength of character and conviction. I have attempted to portray Reiyukai in a way that will be both recognizable to its members and intelligible to those on the outside; I hope I have served Reiyukai Kyodan well.

In particular I wish to express gratitude to the president of Reiyukai, Kubo Tsugunari. President Kubo graciously extended to me the services of his headquarters staff, and without their assistance I could never have collected the data on which this study is based. Among the headquarters staff to whom I am most indebted are Mr. Kawabata and Mr. Torii of the Overseas Department. Also, Dr. Yuyama and Dr. Ejima of Reiyukai's International Institute for Buddhist Studies (formerly the Reiyukai Library) gave me substantive advice and assistance.

To the leaders and members of the Eighth Branch of Reiyukai I owe a special debt of gratitude. Branch Leader Masunaga Sadako gave me the original opportunity to live among Eighth Branch members when she invited me in 1975 to come to Osaka. She and her husband, Branch Leader Masunaga Tadashi, arranged that I reside in their facilities for eight months. It was through this experience that I was able to understand something of what Reiyukai means in the lives of its believers. I wish to thank my roommates and daily companions there for their endless patience in answering a steady barrage of questions, for explaining their beliefs, and for sharing their deepest feelings. The three who bore the brunt of my company were Date Katsuko, Wada Akiko, and Okada Mitsuko.

My teacher at the University of Chicago, Joseph M. Kitagawa, is responsible for the absence of many errors that would otherwise have appeared here, though needless to say I have only myself to blame for any that remain. During the years I was in Japan working on this project, his letters of detailed comment and criticism were an invaluable source of advice and encouragement. Since that time as well, I have continued to benefit from his guidance in completing this study.

From the members of the Department of Religious Studies at the University of Tokyo I received much-needed advice. I would particularly like to thank Professors Wakimoto Tsuneya, Nakamura Kyōko (presently of Kawamura Women's College), and Inoue Nobutaka (presently of Kokugakuin University).

I received many useful suggestions from Professors John F. Wilson and Martin Collcutt of Princeton University and wish to thank them for their careful reading of an earlier draft of this manuscript. I benefited much from discussions with Professor Ann Waswo of the Nissan Institute of Japanese Studies at Oxford University regarding the history of Reiyukai in the early twentieth century.

My parents continue to be my best critics and most ruthless editors. They have invested in this manuscript hundreds of hours, since the days when it was a dissertation. For lack of any adequate means of expressing my gratitude, this book is dedicated to them.

Research for this project was generously supported by the Social Science Research Council and a Fulbright-Hays Doctoral Dissertation Abroad Fellowship. To say nothing of the financial aspect, I am also grateful to the staff of the Tokyo office of the Fulbright Commission, particularly Carolyn Yang and Satō Etsuko, for many happy hours. I also wish to express my gratitude to Yōko Suemoto for her help in proofreading this manuscript.

The friendship of P.L.B. and S.Y. continues to be quite literally a sine qua non.

January, 1982   *Princeton, New Jersey*

Lay Buddhism in
Contemporary Japan

Introduction

The idea that children owe to their parents a debt of such magnitude that it can never possibly be repaid was expounded by Nakae Tōju 中江藤樹 (1608–1648), a pioneer of Japanese Neo-Confucian thought. Employing in a style typical of his era a single idea as the center of his philosophical system, he emphasized filial piety as preeminent among virtues and spoke of the *on* 恩 owed to parents as "higher than the mountains, deeper than the seas." [1] The phrase appeared in *terakoya* 寺小屋 schoolbooks and remained a standard tenet of morals courses down to 1945. The notion of this irreparable debt strikes a responsive chord in many hearts today, and Reiyukai dedicates itself to the establishment of a Buddhist ethic of filial piety symbolized by rites of ancestor worship and supported by other family-centered values. In so doing it attempts to imbue the concept of *on* to parents and ancestors with new life, to demonstrate its relevance to contemporary Japanese society.

However, the modern history of this traditionalist concept, especially as it functioned in prewar courses on morals (*shūshin*, *dōtoku kyōiku* 修身, 道徳教育), is not altogether a happy one. In that context the notion of the *on* borne by children to their parents was employed for the purpose of inculcating habits of obedience and docility, not only to parents, but to superiors of any kind, and not only in childhood, but throughout life. Here the phrase "higher than the mountains, deeper than the seas" became a platitudinous tool of indoctrination and intellectual homogeniza-

---

[1] Bukkyō shisō kenkyūkai, ed., *On*, Bukkyōshisō 4, 4 vols. (Kyoto: Heirakuji shoten, 1978), 4:222.

tion, worthy of all the scorn heaped upon it and similar sentiments by postwar generations who mourn the mental and spiritual prisons created for their elders by a state intent upon creating compliant subjects.

A phrase that embodies such contradictions would be an appropriate motto for a religion which is itself replete with paradoxes— of liberation from a variety of problems on the one hand, and of ever-deeper entrenchment in a narrow range of family-based values on the other. Reiyukai is serious business, a religion whose members demand that it produce results. They are not much interested in "expressive effectiveness" in the sense of cheap, emotional pap to salve the soul into the conviction that whatever is, is best, nor have they time for polite parlor conversation about bygone saints or the pleasures of a heavenly afterlife. In matters religious, all Reiyukai members come from Missouri, and they are prepared to "show" anyone who inquires what Reiyukai has done for them. It solves family problems, heals sickness, and brings countless other tangible, real-life blessings into their lives. They are not crass materialists, but they demand proof, and they get it. When Reiyukai members undergo the process of making Reiyukai work for them, their thought and manner of conducting their lives change, generally so as to be more in conformity with the traditionalist values the group espouses.

Reiyukai Kyodan, "The Society of Friends of the Spirits," is a contemporary Japanese religion deriving from the Nichiren tradition. It has been in existence for some sixty years, though during that time, fourteen bodies have split off, including at least one that has surpassed the parent organization in size and influence. Nevertheless, the groups which have originated by schism have retained much of the doctrine, organization, and ritual of Reiyukai, and it is clear that its general teachings exert a powerful influence over the lives of several million Japanese at home and abroad. The history of this group is dealt with in Chapter 1, and its contemporary activities and organization are treated in Chapter 2.

Ancestor worship is its central practice, and this in an age when Japanese ancestor worship seems to be generally in decline if not dying out. In Reiyukai can be seen many changes from traditional Japanese ancestor worship which seem to have come about in response to changes in Japanese society. Doctrine concerned with ancestors has been developed that transforms the idea of an ancestor itself into a more comprehensive sort of deity than the ancestors of Japanese tradition. This theme is dealt with in Chapters 4, 5, and 6, which treat ritual, witnessing, and the role of women.

The growth of laymen's groups in Japanese Buddhism from the Bakumatsu era (roughly 1830–1868) is clearly exemplified in Reiyukai, which sometimes fostered a frank anti-clericalism. On the one hand this was a negative reaction to corruption and lack of concern for the laity among the priesthood. We can see also a desire to establish a positive religious significance for marriage and the family. This inevitably involved the incorporation of the religious aspirations of women. In Reiyukai women play important roles in the group, and ideas about women, marriage, and the family are at the center of the group's thought and activity. On the one hand, Reiyukai continues women's traditional religious roles in shamanistic practices, but their involvement has also led to qualitatively new developments in doctrine, ritual, and ways of making religion a part of everyday life. These developments have entailed giving women a positive role in ancestor worship. As this came about during Reiyukai's early history, it coincided with a period in Japanese religious history when the state was intervening heavily in religion to manipulate ideas about ancestor worship so as to attach a semi-political, patriotic meaning to ancestor worship.

From the point of view of Reiyukai's significance for the history of religions in general, the group assumes importance as one in which ancestor worship forms the center of a voluntary association. Usually the worship of ancestors is associated with tribal societies or with kinship groups forming the basis of traditional society, as in premodern China or Japan. Examination of Reiyukai can perhaps indicate how the beliefs and practices of ancestor worship change when they are extended beyond kinship bounds and are made the focus of a voluntary association. A general discussion of these and related matters is provided in Chapter 3, "Reiyukai and the Family."

The Japanese new religions have been treated by scholars as having only an expressive sort of significance, and it is almost taken for granted that the main importance of membership is the emotional gratification afforded by joining a group of people with similar problems. There is a tendency to assume that the three problems most commonly faced by members of these groups, namely sickness, poverty, and domestic disharmony, are not, realistically speaking, seriously addressed or altered, in spite of a wealth of testimonial evidence to the contrary. In this study I hope to show that in the case of Reiyukai, in addition to the emotional, expressive significance belonging to the group has for its members, there is also a considerable instrumental effectiveness in solving problems, and that if this were not the case, this group and others like it would not survive.

Since very little research has been done on Reiyukai,[2] it was necessary to collect primary information on which to base this study. In addition to the few published results of academic

---

[2] There are two types of research on Reiyukai in Japanese, journalistic and academic. Leaving aside occasional treatments in the popular press penned purely for sensational value, an excellent journalistic study is Mainichi Shimbun, ed., *Shūkyō o gendai ni tou*, 5 vols. (Tokyo: Mainichi Shimbun, 1976), 2:115–213, a general study of organization and activities, echoing the opinion of most Japanese scholars, to the effect that Reiyukai is in some sense typical of the combination of shamanistic practices, "this-worldly" benefits, and ancestor worship.

In the works of older Japanese scholars on Reiyukai there is an emphasis on biographical studies of the founders, a trend that may be seen in these works: Saki Akio, *Godai kyōso no jitsuzō* (Tokyo: Yagumo shoin, 1970), pp. 23–96; Saki Akio, *Kyōso—shomin no kamigami* (Tokyo: Aoki shoten, 1955); Takagi Hirō, *Nihon no shinkō shūkyō* (Tokyo: Iwanami shoten, 1959). A second line of research traced the historical roots of Reiyukai to mid-nineteenth-century lay Buddhist movements, as in Watanabe Umeo, *Gendai nihon no shūkyō* (Tokyo: Daitō shuppansha, 1950).

The younger generation of Japanese scholars has turned away from general outlines to more specific, usually sociological issues. Kōmoto Mitusgu's works, cited in the Bibliography, address the question of Reiyukai's penetration into rural areas, and the general significance of Reiyukai in gauging more general shifts in Japanese ancestor worship.

Among Western-language works discussing Reiyukai, few are longer than a page or so. Those by H. Neill McFarland and Harry Thomsen, cited in the Bibliography, apparently rely heavily on devotional literature in English issued by the group. The most comprehensive treatment of Reiyukai in Western-language sources is Werner Köhler, *Die Lotus-Lehre und die modernen Religionen in Japan* (Zurich: Atlantis Verlag, 1962), pp. 235–53; this study considers the frequently encountered combination of ancestor worship and shamanism in the new religions.

research on Reiyukai, I used four major sources of information.

Data collected through participant observation among Reiyukai members is the first source. In July, 1975, I contacted the Los Angeles office of Reiyukai and became a member of the group. I let it be known that I was seeking an opportunity to study the group in Japan, and soon thereafter was invited to go to Habikino City, Osaka Prefecture, where the headquarters of the Eighth Branch is located, and to live with members employed by the branch in exchange for teaching English there. I accepted this offer by the branch leaders of the Eighth Branch, Masunaga Sadako and Masunaga Tadashi. I had met Branch Leader Masunaga in Los Angeles where she was visiting her daughter, whose husband is head of the Los Angeles office. From July, 1976 through February, 1977 I lived with members of Reiyukai's Eighth Branch in a dormitory operated for branch employees and went to the branch office on a daily basis, where I observed the full range of Reiyukai meetings and activities, learned about the management of the branch, and was in daily contact with many Reiyukai members.

Although I was careful to explain to my Reiyukai hosts and informants in Osaka that I was conducting academic research, I was at the same time a member of the organization and participated fully in ritual and other activities. This ambiguity in my position probably was the deciding factor in my being able to collect a great deal of information not readily disclosed to outsiders under other circumstances, but at the same time it encouraged the false hope that I might one day become an evangelist for the group.

In March, 1977 I changed my research site to Tokyo in order to carry out a survey, the second major source of data, administered to a sample of 2,000 members from all branches of Reiyukai in Japan. Carrying out a project affecting all the branches necessitated the approval and assistance of the Tokyo headquarters, and completion of survey design and administration required the better part of the following year, until the spring of 1978. Results of the survey are discussed in Chapters 2 and 3, and a complete text and translation, plus more detailed statistical data, appear in the Appendix.

In Tokyo I presented myself to the headquarters staff and to the president of Reiyukai, Kubo Tsugunari, through an introduction from the chairman of the Department of Religious Studies at the University of Tokyo, the president's alma mater, which left no doubt that I was to be considered an outside researcher. This unambiguous position facilitated my survey research while putting an end to my former use of the method of participant observation.

A third source of data, detailed interviews of twenty-two Reiyukai branch leaders, was carried out in Tokyo during the summer of 1978. Inasmuch as my interviews were arranged through the Tokyo headquarters, it was necessary to submit first a list of questions I would ask. Some of the questions I would most have liked to ask had to be deleted at the request of the headquarters as too sensitive politically or in other respects, and thus the questions and interviewees' initial responses were rather stereotyped. Since in addition the organization requested that an official of the Overseas Department be present at all interviews, interviewees often seemed to feel somewhat constrained and under pressure to give the "right answer." However, in most cases it was possible to establish sufficient rapport to overcome these various factors curtailing free expression at least to some extent; and particularly in the case of female branch leaders, the rather dry list of "official" questions was quickly left behind as interviewees expanded on their experiences as believers and leaders of Reiyukai. I found that questions concerning marriage, the family, and the religious possibilities open to women provide the heart of leaders' thought and concern, and these problems are dealt with in Chapter 6.

The fourth major source of information upon which this study relies is members' testimonies. Existing works on the new religions for the most part tacitly assume that the often extravagent claims of healing and other "this-worldly" benefits cannot be taken seriously except as signifying the psychological, emotional, expressive satisfaction which membership provides, and from this perspective testimonials become inadmissible as a source of information on actual events. Nevertheless, testimonies are continually produced in great number, and the act of presenting a testimony before a group is an important part of group membership. In contrast to existing research, this study assumes that testimonies provide invaluable data for the investigation of doctrine, organization, and religious experience. In Chapter 5 a collection of Reiyukai testimonies is examined thematically with the purpose of showing how membership often results in genuine instrumental effectiveness in solving members' problems.

Chapter One

The History of Reiyukai

Part 1: The Role of Crisis

 Most studies on the Japanese new religions explain their origins as the result of crisis. While a crisis may explain (in some weak sense of that word) why groups form at a particular time, it does not account for their persistence once the time of crisis has passed. The earthquake of 1923 played a role in the founding of Reiyukai, but neither its origin nor its continuation can be explained solely by reference to this crisis. To say of Reiyukai that it represents a reaction to crisis would ignore its positive attempts to address the problems of Japanese society and also its inheritance of concepts, beliefs, and rites of Japanese Buddhism. Through the lens of the crisis explanation, we focus necessarily upon reaction and response. The following account, however, emphasizes the founders' positive initiative in formulating a creed and their purposeful transformation of traditional elements to match new circumstances.

Kubo Kakutarō 久保角太郎, as he was known after his marriage and adoption into the Kubo household, was born Matsutaka Kakutarō in the village of Kominato, Awa-gun, Chiba Prefecture, in 1892. He was the family's third son, and the fact of his having been born in the birthplace of the medieval saint Nichiren 日蓮 later inspired him to think of himself as the Nichiren of the Taishō era (1912–1926). At the age of twenty he left home and went to Tokyo where he worked as a carpenter's apprentice during the day and attended Nihon University at night, studying architectural draftsmanship and engineering. His work took him to the Imperial Household Ministry (Kunaishō 宮内省), and his diligence and seriousness there attracted the notice of Sengoku Masayuki 仙石政敬, a high official in the ministry.[1]

Former retainers of Sengoku, the Kubo household were at that time without an heir. Kubo Shin 久保シン, a widow in her fifties, prevailed upon Sengoku to help find a suitable husband for her daughter, who would take the Kubo name and perpetuate the line. Sengoku arranged for Kakutaro to marry into the Kubo house, and it was then that Kakutaro gave up the name of Matsutaka and became known as Kubo Kakutaro. The practice of second and third sons becoming "adopted husbands" (*mukoyōshi* 婿養子) was an accepted one and not particularly exceptional. In fact, one of Kakutaro's elder brothers, Kotani Yasukichi 小谷安吉, had also been adopted, into the Kotani family. Kubo became a full-time employee of the Imperial Household Ministry after his marriage.[2]

Kubo's mother-in-law Shin was an ardent devotee of the Lotus Sutra, and she insisted that Kakutaro be trained by one of the many ideologues of Nichirenshugi, Masuko Yūkichi 増子酉吉. Masuko was a follower of Tanaka Chigaku 田中智学,[3] one of the leaders of the Nichirenshugi (literally "Nichirenism" 日蓮主義) movement which was highly influential through the early twentieth century, enjoying its heyday in the Taisho period, when it fuelled the fires of militant nationalism. Nichirenshugi, a term created by Tanaka in 1901, refers to a nationalistic, political

[1] Sengoku Masayuki (1872–1935), a Taishō bureaucrat, worked in the Kunaishō, the Kizokuin, and the Ōkurashō. He was elected to the House of Peers in 1920. On Kubo's early life, see Watanabe Umeo, *Gendai Nihon no shūkyō* (Tokyo: Daitō shuppansha, 1950), pp. 298–302; and Saki Akio, *Kyōso—shomin no kamigami* (Tokyo: Aoki shoten, 1955), pp. 212–16.

[2] Saki Akio, *Godai kyōso no jitsuzō* (Tokyo: Yagumo shoin, 1970), pp. 34–42.

[3] Tanaka Chigaku (1861–1939) was originally a priest of Nichiren Buddhism but left the order after a disagreement with an abbott who did not accord sufficient importance, in Tanaka's opinion, to *shakubuku* ("forceful proselytization") and Nichiren's patriotic writings. On Tanaka's life and thought, see Edwin B. Lee, "Nichiren and Nationalism: The Religious Patriotism of Tanaka Chigaku," *Monumenta Nipponica* 30, No. 1 (Spring, 1975), 19–35; and the biography of Tanaka by his son, Tanaka Kōhō, *Tanaka Chigaku* (Tokyo: Shinsekaisha, 1977).

interpretation of Nichiren's thought. It was created to distinguish
the movement led by Tanaka from sectarian Nichiren Buddhism.
Tanaka accorded special importance to Nichiren's *Risshō anko-
kuron* 立正安国論 and the idea of *shakubuku* 折伏 (forceful proselytization) in creating a number of laymen's groups, the most
notable of which were the Risshō Ankokukai 立正安国会 and
the Kokuchūkai 国柱会 , The Nation's Pillar Society.[4] Tanaka
stressed the unity of Nichiren Buddhism and State Shinto ideology. His thought moved increasingly to the right through the
twenties, in opposition to the growth of labor and tenants' unions,
political parties, and such religious groups as Ōmotokyō 大本教,
(founded in 1892 by Deguchi Nao 出口ナオ), which he thought
infringed on state religious ideology. He advocated increased state
control of religious bodies through unification of objects of worship, and eventually he proclaimed that the emperor should be the
supreme object of worship for everyone.[5]

For Tanaka and Masuko, true Buddhism is inherently political,
and genuine followers of Nichiren should create a Buddhism
useful in the support and protection of the state. The sympathies
of those who subscribed to Nichirenshugi were with the ruling
class. Their main concern with respect to the rest of society was
that it be orderly, obedient, and loyal. They were not interested in
its problems.

During the Taisho era Nichiren's thought was under re-
examination from two very different perspectives. One sought to
forge a bond between the impassioned patriotism of the medieval
saint and the notion of the absolute authority of the emperor and
the national polity (*kokutai* 国体). The ideologues of this persua-
sion, who included Kita Ikki 北一輝 and others associated with
militarists and the right wing, perceived a threat in religious and
political pluralism. They tended to support the fascist notion that

---

[4] On the various religious groups founded by Tanaka, see Watanabe Hōyō,
"Tanaka Chigaku no shūkyō undō ni tsuite," in *Kindai Nihon no hokke bukkyō*, ed.
Mochizuki Kankō (Kyoto: Heirakuji shoten, 1968), pp. 129–58.

[5] On Nichirenshugi see Ikeda Eishun, *Meiji no bukkyō—sono kōdō to shisō*,
Nihonjin no kōdō to shisō, vol. 31 (Tokyo: Hyōronsha, 1976), pp. 132–42; and
Togoro Shigeki, *Kindai shakai to Nichirenshugi*, Nihonjin no kōdō to shisō, vol. 18
(Tokyo: Hyōronsha, 1972), pp. 113–42.

a subject must ground his every thought and action in his duty to the nation, submitting unconditionally to the imperial will. On this view, the only justification for the existence of a voluntary religious group is its promulgation of a message of patriotism. While one may recognize the existence of degrees of extremism in the propagation of Nichirenshugi, Tanaka Chigaku and his ilk represented the far right of the spectrum.[6]

Kubo was steeped in the sentiments of Nichirenshugi through his training under Masuko, and at the Imperial Household Ministry he imbibed further the air of reverence for the emperor. This experience was a formative influence upon the development of his religious thinking, but there was another aspect of Taisho thought about Nichiren that he found more persuasive and congenial.

Kubo learned about Nishida Toshizō 西田俊蔵 from his brother Kotani Yasukichi around 1919, and although Kubo and Nishida never met, Kubo appropriated many of Nishida's ideas and practices. Nishida was a fuel dealer in Yokohama who took up a religious life after the deaths of his wife and two children in circumstances of terrible poverty. He took the religious name Mugaku 無学, meaning, in his interpretation, "having nothing further to learn." He identified himself with the bodhisattva Jōfukyō 常不軽 (Skt: Sadāparibhūta), a figure in the Lotus Sutra's twentieth chapter whose appearance is promised when the Law has almost been extinguished. He comes as a beggar, but with power to save all beings. Like other contemporary religious figures, Nishida called upon Buddhism to provide ethical guidance in the midst of the confusion of Taisho cultural pluralism. Finding no response from the clergy, he appealed to laymen, proclaiming that the nation must be saved through the power of the ancestors.[7]

---

[6] Togoro, *Kindai shakai to Nichirenshugi*, pp. 113–42.

[7] Nishida was apparently independent of any other religious group, and he did not establish any group for the propagation of his teaching. However, some of his followers customarily assembled in a house distantly connected to the Matsutaka house. Through this connection Yasukichi learned of Nishida's teaching and told Kubo about them. What became of Nishida after that time is not known. He left no writings, and sources on his ideas are few. See Watanabe Umeo, *Gendai Nihon*, pp. 295–98; Saki, *Kyōso*, pp. 213–15; and *Godai kyōso*, pp. 38–41.

Nishida developed a distinctive concept of ancestors later incorporated with few changes by Kubo. Nishida said,

> The living individual is the body left behind by the ancestors in this world,
> so we should treat our ancestors as if they were our own bodies. . . . In our
> hearts we have the seed of buddhahood, which also remains in the
> ancestors' souls, so we must protect it for our own salvation. The salva-
> tion of the ancestors is our own salvation, and our salvation is the
> ancestors' salvation.[8]

In other words, ancestor worship is necessary for the individual's
salvation. Care of the ancestors must not be entrusted to priests.

An important part of Nishida's ancestral rites was the posthumous name, the *kaimyō* 戒名. Although it was customary for
posthumous names to be written for the deceased by a priest for a
substantial fee, Nishida held that this essential requirement for
salvation should not be withheld for lack of money, and that it was
immoral for priests to encourage mistaken ideas about the matter.
A posthumous name is considered necessary for salvation in
Japanese folk belief. The spirit requires a new name upon taking
up residence in the other world, and it is also thought that without
such a name the spirit cannot be called by the buddhas to come
forward to hear the sermons and spiritual instruction necessary
for salvation.[9]

---

[8] Nishida's assertion that priests must not be entrusted with the care of ancestral
spirits derives from the anti-clericalism of the period in which he lived on the one
hand, but in addition it grows out of a doctrinal dispute within Nichiren Buddhism,
originating in the Meiji period, known as the *sanzu jōbutsuron* 三途成仏論. This
debate was an important element in the founding of the earlier lay group,
Butsuryūkō 仏立講. In this debate the traditionalist side held that priestly ritual to
transfer merit to beings in the lowest three realms of existence (the *sanzu* 三途 : the
hells, the animal world, and the realm of the hungry ghosts) is sufficient to release
them from their sufferings, but the reformist side held that priestly merit transfer
was null and void in the latter days, following Nichiren, and that only individual
faith and spiritual discipline could release them. Thus if an ancestor happened to be
in such a realm, priestly rites would be ineffective in bringing about his rebirth. See
Murakami Shigeyoshi, *Butsuryūkō kaidō Nagamatsu Nissen* (Tokyo: Kōdansha,
1976), pp. 52–55.

[9] Nawata Sanae, "Reiyukai," in *Reiyukai, Risshōkōseikai, Sōkagakkai*, Shinshūkyō no sekai, vol. 2 (Tokyo: Daizōkan, 1979), pp. 30–32.

Nishida also developed the practice, retained in Reiyukai, of inscribing a type of posthumous name (signifying not death but entry into a religious life, as a novice monk receives a religious name upon entering the clergy) on a single tablet for worship in the domestic altar. This name, the *sōkaimyō* 総戒名 (posthumous name for all the ancestors of a household) incorporated not only the husband's name, but the wife's maiden name, thus becoming the object of worship for the household formed around their marriage. The tablet represents all of the couple's ancestors traced bilaterally. This practice encouraged the idea that husband and wife form a natural ritual unit, and that their salvation results from their joint religious practice, thus forming a nucleus in ritual symbolism around which to build positive interpretations of the religious significance of marriage.[10]

Nishida held that natural disaster and social unrest arise from a failure to worship the spirits correctly. He was particularly concerned with the *muenbotoke* 無縁仏 ("spirits without relations"), spirits of the dead who leave no descendants to enshrine and worship them properly. He used to clean the graves of these spirits, write posthumous names for them, and enshrine them in his own house.[11]

Nishida believed that people become sick or poor due to their karma. Part of one's karma is made by one's own actions, and another part is inherited from the ancestors. He held also that people have the particular spouses and children they do because of karma they inherit from the ancestors. Kubo incorporated the beliefs and practices outlined here more or less without change.[12]

Under the influence of Nishida, Kubo's thinking developed along lines antithetical to the chauvinistic patriotism of Nichirenshugi. He became dedicated to founding a society for laymen to address the problems of modern society through Buddhism. His era, he believed, was floundering for lack of ethical guidance. Because the Buddhist clergy was content to draw an income from the performance of ancestral and funeral rites, they took no initiative in aiding their parishioners' desire to lead ethical

[10] Ibid.
[11] Ibid.
[12] Ibid.

lives. Further, because parishioners entrust the care of their ancestors to the temples, the world is full of war and calamity, and
society is in turmoil. Each person must worship his own ancestors
and take responsibility for their salvation through reciting the
Lotus Sutra for them, without clerical intervention. In this
message there was the intent to address Japan's social problems,
but there was little mention of the sancta of Nichirenshugi: emperor and kokutai.[13]

Kubo combined his stress on lay ancestor worship and its
accompanying anti-clericalism with another element traditionally
important in Nichiren Buddhism: faith healing. He underwent
ascetic training at a Nichiren temple known for shamanistic
healing, the Nakayama Hokekyōji 中山法華経寺 of Chiba
Prefecture.[14] This aspect of Kubo's lay Buddhist practice had
nothing in common with Nichirenshugi.

At this temple Kubo met Wakatsuki Chise, 若月チセ an independent spiritualist. She was about forty at the time. In *kami-
gakari* 神がかり, or spirit possession, she relayed revelations from
various spirits. She and Kubo attempted to found a layman's
group, Rei no Tomo Kai 霊の友会 (Friends of the Spirits) in 1919,
and it is from this time that the present group Reiyukai dates its
official founding, though actually this first attempt failed to attract
a following, and the group soon dissolved.[15]

Nevertheless, the association of Kubo and Wakatsuki continued, and when Kubo Shin was taken ill with a nervous ailment
interpreted as possession by a spirit, Kubo had her treated by
Wakatsuki. Shin was cured, and the event undoubtedly en-

---

[13] *The Reiyukai, Its Aim and Practice* (Tokyo: Reiyukai, n.d.); Kotani Kimi, *Watakushi no shugyō seikatsu, sanjūgo nen* (Tokyo: Reiyukai, 1958), pp. 1–20. The autobiographical writings of early leaders touch upon various aspects of Kubo's teachings. It seems that he never systematized them in credal form but instead evolved them somewhat eclectically. See Kusada Isaburō, *Konjō o naose*, Taiken no bukkyō, vol. 6 (Tokyo: Hotoke no sekaisha, 1974), chaps. 2 and 3.

[14] See sources in note 13. On the Nakayama Hokekyōji see Nakao Takashi, *Nakayama Hokekyōji shiryō* (Tokyo: Yoshikawa kōbunkan, 1968); and Uchino Kumiko, "Kishimojin shinkō ni miru minshū no inori to sugata," in *Nichirenshū no shomondai*, ed. Nakao Takashi (Tokyo: Yūzankaku, 1975), pp. 307–321.

[15] Murakami Shigeyoshi, *Nihon shūkyō jiten* (Tokyo: Kōdansha, 1978), pp. 414–15.

couraged Kubo to persevere in developing his ideas independently of Masuko. However, this was the last straw for the already strained relation between Masuko and Kubo. Masuko could not sanction faith healing as a legitimate part of Nichirenshugi, and so the two parted company.[16]

The split between Masuko and Kubo points to an enduring division among Nichiren-derived groups between a nationalistic and a spiritualistic emphasis. Those for whom the idea of Buddhism as protector of the state is central cannot accept the inclusion of this-worldly benefits such as healing. Adherents of nationalistic Nichirenshugi take an authoritarian stance in which the interests of Buddhism as an institution are seen to lie with the state in the suppression of independent sources of authority—religious, political, or both in combination.[17]

While Meiji and Taisho regimes upheld the gods of Shinto as supreme, a faith healer claiming inspiration from deities outside the state pantheon put him- (more often her-) self outside the sphere of state ideology. Well-publicized cures have readily found believers, and the ability to heal gives the curer a charisma which is difficult for the state to undercut with credibility. Spontaneous spirit possession combined with a talent for organization can lead to the formation of groups claiming a source of legitimacy in the authority of a deity and that deity's messenger in this world, as was the case in Tenrikyō 天理教 and Omoto, to name only two examples. The Japanese state and its allies in the religious world have seen potential enemies and sources of potential revolt in such groups and have tried to suppress them. In the background of the final separation of Kubo from Masuko lay this issue of the locus of religious authority.[18]

[16] Ibid.

[17] A similar schism concerning the contrasting interpretations, religious and political, of Nichiren Buddhism occurred within Butsuryūkō in the Meiji period. The group split into two factions over the issue of healing. The side that was more interested in politics dissolved at the death of its leader, while the party interested in healing, in which women took prominent roles as healers, has endured to the present. Murakami, *Butsuryūkō*, pp. 77–78 and 92–96.

[18] Much of twentieth-century Japanese religious history is the story of the rise and suppression by the state of groups whose central practice is healing. See Murakami Shigeyoshi, *Nihon hyakunen no shūkyō* (Tokyo: Kōdansha, 1968).

It was not until 1925, in the aftermath of the catastrophic earthquake of 1923, that Kubo was able successfully to establish a Buddhist layman's group in accordance with his ideals, and then it was less he than his sister-in-law Kotani Kimi 小谷喜美 who was responsible for converting the original members. Taisho Japan before 1923 witnessed considerable intellectual, political, and social ferment, not all of which was to Kubo's liking.

Japanese culture of the Taisho era extolled individualism and internationalism in a new way. In art and literature a new dedication to art for its own sake arose apart from the didactic motive of edifying the populace, and the birth of individualism rejected the limitations of the idea that a Japanese artist must produce something "uniquely Japanese." Zola and the naturalists were translated and imitated, and a variety of literary styles flourished. In sculpture Rodin was admired, and Mallarmé was influential in poetry. Sōseki warned the state to adopt a broad policy of cultural support rather than narrowly recognizing only that which was compatible with patriotic platitudes.[19]

The great industries of mass culture appeared, and a newly literate society became its avid consumers. Before Taisho there was little idea of an independent press, as it had been assumed that journalism existed largely to promulgate the will of the state. Now, however, the French printing machines producing Japanese newspapers were constantly humming as circulation increased rapidly, and newspapers began to be regarded as businesses. Their content expanded to include news, entertainment, and advertisement. The distribution of newspapers of course depended upon widened nationwide channels of communication, and especially after the Russo-Japanese War, a heightened desire for news. Newspapers, in spite of the existence since 1908 of local editions, had a homogenizing, leveling effect. It is noteworthy also that the standard "level" was a high one. In addition to serializations of the novels of Soseki and others, it included the world's longest novel, *Daibosatsu tōge* 大菩薩峠, and works of serious social criticism, such as Kawakami Hajime's 河上肇 *Bimbō monogatari* 貧乏物語 (A tale

[19] Minami Hiroshi, *Taishō bunka* (Tokyo: Kyōsō shobō, 1965), pp. 41, 44–46, and 97–98.

of poverty) in 1917, which attacked the growing gap between rich and poor on humanitarian grounds, and Kagawa Toyohiko's 賀川豊彦 *Shisen o koete* 死線を越えて (Crossing the line of death), which was similarly critical of social inequality. The content of Japanese newspapers helped produce a layman learned in social, political, and even philosophical issues.[20]

Kubo was sufficiently influenced by Nichirenshugi and the patriotic bureaucratism of the Imperial Household Ministry to react negatively to individualism and social criticism. To him the liberal sentiments of Taisho culture threatened tradition, and he thought the proliferation of political opinion produced a confusing morass of conflicting values in which there were few signposts to guide the individual in discerning the truth and the right way to live. To him the solution lay in a return to the worship of ancestors and in strengthening the family system. He and his followers saw the family and the values implicit in ancestor worship especially endangered by the woman's culture that first appeared in Taisho.[21]

A woman's movement pressing for suffrage and changes in the Civil Code applying to the position of women emerged in Taisho and published a number of journals, of which *Seitō* 青鞜 (Bluestocking) was the most celebrated.[22] Women socialists such as Itō Noe 伊藤野枝 and others were active at this time.[23] This was the first serious political activity by Japanese women to unite and improve their condition. Their critiques of existing social institutions inevitably involved criticism of the family system, especially the investiture of great power over other members in the head, the *kachō* 家長.[24] Inasmuch as the family was the unit for

[20] Ibid., pp. 44, 94–96, and 118–36.

[21] Writers such as Watanabe and Saki, cited above (n. 1), have said that Kubo developed his ideas in reaction to Westernization. He certainly had no great love for foreign culture, but it is perhaps more accurate to say that he mounted active opposition only to elements he believed threatened the family.

[22] *Seitō* was founded in 1911 by Hiratsuka Raichō.

[23] Ide Fumiko and Esashi Akiko, *Taishō demokurashii to josei* (Tokyo: Gōdo shuppan, 1977), chaps. 5 and 6.

[24] Nakano Tadashi, "Ie no kōzō to ishiki oyobi henyō," in *Shōka dōzokudan no kenkyū*, ed. Nakano Tadashi (Tokyo: Miraisha, 1974), pp. 155–59; Fukutake Ichirō, *Nihon kazoku seido shi gaisetsu* (Tokyo: Yoshikawa kōbunkan, 1972), pp. 199–205.

the performance of ancestor worship, an attack on the one constituted a threat to the other, as Kubo no doubt perceived.

Women's political activities during Taisho went directly counter to the values Kubo espoused, and he must have opposed them.
However, women were being drawn into the public realm as never
before, and once the industries of mass culture perceived in
women a new group of consumers, changes in women's conscious-
ness became inevitable.

It was in 1900 that Mitsukoshi Dry Goods became Mitsukoshi
Department Store, and from that time on its advertising staff set
about shaping the tastes of the women of Japan. There had been
fads and fashions in Meiji, but in Taisho fashion became big
business, and Mitsukoshi and others hoping to attract the pur-
chasing power of urban women began to conduct scientific research to increase the psychological effectiveness of advertising.
One of their great successes was a three-year vogue for the
"Genroku-look" in kimono and accessories.[25] In publishing, the
Kōdansha corporation took the lead, establishing in 1920 the
women's magazine *Fujin kurabu* 婦人倶楽部 (The Women's
Club). Iwanami, the second leading publisher, was not to be
outdone and published the popular *Shufu no tomo* 主婦の友 (The
Housewife's Friend) from 1917 and also *Shufukōron* 主婦公論
(The Housewife's View). For the more intellectual, but not necessarily political stratum, there was *Josei kaizō* 女性改造 (Women's
Reconstruction), echoing contemporary calls for "reconstruction" and reform in social thought and awareness.[26] These popular magazines reached a wider audience than more critical, political journals like the feminist publications *Seitō* and *Sekai fujin*
世界婦人 (Women of the World), founded in 1907 by the socialist
Fukuda Hideko 福田英子, advocating radical social change in the
family system and the legal status of women.[27]

While the popular press's messages to women generally did not
seriously challenge the status quo, subtle changes crept in that

[25] Minami, *Taishō bunka*, pp. 162–72.

[26] Ibid., pp. 128–29.

[27] Ibid., pp. 129–30; Ōhara Takashi, "Fukuda Hideko ni miru fujin kaihō shisō
no hatten; *Sekai fujin* o chūshin ni," in *Kindai Nihon shisōshi no kiso chishiki*
(Tokyo: Yūzankaku, 1975), pp. 144–45.

were not entirely in harmony with tradition. For example, the notion that "love" and "marriage" were opposite spheres, that "love" threatened the family, was little questioned by the popular press (though free love was idealized by some of the political women's journals).[28] However, this received wisdom was not completely at ease with the barrage of fashion advertising directed at married women to convince them that beauty was not undesirable in the home, and that expenditures on their wardrobes and hairstyles were not at odds with their roles as *ryōsai kenbo* 良妻賢母, "good wives and wise mothers," the only legitimate aspiration for women according to the educational system. Although the equipment for permanents came in during early Taisho, short hair still produced shocked reactions, and cosmetics still had to be marketed under pretense of their medicinal value.[29] However, these superficial changes constituted a subtle threat to traditionalists like Kubo.

On September 1, 1923, Tokyo and the surrounding Kantō area were struck by an earthquake of 7.9 degrees of magnitude. On that day there were 222 smaller quakes; on the next day 323, and on September 3, there were 181 tremors. One hundred thirty-eight thousand people died, mainly in the fires that raged over Tokyo on September 1 and 2. Four hundred ten thousand houses were burned. After the initial quake, communication lines of all kinds were cut, and only when an enterprising Kanagawa policeman swam out to a fishing boat and used a marine radio did the rest of Japan learn that its capital and center of culture was being destroyed.[30] Thanks, however, to regional presses and recent technical innovations in photography, the nation was given quick written and photographic accounts of the destruction.[31] Tokyo was placed under martial law on September 2, whereupon the police and the military took over. The emergency situation provided the ideal pretext for rounding up dissidents and others, notably Korean immigrants, for quick dispatch. Socialists such as Ōsugi Sakae 大杉栄 and his wife Ito Noe were executed without

---

[28] Minami, *Taishō bunka*, pp. 255ff.
[29] Ibid., p. 255.
[30] Nakajima Yōichirō, *Kantō daishinsai* (Tokyo: Yūzankaku, 1973), pp. 29–30.
[31] Ibid., pp. 27–30.

trial by the police, and many other socialists, communists, and anarchists were arrested though they had committed no crime. According to police accounts, forty Koreans were executed without trial; the actual figure was probably much higher. The government did nothing to suppress false rumors that Koreans were poisoning the wells.[32] The earthquake precipitated a situation of general crisis and ushered in an era of suppression of the liberalism of the earlier Taisho period.[33] While the earthquake alone was not entirely responsible for fiscal and labor crisis or for the end of liberalism, it marked a watershed, one that was especially influential in the founding of Reiyukai.

Economic crisis following World War I had been deepening since 1920, but the earthquake greatly worsened it and added to the atmosphere of fear. In the earthquake five billion yen worth of property was lost, causing the closure of many small banks. In Tokyo and neighboring Kanagawa Prefectures, 85 percent of the factories were seriously damaged, and as a result 68,866 persons lost their jobs. Moneylending came to a halt, and the stock market fell. The government proclaimed a moratorium on debt repayment, suspended many taxes, and issued low-interest loans to aid in recovery. Nevertheless, conditions of acute crisis continued, and these were felt most severely by the urban poor.[34]

Even before the earthquake, industrialization, the spread of the factory system, housing shortages, and widening gaps in the distribution of wealth, not to mention the hardships caused by repeated wars, all contributed to the burden of the urban poor.[35] Migrant workers (*dekaseginin* 出稼ぎ人) were pouring into the cities from the countryside, particularly into northern Tokyo, where Kotani Kimi made Reiyukai's first converts. This area had historically

[32] Ibid., chap. 4 *passim*.

[33] Ibid., chap. 2 *passim*.

[34] Ibid., pp. 18–22.

[35] On the social consequences of industrialization and urbanization, see Thomas O. Wilkinson, "Family Structure and Industrialization in Japan," *American Sociological Review* 27 (1962), 678–82; Irene Taeuber, "Family, Migration, and Industrialization in Japan," *American Sociological Review* 16 (1951), 149–57; Ōhashi Ryūken, *Nihon no kaikyū kōsei* (Tokyo: Iwanami shoten, 1977), pp. 13–76.

held a large population of *burakumin* 部落民 (outcastes),[36] engaged in occupations traditionally considered polluting: tanning,
slaughtering, and cremation. People in these slum areas were
employed in the factories of the heavy industries if they were
lucky, and less fortunate men and women lived on day labor,
doing such work as sewing parachutes, making matches, construction work, and ragpicking. They lived in rental housing for
the most part, often the "long houses" (*nagaya* 長屋) where many
people were squeezed into a small section of a large dwelling for
which they paid a daily fee. Their food was the spartan fare of rice
and salt, or when that was unavailable, they could buy leftovers
from military barracks or from schools, purveyed by dealers in
such commodities.[37] It was from this stratum of society that
Reiyukai's first converts came.

Kubo finally gained a public through his sister-in-law Kotani
Kimi. It was she who organized a group to propagate his ideas,
and without her he might have died an unknown street preacher.
Kimi was born on January 10, 1901 in Miura-shi, Kanagawa
Prefecture. At birth she was so severely underweight that her
mother made monthly pilgrimages to the deity of the Nakayama
Hokekyoji to pray for Kimi's health. Kimi's childhood was spent
in extreme poverty as her father had died when she was very
young. She was able to complete only five years of primary education. She married a fisherman who was soon lost at sea, leaving
her a widow while still in her teens. At seventeen she went to Tokyo
to work as a maid and married Kotani Yasukichi in 1925.[38]

Yasukichi ran a boarding house, and in addition, he was employed sometimes in the Kubo household, where he came under
the religious influence of Kubo Shin. In fact, he was in the house
when the earthquake occurred. As Kakutaro and Yasukichi
began to study the Lotus Sutra together, they realized that the
"evil, evil world of the five impurities would surely come, and no

---

[36] Nakamura Masanori, "Toshi kasō shakai," in *Kindai Nihon no kiso chishiki*
(Tokyo: Yūzankaku, 1972), pp. 162–63.

[37] Ibid.

[38] Kotani, *Watakushi no shugyō*, pp. 21–23 and Murakami, *Nihon shūkyō jiten*,
pp. 414–15.

matter what the obstacle, they must worship the ancestors." The advent of the world of the five impurities (*gojoku akuse* 五濁悪世) was prophesied in the second (*Hōben hon* 方便品) chapter of the Lotus Sutra.[39] The occurrence of the earthquake while the two were actually studying the prophecy undoubtedly convinced them of its truth and imminence.[40]

Two days after Kimi's marriage, her husband informed her that worship of the ancestors was the custom of the household and that she should begin reciting the *daimoku* ("Hail to the Lotus Sutra" 題目) and the Lotus Sutra. However, she had been raised in the Pure Land faith, and was unable to believe in the Lotus. She had never seen a sutra before, nor held a rosary. This being the case, it was agreed that simple recitation of the daimoku would be sufficient for the time being, and this she began.[41]

However, before half a year had passed, Yasukichi was suddenly taken ill. This sickness became the occasion for Kimi's conversion to Kubo's teaching and active proselytization. Yasukichi wanted to have Buddhist priests perform rites for his ancestors on their memorial day, and he had written a letter requesting ceremonies and enclosing the requisite fee. He had asked Kimi to post the letter, but just as he stood up to hand it to her, he was stricken by a terrible pain in the hips. He was in so much pain that he sent Kimi for a doctor instead of to the post office. The doctor came and administered injections, but their effect soon wore off, and again Yasukichi was overcome with agony. About a week later, when he was no better, Kubo paid him and Kimi a visit. He displayed no sympathy:

Just what do you two think you're doing? You weren't born in this world just to make money. You got sick because you don't worship your ancestors. Because of that, you're clinging to doctors, having shots, and

---

[39] Kotani, *Watakushi no shugyō*, p. 20. For the Lotus Sutra's dire prophesy, see Taisho 9.7. The five impurities with which the world will be afflicted are 1) corruption of society; 2) the proliferation of mistaken thought; 3) the proliferation of the passions; 4) withering of the fortunes of men; 5) reduction of the span of human life to a mere ten years.

[40] Ibid.

[41] Ibid., pp. 20–21.

taking medicine. Recite the daimoku! And because this woman here [Kimi] is a terribly obstinate woman, her karma is very bad.[42]

So saying, he exhorted Kimi to convert to his views, saying she could quit if Yasukichi failed to be healed. In Kubo's opinion, Kimi's original refusal to worship the ancestors as he and Yasukichi had instructed her was part of the reason for Yasukichi's illness. Another reason was that Yasukichi had gone against Kubo's teaching by attempting to pay a priest for ancestral rites. He should have realized that only descendants are qualified to set the ancestors at rest.[43]

Kimi began ritual as Kubo directed, but after another week Yasukichi still could not stand, nor could he sleep. Kimi was distraught and began to contemplate divorce. Her mother and Kubo accused her of being callous and cold, and Kubo told her that if her lack of human feeling went so deep, she must purify herself through cold water austerities, praying for Yasukichi's recovery. He ordered her to continue this regimen until Yasukichi regained his health, and if after that she still wanted a divorce, he (Kubo) would no longer stand in the way. Kimi began performing cold water austerities, pouring icy buckets of water over her body five or six times a day, as well as reciting the daimoku and the sutra. The result was that Yasukichi was cured. This healing convinced Kimi once and for all of the truth of Kubo's message, and from then on she became ardent in its propagation.[44]

She began preaching on the streets, going all over Tokyo to spread the word that everyone must worship the ancestors as crises even worse than the earthquake were in store. She moved several times and reports that she was living in nagaya, which suggests that she was very poor. In her account of this activity it is not clear whether Yasukichi followed her or whether she left him in the care of his children by his former marriage, nor are the dates clear, but it appears from the account given in her autobiography that she was alone much of the time, and that her first successful conver-

---

[42] Ibid.
[43] Ibid.
[44] Ibid., pp. 21–22.

sion of large numbers occurred between late 1925 and late 1931, when Yasukichi died.[45]

In the following account of Reiyukai's first converts, Kimi speaks of them as "ragpickers," *kuzuya* 屑屋. From details of her description, it is clear that the term may be understood literally as people who made a living collecting and reselling waste materials, but the word *kuzuya* and its more polite form, *kuzuya san* 屑屋さん, were also contemporary euphemisms for burakumin, the outcaste group known to be numerous in the Arakawa Ward of northern Tokyo.[46] Thus it is highly likely, though impossible to document with certainty, that the original members included burakumin. At any rate, it is certain that they were an urban proletariat living in extreme poverty. Kotani describes how she gained these converts:

I began walking all over Tokyo, barefoot and without riding the trains. That's the kind of life I was living. I lived in Asakadachō.... At first I lived in a boarding house in Aoyama, but I moved to Senju for ascetic training, to the neighborhood called Umeda, around the great bridge [across the Arakawa River]. I lived there for one hundred days of spiritual training. There used to be a big Tenrikyo church there. For those hundred days I did cold water austerities in the river, worshipped the morning star, and prayed. While I was praying, I was told [by spirits] that come what may, I must make converts.

In just that neighborhood there were some six hundred families of ragpickers. In three-mat rooms (9' × 6') there might be a family of four, or in the case of large families they sometimes lived seven in a three-mat room; these were the conditions in which these six hundred families were living. I spent the days visiting them, talking to them and telling them about the teaching of worshipping our ancestors. When I tried to proselytize them, I found that they didn't have the money to buy a sutra, and if I invited them to worship at my place, they didn't have decent clothes to wear, so of the ten *yukata* 浴衣 [summer kimonos] I started out with, I gave away about five, but soon there were more and more converts, so I had to give one person only half a yukata and make that cloth into a kind

---

[45] Ibid., pp. 24–25.

[46] The high concentration of crematoria in the area provided the burakumin employment; see Matsudaira Yasuo, *Arakawa-ku no rekishi*, Tokyo furusato bunkō, vol. 19 (Tokyo: Meichō shuppan, 1979), chaps. 6, 7; and Tokyoshi Arakawa-ku yakusho, *Arakawa-ku-shi*, 2 vols. (Tokyo: Kawaguchi insatsujo, 1936).

of short coat so they could come and worship. In this way I was able to work for the ancestors. Some of them had such bad cases of lice that they couldn't move.

Every day the landlords would come and collect the daily rent of twenty-five or fifty sen, or whatever they were charging, and they came every day in the evening to get whatever money the ragpickers had made at work that day. If they were sick, the ragpickers couldn't even afford rice gruel. I was doing cold water austerities every morning, and every day about daybreak produce trucks passed along the road steadily, like the beads in a rosary, and cabbages and greens fell as they went by. I'd pick them up and wash them in the river and take them to the sick ragpickers who couldn't get out of bed and cook them in salt or make soup, and we'd eat them together. That's how I spent my days. I didn't care about money; I wanted to heal their sickness.

. . . .

For a number of years I hadn't bathed in hot water; I was doing cold water austerities several times a day. When summer came I couldn't buy new clothes, so I started doing take-home work like blowing up balloons, stuffing envelopes, or making parachutes. I had to earn twenty-five sen per day, and then I had to pay for gas, electricity, and charcoal. Besides that I spent seven sen a day for incense to light when I visited the ragpickers' homes and worshipped their ancestors. For an altar they had only an orange crate or a shelf made out of a board on which they put only the death register and the sutra. They couldn't afford incense, and of course candles were out of the question. They were so badly off that I would take incense with me to worship. At the end of my hundred days there, almost all of them had converted.[47]

The conversion of these families was a milestone for Kotani. In one hundred days she proved her ability to organize and lead. She provided Kubo with a following, and more importantly, she established her competence as a healer. Success in healing must have convinced her once and for all that worship of ancestors is the true path to salvation and must have persuaded her converts of her spiritual powers. It was through the conversion of these six hundred families that the public career of Kotani and the organization of Reiyukai were launched.

Kotani made common cause with the original followers by sharing their poverty and introducing a ritual and beliefs supposedly capable of improving the conditions in which they lived.

[47] Kotani, *Watakushi no shugyō*, pp. 23–25.

Combined with ancestor worship performed through recitation of an abridged version of the Lotus Sutra was the idea that a genuine change of heart and repentence would surely lead to benefits in this life, such as healing of physical illness and improvement of economic condition. Kotani's sincerity made her message convincing.

Kotani does not relate how the healings she worked occurred, but from the context we may suppose that an important part of it lay in the improvement of diet and hygiene. She provided vegetables for these converts, rare delicacies according to contemporary accounts of slum life which hold that rice and salt were the staples. For those afflicted with body lice to the point of debilitation, a bar of lye soap alone would constitute a cure. For people living so close to the edge of survival, relatively simple innovations such as these produced major improvements in the quality of life.

But healing is a more complicated matter. Kotani addressed the problem of self-respect and self-worth directly by denying the contemporary notion that a ragpicker's trade is unclean.

Those people worshipped their ancestors; their trade is not unclean. They remanufacture things others have thrown away and play an important role in society. Some people grow crops in a field, some grow timber in the mountains, or run a business with their own financial means. Ragpickers have no financial means, but they pick up the things other people have thrown away and make them into new things and so play important roles in society. I realized that not just anybody can do the work they do.[48]

A doctrine of social equality was from the very beginning an important element of Reiyukai's teaching. To deny the notions that stigmatized ragpicking and the other trades traditionally performed by burakumin was a radical statement requiring considerable courage in Taisho Japan. Kotani's encouraging these early converts to take pride in themselves and their work also played a part in healing.

In organizing these converts, it is probable that Kotani depended initially on women converts. It would have been difficult for a woman to approach men directly as potential converts, without alienating the women in their families. However, if the

[48] Ibid., p. 24.

cooperation of women in the household were secured, there would be no problem in approaching the men through their mediation. Other women would take for granted that Kotani would have more in common with them, and that her teaching would have special relevance for them. In fact, since much of the teaching bore on the norms and values of the family system, its relevance *was* slanted toward women, because the family system is thought to represent a greater part of their lives than men's, as men are assumed to have a sphere of life outside the home (work) which women do not share.[49]

In accounts of a 1927 healing, Kotani shows how she depended on organizing a group of women to guarantee the success of proselytization of an area around Kubo's birthplace. Word came from Kominato that the wife of an old friend had become insane and been put away in a padded cell. Kimi had a dream that something precious was buried behind that family's house. She traveled there to investigate, and it soon came out that an ancestor of theirs had been the first priest of Tanjōji 誕生寺, the temple where Nichiren had taken the precepts. In this priest's old age, he had collected river stones and written the entire Lotus Sutra on them, accumulating tens of thousands of these stones. Kotani had a second dream in which it was revealed that the stones were the buried treasure of the first dream, and that they should be dug up. A large number of village people collected to unearth them, and an air of great excitement prevailed for three days of excavation. When the stones were fashioned into a monument, the insane woman was cured by worshipping it, implying that the merit of spreading the Dharma by bringing the sutra into the world again in this new form had returned the woman to sanity. Kotani had the woman's fellow inmates at the asylum worship the monument, and they also were cured. All of them were women who had married into the locale from elsewhere and thus were "utter stran-

---

[49] Murakami Shigeyoshi, *Kindai minshū shūkyō no kenkyū* (Tokyo: Hōzōkan, 1972), p. 21. Murakami discusses the traditional role of women in leading popular religious movements based on healing. See also Oguri Junko, *Nihon no kindai shakai to Tenrikyō*, Nihonjin no kōdō to shisō, vol. 7 (Tokyo: Hyōronsha, 1976), chap. 1; Yasumaru Yoshio, *Deguchi Nao* (Tokyo: Asahi shimbunsha, 1977), chaps. 1–4.

gers." They became converts and helped in the conversion of the area.[50]

Studies of the Japanese new religions have relied almost without exception on the notion of social crisis in interpreting the emergence and continuation of these groups. It is argued that conditions of social crisis have existed since roughly the beginning of the Meiji era (1868–1912) to the present, and that the groups known as the new religions arose successively in response to those conditions. H. Neil McFarland writes that from the middle of the eighteenth century to the present, frequent changes of political power and government policies increased the oppression of the common people who, in reaction

sought aid and security in . . . their religious tradition. . . . The anxieties of those who have accepted the solutions proferred by the New Religions have stemmed from poverty, illness, powerlessness, and confusion of values, especially those governing personal and familial relations. . . . The New Religions arose primarily to shelter the masses from the impact of a threatening world. . . . Initially they functioned as crisis religions.[51]

While a general correlation between the appearance of religious groups and social crisis is easily recognized, the momentary sense of the idea of crisis is strained by the proposition that the crisis has lasted from the mid-eighteenth century to the present. It seems improbable that the heightened intellectual and emotional states these authors associate with crisis could be sustained over generations or that the various changes and crises occurring during this period would have a uniform influence upon religious groups. Furthermore, while the word "crisis" could readily be applied to the immediate postwar period, it is clearly inapplicable to con-

[50] Kotani, *Watakushi no shugyō* pp. 43–45.

[51] H. Neil McFarland, *The Rush Hour of the Gods* (New York: Harper Colophon Books, 1967), pp. 11–15. The term "crisis religion" is not further defined. The view that the new religions have arisen in response to social crisis is endorsed by these authors, among others: Togawa Isamu, *Gendai no shinkō shūkyō* (Tokyo: Taiyō, 1976), pp. 7–10; Anesaki Masaharu, *The Religious Life of the Japanese People* (Tokyo: Kokusai Bunka Shinkōkai, 1970), p. 96; Takagi Hirō, *Nihon no shinkō shūkyō* (Tokyo: Iwanami shoten, 1959); Saki, *Godai kyōso*; Murakami, *Nihon hyakunen no shūkyō*.

temporary Japan. "Crisis" is seldom defined precisely, and thus various senses of its vernacular usage are applied rather indiscriminately.[52]

Often associated with the view that the new religions are "crisis religions" is the assumption that their significance is therefore expressive rather than instrumental, that they allow people to make an immediate, emotional response to the problems of the crisis, but are not, realistically speaking, appreciably effective in solving those problems. As McFarland continues, describing the members of the new religions,

[They are] those who feel the great pressures of life in the modern world but who have too little discernment to be fully aware of the real complexity of current issues. To such persons, the prospect of finding immediate solutions to persistent problems seems not only attractive, but quite feasible. The causes of crisis, they suppose, must be knowable and susceptible to some kind of direct counteraction.[53]

In other words, members of the new religions are seeking quick, emotionally satisfying solutions to problems whose nature they do not correctly understand. Based on these mistaken assumptions, the solutions are bound to fail in all but immediate, emotional gratification. Virtually all scholars who have written on the new religions have accepted this view, tacitly or with frank approbation.[54]

It seems likely that the crisis precipitated by the 1923 earthquake and the general sense of urgency it created may have made it easier for Kotani to collect followers than it was when Kubo tried and failed in 1919. The mood of Japan after the earthquake was apocalyptic, and religious interpretations of the disaster found acceptance. Kubo believed that the earthquake

[52] See sources in note 51, above.

[53] McFarland, *The Rush Hour of the Gods*, pp. 11–15 and *passim*.

[54] Notable exceptions to this generalization are the writings of Japanese *minshūshi* ("People's History") scholars such as Yasumaru Yoshio and Kano Masanao, who treat the new religions in the context of social and intellectual history. See Kano Masanao, *Shihon shugi keisei ki no chitsujo ishiki* (Tokyo: Chikuma shobō, 1969) and Yasumaru Yoshio, *Nihon no kindaika to minshū shisō* (Tokyo: Aoki shoten, 1974).

resulted from the release from hell of evil spirits into the human world. He said that future disaster could be avoided by enshrining these spirits in the same manner as ancestral spirits and by carrying out rites for them. Early converts expressed their acceptance of his views by joining Reiyukai. But they went on to make constructive efforts to cope with the situation. Expressive effectiveness of emotional comfort in the face of crisis was complemented by genuine instrumental effectiveness in improving the lives of early members. Had this not been the case, the group would not have outlived the original crisis situation.[55]

Kotani writes of her original converts that those whom she found living in three-mat rooms soon were able to move to larger houses, and that by dint of frugality, hard work, and mutual aid, many were able substantially to improve their standard of living.[56] Sociologists of religion have often remarked on the tendency for religious groups to facilitate upward social mobility, a form of instrumental effectiveness also seen in Reiyukai.[57] Members combined religious practice with economic mutual assistance, following the customs of religious groups called *kō* 講, "confraternaties," which have existed since the medieval period.[58] By the end of the war Reiyukai's membership was no longer composed mainly of those in dire economic straits, but was concentrated among the self-employed, owners of small businesses or family businesses, small-scale manufacturers, and the like.[59] There was therefore a significant elevation of class status. Although Reiyukai was founded in Arakawa Ward, site of some of prewar Tokyo's worst urban poverty, the first headquarters building was con-

---

[55] It is undoubtedly true that Reiyukai and other new religions have devoted much attention to providing emotional support to the membership, but this aspect has tended to be overemphasized in accounting for their emergence and persistence.

[56] Kotani, *Watakushi no shugyō*, p. 25.

[57] A number of Reiyukai's first-generation leaders have recorded their experiences in autobiographical form. All of them came from the class of the self-employed or owners of small to medium-scale businesses. See the thirteen-volume series of their writings, *Taiken no bukkyō*, published by Reiyukai.

[58] On the historical background of *kō*, see Sakurai Tokutarō, *Nihon minkan shinkōron* (Tokyo: Kōbundō, 1973).

[59] Kotani, *Watakushi no shugyō*, p. 25; see n. 57 above.

structed in 1930 in the more "respectable" Akasaka area, and Reiyukai seems to have left no trace in Arakawa. Thus Reiyukai was able to contribute to members' financial stability and to their upward mobility through its ethic of frugality and restraint of individual desire in the context of family groups united by a common religious practice.[60]

The question why Kotani succeeded where Kubo failed finds an answer not only in the air of crisis which may have facilitated Kotani's attempt but also in the emerging division of labor between them. Kubo was the theorist while Kotani was the charismatic healer skilled in organization. She succeeded in marshaling the considerable energies of women converts to go out on the Tokyo streets to proselytize. No bureaucratic concerns such as may have restrained Kubo, now an employee of the Buildings and Grounds division (*eizenka* 営繕課) of the Imperial Household Ministry, held back Kotani, nor did the necessities of full-time employment. From the time of her conversion, furthering the spread of Reiyukai was her first priority, to which she dedicated the rest of her life. Continuing to accept Kubo's guidance in the area of doctrine, she supervised growing networks of converts in active proselytization. While he addressed public meetings, she worked behind the scenes to coordinate and increase the membership.[61]

The inadequacy of the crisis explanation to account for the origin and persistence of Reiyukai is most acute where it fails to encompass the historical character of the group and its message. To label Reiyukai a reaction to the earthquake would ignore Kubo's intent to found such a group even before 1923, and it ignores the influence upon him of the ideology of Nichirenshugi and the Nichiren-derived spiritualism of Nishida Toshizo. Further, the crisis explanation ignores the inheritance by Reiyukai of such traditional elements of Nichiren Buddhist practice as use of the Lotus Sutra and the daimoku, albeit with purposeful, systematic

---

[60] Reiyukai's earliest code of rules, *Seigyō* 正行, first promulgated in 1934 in the *Reiyukaihō*, specified that members were not to lend or borrow money within the group. On mutual assistance among members of *kō*, see Sakurai, *Nihon minkan shinkōron*, pp. 159–202.

[61] Kotani was officially named president of Reiyukai, and Kubo was its director.

transformations. Lastly, the crisis explanation fails to take seriously the group's intent to address contemporary problems it
perceived in Japanese society, such as the ethical confusion Kubo
perceived well before the earthquake. While the earthquake and
attendant crisis provided the opportunity to effect substantive
innovation and transformation of traditional religious practice,
the impetus to do so and the elements on which changes would be
wrought were present before the crisis, which at most facilitated
organization and recruitment.

Part 2: Expansion under State Supervision

Reiyukai was founded in a period in which the state exercised
increasing supervision over the activities of religious organizations. The passage in 1925 of the Peace Preservation Law granted
the state sweeping powers over religious groups, enforced severely
by the special police forces.[62] Thus Reiyukai and other groups of
the period had to tailor their intellectual development and social
organization to the limits of state tolerance. These limits were
progressively narrowing. Compromise was the price of survival.
From the early 1930s until 1945, Reiyukai behaved increasingly
like one of the bureaucratically inspired, semi-voluntary groups
espousing a patriotic message, such as reservists groups, patriotic
women's societies, and youth groups.[63]

   Reiyukai began printing its periodical *Reiyukaihō* 霊友会報 in
1934, and from the time of its founding until the first issue of this
bulletin there are few sources of information available about the
group. However, in Kotani's autobiography many events of this
early period are recorded, though their sequence and dating is not
always clear. Nevertheless, from this source and from autobiog-
raphies of other early leaders we learn that it was during this
period that Reiyukai grew from a small cult to an organized
religion and established its principal rituals, texts, and beliefs.

   The sutra used in morning the evening worship, the *Aokyōkan*

---

[62] The Tokubetsu Kōtō Keisatsu, established to deal with thought crime and
administered by the Home Ministry, was abolished after 1945.

[63] Kotani, *Watakushi no shugyō*, p. 59.

青経巻, "The Blue Sutra," was codified and distributed in 1931. This work, described in detail in a later chapter, is an abridgement of the Lotus Sutra. Kotani notes that it was decided in 1930 to include in the Blue Sutra additional chapters from the Lotus, with the result that daily recitation took as long as two hours. Later editions shortened the length of time required to about thirty minutes.

Also during this period the ritual of ancestor worship, *senzo kuyō* 先祖供養, was formalized. Sutra recitation is the major element of the rite, performed while wearing a white sash, with the daimoku and the believer's name written on it. Related practices such as offerings of water on the altar, construction of the altar from white wood, and the recitation of formal greetings morning and night before it were established.[64]

A headquarters building established in 1930 in Akasaka was replaced by a larger building on the site of the present headquarters in Azabudai. It is not clear whether there was sufficient revenue at this time to employ believers to handle the administration of the group, though there was a custom of early leaders going daily to the headquarters.[65]

In 1931 Kubo, Kotani, and a small group of early leaders made a formal pilgrimage to the Ise Shrine to declare the group's purpose to the imperial deities and to make a vow to establish a universal ordination platform, a *kaidan* 戒壇. The proof of a school's independence in Buddhism is its qualification to ordain clerics independently of whatever larger group from which it originated. The place in which the ordination platform is located becomes the sacred center of the new group. Kotani describes the events of this pilgrimage by saying that the group followed in the steps of Nichiren when he made an Ise pilgrimage, doing cold water austerities at the same locations and, after midnight, kneeling in the shrine precincts vowing to establish the ordination platform to improve society and the world. The fact that Reiyukai made such a vow at Ise signifies the intention to establish a group dedicated to the nation and to patriotic goals. This promise was

---

[64] This ritual is treated in detail in Chapter 4.

[65] Kusada, *Konjō o naose*, chap. 2.

eventually redeemed in the construction of Mirokusan 弥勒山 in 1964.[66]

Because Reiyukai advocated ancestor worship and a familistic ethic quite similar to what everyone in Japan was taught through the schools, the armed forces, state-sponsored semi-voluntary organizations such as youth groups and the like, its message was not perceived as dangerous or deviant. Further, State Shinto ideology itself was explicitly linked to ancestor worship. Consequently, Reiyukai's mixture of ancestor worship and familistic values was acceptable even within a world of thought controlled by State Shinto.

State Shinto was an artificial creation which had little relation to the religious practice of the people, but which, through skilful utilization of the educational system and other institutions was able to promote a world view and ethic suited to the state's goal of creating an orderly, obedient populace supporting the goals of modernization and territorial expansion. State Shinto depended heavily upon the family system for early training in obedience to the authority of elders and more generally the duty to obey superiors. State textbooks, centrally authored after 1908, dwelt heavily on the duty of children to repay to their parents the debt (*on*) that is "higher than the mountains, deeper than the seas." Duty, filial piety, and obedience were made supreme ethical principles. Loyalty and filial piety were equated in order to promote the idea that the nation was a great, single family united in its mission, with the emperor at its head. That is, the attitude of filial piety toward parents is to be transferred to superiors outside the home. Ancestor worship is the proper religious expression of loyalty and filial piety. Elaborate rites centering on the Yasukuni Shrine 靖国神社 to worship spirits of the war dead constituted ancestor worship on a national scale, paralleling domestic ancestor worship in which families were required to enshrine talismans from the Ise Shrine, sacred center of the imperial cult.[67]

---

[66] Kotani, *Watakushi no shugyō*, p. 62.

[67] Murakami Shigeyoshi, *Kokka shintō* (Tokyo: Iwanami shoten, 1970); Kishimoto Hideo, *Japanese Religion in the Meiji Era*, trans. John Howes, vol 2: *Japanese Culture in the Meiji Era* (Tokyo: Ōbunsha, 1956), pp. 5–74; Yasumaru Yoshio, *Nihon nashionarizumu no zen'ya*, Asahi sensho, vol. 94 (Tokyo: Asahi

The notion of the Japanese as a single family, presided over by the emperor as patriarch, in which role expectations and obligations were parallel inside and outside the home, presented a view of society as a smoothly working hierarchy of complementary functions, without divisive cleavages of interest or opportunity. This view was in radical opposition to emerging Japanese socialist and communist interpretations of society as composed of antagonistic forces, stratified by class and inevitably opposed. The usefulness of the state's familistic view of society to its goal of creating a manageable populace is obvious. The family and the workplace (or military service) were considered complementary spheres between which there was no real conflict; employers or other superiors were, on this view, parental figures who rightfully took a paternalistic attitude toward subordinates. Toward superiors, subordinates should be grateful, loyal, filial. Workers and capitalists should join together to carry out the will of the emperor.[68]

The proper expression of subjects' loyalty and filial piety was ancestor worship, which paralleled the emperor's worship of the imperial ancestors, expressing the union of nation and family. As the individual was to the family, so was the family to the nation, yielding the proposition that the structure of the family replicates the structure of the nation. Ancestor worship was used as a symbolic expression of the analogy and thus was given a political meaning in State Shinto. This political meaning was lacking in common conception and domestic practice before the advent of State Shinto.[69]

State Shinto had a militaristic component which included the

---

shimbunsha, 1977), pp. 38–81; Gotō Yasushi, "Meiji no tennōsei to minshū," in *Tennōsei to minshū*, ed. Gotō Yasushi (Tokyo: Tokyo daigaku shuppankai, 1976), pp. 111–30; Robert K. Hall, *Shūshin, the Ethics of a Defeated Nation* (New York: Bureau of Publications, Teachers' College, Columbia University, 1949), pp. 11–17; Maruyama Masao, *Thought and Behavior in Modern Japanese Politics*, expanded ed. (London: Oxford University Press, 1969), chaps. 1, 2, 4; David C. Holtom, *Shinto, National Faith of Japan* (London: Kegan Paul, Trench, Trubner, 1938); and Holtom, *Modern Japan and Shinto Nationalism* (Chicago: University of Chicago Press, 1947).

[68] Murakami, *Kokka shintō*, chap. 3 *passim*.
[69] Ibid.

idea that Japan has a sacred mission to spread its way of life to other Asian nations and to establish the Greater East Asia Co-Prosperity Sphere, an idea based on notions of racial superiority. This component of State Shinto ideology had only passing and peripheral influence upon Reiyukai.[70]

There is little doubt that many Japanese found the ideology of State Shinto unconvincing and the authoritarian manner in which it was forced upon the people repellent. Nevertheless, it was so inescapably pervasive that it inevitably shaped the thought of millions. Its competitors were so completely suppressed by the mid-1930s that it was accepted by those lacking exposure to alternative systems of thought. Certainly it was the most influential ideology of Reiyukai's early history.[71]

Reiyukai's founders grew up in a society dominated by the world view of State Shinto, and they had little or no contact with any other philosophical views. We find no hint of influence from the leftist political parties or ideologies of the period. As for most Japanese of the times, the idea of the nation as a single family, the idea of a diffuse obligation, *on*, owed to all superiors, duty as the supreme ethical principle, and the importance of ancestor worship in repaying obligation were taken by the founders as inherent in the order of the world, not matters of scrutiny or debate. The founders were not actively interested in the political component of State Shinto. Focusing on the family and ancestor worship, they assumed that when people live in accordance with familistic ideals they will be in harmony with the world order and therefore will be happy, healthy, and moderately prosperous.

---

[70] During the 1930s and continuing through 1945, all religious groups had to pay lip service to the state cult. Reiyukai was no exception to this rule, and the nationalistic rhetoric that appears in its pre-1945 publications is not particularly more extreme than comparable writings from other groups of the period.

[71] Yasumaru, *Nihon no kindaika*, pp. 4–7. Yasumaru discusses the power over the minds of the people held by the ethical ideas of State Shinto and shows how difficult it was for most people to escape the web of concepts so deeply embedded in popular ethical thought. Western writers, on the other hand, such as Edward Norbeck, *Religion and Society in Modern Japan* (Houston: Tourmaline Press, 1970), p. 59, have written that it is caricature to assume that all Japanese believed in the ideas of State Shinto. However, the influence of the system on society was immense, and for many people today the familistic image of society promoted by State Shinto remains unquestioned.

The 1930s saw major suppression of religious groups under the Peace Preservation Law on charges of "disrespect" to the throne, lese majesty. Long the object of government suspicion, Omotokyo promulgated an independent formulation of agrarianism (*nōhon-shugi* 農本主義) to counter government policy. This was taken to be an incipient *coup d'état*, and in December 1935, 550 police descended on Omoto headquarters and destroyed it entirely, arresting group members all over the country. Many died in prison. Hitonomichi ひとのみち had consistently toed the government line by advocating worship of the emperor in order to avoid persecution. However, the group was charged with holding a "vulgar" interpretation of national mythology, and in 1936 it was branded an "evil religion" (*jakyō* 邪教) and its leaders imprisoned. In 1938 Honmichi ほんみち, a pacifist schism from Tenrikyo, was proscribed and 1,000 of its members rounded up when the leader Ōnishi Aijirō 大西愛治郎 published a pamphlet warning the nation of impending disaster. Onishi was jailed and died in prison. Seichō no Ie 生長の家, which had split off from Omoto in 1929, fared better largely because it wholeheartedly endorsed state propaganda. Seicho no Ie and Reiyukai in fact were the religious groups suffering least damage in the thirties and forties. However, Kotani was once jailed for distributing pamphlets, and this incident made acute the need to find a means of coexistence with the state.[72]

Kubo continued working at the Imperial Household Ministry for some time after the founding of Reiyukai and thus did not devote full time to it. He abridged the Lotus Sutra for daily recitation and codified doctrine and ritual, while Kotani concentrated on proselytization. He also maintained important contacts with the nobility through the Kubo and Sengoku houses, which were of use in avoiding government suppression.[73]

Clear trends in Reiyukai's thought emerged in the 1930s. A strong anti-clerical philosophy asserted the legitimacy of layman's Buddhism and emphasized personal experience of the truth of ancestor worship and the effectiveness of ancestral rites in healing.

---

[72] Murakami, *Nihon hyakunen no shūkyō*, pp. 122–35 and Kotani, *Watakushi no shugyō*, p. 53.

[73] In particular, Kubo enlisted the Nichiren Buddhist nun and member of the nobility, Kujō Murakumo 九条村雲. See Murakami, *Nihon shūkyō jiten*, p. 417.

Many testimonies were published, and a great proportion of the articles in the *Reiyukaiho* were devoted to the theme of women's role and mission. Approximately half of the articles were written by women, and it is quite apparent that women were taking the lead in proselytization. As time went on, however, and especially after the declaration of war, the number of articles about Reiyukai's teaching decreased markedly, replaced by State Shinto thought stressing the value of loyalty and filial piety with scarcely any mention of the Buddhist themes seen in earlier years.[74]

Each issue of *Reiyukaiho* featured a sermon by Kotani or Kubo, followed by a statement of the group's mission. Just below these were articles explaining why laymen must conduct their own ancestral rites, without priests. The second and succeeding pages were taken up by articles on such topics as the mission of Japanese women, the true Japanese spirit, or by testimonies. Sometimes continuing articles on some theme appeared. All articles were accompanied by phonetic script (*furigana*), for those unfamiliar with more complicated Sino-Japanese characters. Periodic mention of newly founded chapters of the group indicates that the group was growing very fast, though exact statistics for this period are unavailable.[75]

The statement of mission, repeated in each issue, shows how the group hoped to put itself at the service of the nation.

The Mission of the Dainippon Reiyukai

Following the laws of the universe;
Reverently accepting the sacred teachings of the Great Japanese Empire;
Adapting ourselves to the times in accordance with change;
Faithfully following the highest aspiration of mankind;
Expounding the True Law;
Extending it widely to mankind;
Preserving the divine pronouncement of myriad ages past;
Without sparing our lives in so doing;
Setting aside many sorrows and brightening the darkness of mankind;

[74] The space allotted to ideas uniquely Reiyukai's decreased even more rapidly after 1940.

[75] *Reiyukaiho*, No. 1 (Sept. 8, 1934), p. 3; No. 3 (Dec. 9, 1934), p. 2; No. 93 (April 31, 1938), p. 2.

Completing the establishment of the one, great ordination platform;
Erecting upon a changeless foundation with ten trillion hurrahs;
The pure, single, and wondrous nation of the ancestors and buddhas;
Such is our purpose.[76]

Ancestor worship was erected as the central practice by the early Reiyukai leaders, who conceived that the rites could adequately be performed by individual families. In upholding the priesthood of all believers, the group poured scorn on the Buddhist clergy. These were accused of mediocrity, of encouraging vice, and of being mercenary. If each family would correctly worship its ancestors according to the teachings of Reiyukai, Japan would escape destruction and be saved. The ancestors cannot achieve salvation through priestly ritual; the solution is for each family to care for its own ancestors. The temples are useless and should be turned into nurseries and kindergartens. Parishioners should cease paying contributions to the temples. All the clergy is good for is guarding the bones of the dead. This message was sounded repeatedly and with increasing volume.[77]

Perhaps in reaction to the liberalism of early Taisho and the new women's movement, many articles in *Reiyukaiho* were devoted to the mission of women to be good wives and wise mothers of children who will grow up to be good subjects. It is their duty to "protect" the home and raise their children to be loyal and filial. They are the pillars of the family, and they must uphold its ideals. These ideas are given Buddhistic coloration by being mixed with ideas about women's karma, which women must expiate in order to fulfill their duty in society. Women must uphold the Imperial Rescript on Education and teach virtue in the home, and in so doing they can achieve salvation (*nyonin jōbutsu* 女人成仏). Women should cultivate mercy, modesty, and restraint in speech and action as well as fidelity, simplicity, and personal cleanliness. Conquests of defects in women's nature due to karma and pollution can be overcome in Reiyukai, and this personal victory has a patriotic meaning. One woman writes: "Through this religion, namely the spirit of the Lotus Sutra, I have realized that I can

[76] *Reiyukaiho*, No. 1 (Sept. 8, 1934).
[77] Ibid. These ideas are found in virtually any issue of the periodical.

throw away my weak female nature and stand up for my country like a man." [78]

Another woman gives her views on how women must protect the home front during the war. She says that since women go to other families as brides, it is only natural that they have their own hopes and desires. Yet there are some who wonder whether the ancestors of the household into which they marry are their ancestors as well. This is willful and selfish. The woman who becomes a bride in the new household takes on its ancestors as her own, starting with the husband's mother and father. It is unfilial to think otherwise. To realize this is the beginning of serious thought about the nation. Women on the home front must perservere and join their hearts with the brave soldiers at the front. To do this they must save their ancestors; this is the meaning of loyalty and filial piety. [79]

Once into the 1940s it became apparent that Reiyukai had put itself at the service of state ideology, as the following article shows.

Respect for the Gods, Ancestor Worship, and Buddhism

Respect for the gods and the worship of ancestors is natural; it is true *senzo kuyo*. Respect for the gods and worship of ancestors is not a concept, it is a way of life. It is not a custom, but training for true human life.

In Japan, philosophy is respect for the gods and ancestor worship. This is Japanese history. Our national polity has always been built upon it, and accordingly it is the basis for growth and development.

Professor Kubo fought a solitary battle on a thorny path with no support and no place of refuge, alone, by his own flesh and blood, always in silence, spreading the true teaching for Tenshō Daijin 天照大神 [better known as Amaterasu Ōmikami, the sun goddess, apex of the State Shinto pantheon] and the worship of ancestors ... with a deep realization of Japan's mission.

Loyalty and filial piety are the basis of a truly Japanese humanity; they are the Japanese way. Speaking of this in a Buddhist way, it is the true practice of layman's ancestor worship. Japanese Buddhism is actually Buddhism for the protection of the state. Buddhism in our country exists

[78] Kiyota Nuhiko, "Katei seikatsu to fujin," *Reiyukaiho*, No. 160 (June 12, 1943), p. 2.

[79] Miki Takako, "Fujin no tachiba," *Reiyukaiho*, No. 159 (May 12, 1943), p. 4.

for the purpose of promoting loyalty and filial piety, and for protecting the nation.[80]

This and many other similar articles show how completely the group had to subordinate its own development to the demands of the state cult. As the war went on, a large volume of articles was devoted to diatribes against England and the United States, with predictable wartime rhetoric to the effect that the inhabitants of those countries have no conception of familial relations or the Japanese way, that they are cannibals, little better than animals or even vegetables, and so on. Japan must by all means win the war, establish the Greater East Asian Co-Prosperity Sphere, and thus fulfill its divine mission. Needless to say, this type of writing disappeared completely after 1945.[81]

Until the end of the war, the women's group under Kotani conducted a series of public service projects to aid the war effort, collecting money, making comfort kits for the soldiers, providing free medical consultation and treatment, and forming a service corps to work in the gardens of the Imperial Palace. They also held public lecture series. All these activities helped the group escape suppression.[82]

Although everyone in Japan was taught the values of the family system through State Shinto, its agencies of indoctrination such as reservists groups, women's groups, youth groups, and others, were much stronger in the countryside, where they dovetailed with previously existing cooperative societies in the villages. They were comparatively less effective in the cities. Reiyukai's original followers, lacking exposure to alternative systems of thought, were probably rather easily drawn into a group that combined many elements of government ideology while promising a release from sickness and misfortune. Reiyukai called for no fundamental revolution of thought nor for any opposition to the forces of order or the prevailing ideology. Had it done so, it would quickly have

---

[80] Naganuma Masao, "Keishin sūso to bukkyō," *Reiyukaiho*, No. 134 (April 12, 1941), p. 1.

[81] *Reiyukaiho*, No. 171 (Dec. 5, 1944), p. 2.

[82] These activities are given prominent coverage in each issue of *Reiyukaiho*.

been silenced. Its message carried a strong sense of personal relevance and urgency through the elements of healing and the notion that performing ancestor worship leads to a release from suffering. At the same time, the group increasingly aligned its ideals and activities with State Shinto ideology, thus drawing Reiyukai members, for better or for worse, into the mainstream.[83]

Part 3: Reorientation and Renewal

The end of the war was for Reiyukai as for all Japan a period of great trial and suffering. Kubo died in 1944, and Kotani succeeded him. At the end of the war, the great cities of Japan were evacuated, and many Reiyukai members went out to the country-side and made large numbers of converts, though previously there had been few members in rural areas.[84] Their proselytization on all fronts was very successful, and by 1945 Reiyukai was nearly the largest of the new religions.[85] However, disengaging from a long period of state supervision was not easy and required con-siderable reorientation. Problems in setting a new course were aggravated by strife surrounding Kotani's succession and by nu-merous schisms, all related to her authoritarian style of leadership, which was more in keeping with the mores of prewar Japan. To make matters worse, the group became entangled in highly dam-aging legal battles which for a time badly tarnished the group's public image and put an end to its high rate of growth. When

---

[83] On the role of such bureaucratically inspired groups in prewar Japanese society, see Shimamura Atsuki, "Daitoshi ni okeru kenryoku to minshū no dōkō," in *Taishōki no kenryoku to minshū*, ed. Koyama Hitoshi (Tokyo: Hōritsu bun-kasha, 1980), pp. 55–72; Kano Masanao, "Meiji kōki ni okeru kokumin soshikika no katei," *Shirin* 69 (Mar., 1964), 18–46; Nakamura Masanori, "Keizai kōsei undō to nōmin tōgō," in *Shōwa kyōkō*, ed. Tokyo daigaku shakai kagaku kenkyūjo (Tokyo: Tokyo daigaku shakai kagaku kenkyūjo, 1978), pp. 197–262; Sasaki Ryūji, "Nihon gunkoku shugi no shakaiteki kiban no keisei," *Nihonshi kenkyū*, No. 68 (Sept., 1963), 1–30; Suzuki Masayuki, "Nichiro sengo no nōson mondai no tenkai," *Rekishi gaku kenkyū*, special issue (1974), 150–61; Richard Smethurst, *A Social Basis for Prewar Japanese Militarism* (Berkeley: University of California Press, 1974), pp. 67–87.

[84] Kotani, *Watakushi no shugyō*, chap. 3.

[85] Ministry of Education, *Shūkyō nenkan*, 1947.

Kotani died in 1971, she bequeathed to her successor Kubo Tsugunari (久保継成) the difficult task of reconciling the old guard with the values of contemporary society, of improving the group's public image, and of formulating a universal message out of the prewar ethic of familism and ancestor worship. His success in these areas has been considerable, and at present the group is growing and facing up to the challenges of the present and future with resolution.

Kotani consolidated her position as Kubo's successor through the allegiance of the women's group in Reiyukai, the Kunitomo Fujinkai 国友婦人会 (Patriotic Women's Society), and by the fact that Kubo had entrusted her with raising his son Tsugunari at an early age. The women's group was headed by Kotani, and until her death it was the most active agency within Reiyukai. She trained other women, who remained loyal to her and thus provided her with a base of power. The combination of this with the guardianship of Kubo's son assured her position, though there were by that time other powerful leaders within Reiyukai.[86]

Reiyukai is organized into branches that enjoy considerable autonomy. Each branch leader collects monthly fees and has a direct or indirect proselytization tie to each branch member. There is no such tie between the headquarters and individual members. Thus, their most direct loyalty is to the branch leader, and before the construction of Shakaden 釈迦殿, the headquarters where all Reiyukai members worship a common object, a statue of Shakyamuni, without respect to branch membership, the tie between the branches and the headquarters depended in effect upon the relations between the branch leaders and Kotani, and these were often bad. As a consequence, there ensued a series of schisms, the most significant of which was that of Niwano Nikkyō 庭野日敬 and Naganuma Myōkō 長沼妙佼, who founded Risshōkōsekai 立正佼成会 in 1938.[87] This pair had formerly led a branch in Reiyukai, which developed such distinctive features as doctrinal study groups led by Niwano. Kotani greatly disliked this, and as a result there has never again been a serious doctrinal

[86] Kotani, *Watakushi no shugyō*, chap. 3.
[87] Watanabe Umeo, *Gendai nihon*, pp. 324–37; Saki, *Godai kyōso*, pp. 84–87.

study forum within Reiyukai. Kotani publically criticized Niwano and said he was introducing heretical practices. She demanded absolute obedience from her followers, and those who were not prepared to submit to her authority completely had no lasting place within the group.[88]

After 1945 nationalistic propaganda disappeared from the pages of Reiyukai publications, and like other new religious groups the byword of the early postwar era was world peace. However, the group's vision of society remained largely unchanged, as did the centrality of norms and values derived from the prewar family system.[89]

Reiyukai's message since 1945 has self-consciously been opposed to "individualism" and seeks the meaning of human life in the family system. Human existence, especially women's, is assumed to take place almost exclusively within this framework, and salvation can only be achieved through strict adherence to its precepts. The claims of the family are nearly absolute in Reiyukai; one hears little even of the idea of *ninjō* 人情, "human feelings," which elsewhere in Japanese society is feebly invoked to counterbalance the claims of duty. The absoluteness of these claims is given a religious significance by the Buddhist coloration of the ideas of karma and repentence, and by the deities of the system, the ancestors. Reiyukai saw a threat to this system in the postwar changes in traditional Japanese culture. The call for a return to the values of the family system continues to be the group's major message.

After the war Reiyukai suffered a series of legal embroilments that seem to have been connected with factional strife within the group. In 1946 Reiyukai sponsored the building of a hospital in Tokyo. According to Kotani, some of the doctors involved in the project asked her to store some drugs and gold bullion until the hospital had been completed. Since the headquarters was equipped for safe storage, the request to store drugs was not unnatural, though the question of the bullion is less clear. However, factional strife was rampant at the time, and it appears that some of the

---

[88] Murakami, *Nihon shūkyō jiten*, p. 417.
[89] Ibid., p. 418.

partisans notified the Occupation authorities, who confiscated the material. The press gave highly sensational coverage to the event, implying that Reiyukai was somehow involved in illegal drug and currency traffic, but there was never any hard evidence to prove the charges conclusively.[90]

In 1950 an original calligraphic work in Nichiren's hand was removed from the Kuonji 久遠寺 temple and was later discovered in the Reiyukai headquarters. This event also appears to have been connected with infighting, but again it generated sensational press coverage which greatly damaged the group's image and reduced the membership.[91]

The most damaging incident occurred in 1953, when Reiyukai was accused of embezzling money from the Red Cross in the course of a collection drive, and with tax evasion for not reporting the embezzled funds as taxable income. Kotani and two other leaders were arrested. In the end these two confessed, and charges against Kotani were dropped, though not before the press informally interviewed a number of people willing to testify to such character faults as cruelty and greed, again in lurid detail. The informal allegations so obviously derived from jealousy and resentment that they do not merit serious, literal consideration, but they show that Kotani had many enemies. This incident finally slowed the unimpeded growth Reiyukai had enjoyed since its founding. It was soon overshadowed by other groups.[92]

The women's group continued its activities after the war, donating goods and funds to centers for the aged, orphans, the handicapped, and children. They planted thousands of cherry trees to beautify the bombed cities, and they released great numbers of fish into the lakes in city parks. They tried to aid families to locate

---

[90] Kotani Kimi, *Ten no ongaku* (Tokyo: Reiyukai, 1972); Kotani Kimi and Ishihara Shintarō, *Ningen no genten* (Tokyo: Sankei shimbun, 1969); National Diet Library special clipping file concerning Reiyukai; Saki, *Godai kyōso*, pp. 77–84. It seems that Reiyukai employed as an "advisor" a former head of the Safety Agency (National Police Agency, Prime Minister's Office), Kimura Tokutarō. Witnesses testified that Kimura was paid immense sums and received as presents many valuable works of art from Reiyukai for his role as intermediary between the group and national police and legal agencies.

[91] National Diet Library special clipping file concerning Reiyukai.

[92] Ibid.

Table 1. Reiyukai Membership

Year	Total	Year	Total
1930	500	1972[a]	2,020,353
1937	30,000	1973	2,267,818
1941	100,000	1974	2,304,112
1949	1,815,944	1976	2,477,907
1966	4,198,635	1977	2,528,756
1971	4,259,589	1979	2,838,000
		1982	2,962,880

Source: Statistics Bureau of Reiyukai Headquarters.

[a] In 1972, the method of calculation was changed from counting membership application cards to counting monthly dues received.

missing members and undertook to have the remains of the war dead enshrined in the Yasukuni Shrine. They performed prolonged rites to pacify the spirits of the war dead and bestowed posthumous names upon them.[93]

Significant new construction projects began. The new headquarters, Shakaden, dedicated to the Buddha Shakyamuni, was completed only after Kotani's death, but Mirokusan, dedicated to the Future Buddha Maitreya, was completed in 1964. It was the completion of Mirokusan that fulfilled the promise of Kotani and Kubo to construct an ordination platform. Also in 1964, Meihōgakuen 明法学園, a school including kindergarten through high school, was opened in Higashi Murayama, not far from Tokyo.[94]

Kotani traveled abroad to open overseas missions on a small scale. She was accompanied by Kubo Tsugunari, who has expanded these overseas projects to include South American and Asian nations.[95] As will be seen below, these foreign missions are currently something of a sore subject.

Kotani established connections with politicians of the Right in the Liberal Democratic Party, and Reiyukai became a patron of Ishihara Shintarō 石原慎太郎, a conservative leader.[96] A book of

[93] Kotani, *Watakushi no shugyō*, chap. 3.
[94] Saki, *Godai kyōso*, pp. 88–91.
[95] Kotani, *Watakushi no shugyō*, chaps. 5 and 6.
[96] Kotani and Ishihara, *Ningen no genten*.

Table 2. *Groups Originating as Schisms from Reiyukai*

Year of Founding	Group	Founder
1930	Nihon keishin sūso jishūdan 日本敬神崇祖自修団	Wakatsuki Chise, 若月チセ Betsugi Sadao 別木定雄
1935	Kōdō Kyōdan 孝道教団	Okano Shōdō 岡野正道
1936	Sankai Kyōdan 三界教団	Takahashi Kakutarō 高橋覚太郎
1938	Shishinkai 思親会 Risshōkōseikai 立正佼成会	Ido Kiyoyuki 井戸清行 Naganuma Myōkō, 長沼妙佼 Niwano Nikkyō 庭野日敬
1948	Hakuaidōshikai Kyōdan 博愛同志会教団	Naganuma Ginjirō 長沼銀次郎
1950	Myōchikai Kyōdan 妙智会教団 Busshogonenkai Kyōdan 仏所護念会教団 Kuonkai 久遠会 Hōshikai 法師会	Miyamoto Mitsu 宮本ミツ Sekiguchi Tomino 関口トミノ Hisamatsu Shūtō 久松修等 Saitō Chiyo 斉藤千代
1951	Daieikai Kyōdan 大慧会教団 Myōdōkai Kyōdan 妙道会教団 Daijikai Kyōdan 大慈会教団 Seigikai Kyōdan 正義会教団	Ishikura Matsue 石倉マツエ Sahara Chūjirō 佐原忠次郎 Iwatate Kōkichi 岩楯光吉 Yamaguchi Masae 山口まさえ
1953	Kishinkai 希心会	Iijima Shōkichi 飯島将吉

dialogues between Kotani and Ishihara was published, and its content well illustrates the orientation of Reiyukai under Kotani's leadership.

Kotani: You often hear that old people should obey their children, but children must respect their parents. ... This is what we teach in Reiyukai.

Mothers-in-law and daughters-in-law must live in harmony. When men marry, they tend to dote on their wives, who naturally don't get on too well with the husband's mother. In Reiyukai daughters-in-law get on well with their mothers-in-law. When the daughter-in-law gets up in the morning, she greets the ancestors, saying, "Good morning." Then she also says "Good morning" to her husband and his parents. At night she says, "Good night, Mother," to her mother-in-law, even out in the countryside, in farm families. No mother-in-law can hate a daughter-in-law like that.... No bad children can come from such families.[97]

. . . .

Kotani: Women these days seem to have stopped having many children. Usually they have about two. What do you think about that, Mr. Ishihara?

Ishihara: I think they ought to have five or six, myself.

Kotani: I think so, too. Why is it that women these days won't bear children?

Ishihara: Well, to make a long story short, they're thinking of nobody but themselves. They aren't thinking of mankind as a whole. They have no desire to produce descendants, and in a nutshell, they think only of their own comfort. They think children are a bother, so they put off having them for as long as possible. A concern for humanity is lacking in modern man.

Kotani: If we go on like this, the Japanese people will decrease drastically, as in ancient France.

Ishihara: Well, people talk about a population problem, but when the number of children decreases, I think it's a problem of selfishness on the part of people who ought to become parents. I'm afraid that our great possibilities as Japanese are slipping away. As for me, when my first child was born, for the first time, there were ancestors and descendants, like the links of a chain that had been connected. I felt that I'd become a link in the chain for the first time.

Kotani: That's so true. It's exactly as you say. That's because it is also through children that karma is transmitted. When people do good, good karma is created.[98]

A return to the values of the old family system is thus seen as a panacea for a variety of social problems.

Since Kotani's death in 1971 Reiyukai has been headed by Kubo Tsugunari. He is a graduate of the doctoral program in Buddhist Sanskrit Literature at the University of Tokyo, and his intellectual interests and training have provided new points of

[97] Ibid., pp. 109–110.
[98] Ibid.

departure in leadership. Under his presidency the Youth Group has become the most active agency in Reiyukai, overshadowing the women's group. This enlargement of the role of the Youth Group, which occurred in other new religious groups also, became conspicuous around 1955. The Youth Group now takes the lead in foreign missions. Here and in Youth Group publications, Kubo has tried to change the image of Reiyukai by deemphasizing elements that are easily ridiculed by the press as "superstitious," "irrational," and so on. Thus healing and related practices currently receive less public attention. English slogans such as "Inner Trip" as a code word for Reiyukai are used in mass media advertising, and foreign members are cultivated.[99]

A major test of Kubo's attempt at image-change was a missions campaign directed mainly to North and South America, called Inner Trip, lasting from about 1972 to 1977. Branch offices in Brazil, Canada, Mexico, and the United States attempted to increase membership by offering special tours to Japan with emphasis on Reiyukai establishments, including a trip to Mirokusan where participants underwent a modified version of the training program there. However, most left Japan with only a vague understanding of Reiyukai, and some failed to distinguish it from a discount travel agency. As a result, few of those who enrolled in Reiyukai (one of the requirements for the discounts) remained, and the net gain of members was minuscule. Unfortunately, the group was subsidizing the Inner Trip tours with borrowed money, and went rather heavily into debt to finance this unsuccessful venture. Kubo cannot have risen in the estimation of older, more experienced leaders, who do not readily accept change.[100]

Kubo's image-change has so far been more stylistic than substantive, but there is some reason to think it may encourage more divisiveness. The independence and autonomy of the branches make it possible for a strong local leader to leave Reiyukai, taking all the branch members. The bulk of the membership is now located not in Kantō area and thus under the direct influence of

[99] "Kubo Tsugunari," *Gendai* No. 13 (Dec., 1978), p. 7; Nawata, "Reiyukai," pp. 6–19.

[100] During my fieldwork, I interviewed a number of "Inner Trip" participants and found no one who had an accurate idea of Reiyukai.

the headquarters, but in the Kansai, particularly in the powerful Eighth Branch, Reiyukai's largest.

During my field work at the Eighth Branch, I often heard members describe a widening gap between Tokyo and Osaka. The leaders of the Osaka membership feel that the headquarters' policies are too liberal, straying too far away from the original teachings of Kotani. Many of the sermons of the Eighth Branch leaders are devoted to the theme that democracy, individualism, and excessive rationality are unsuited to Japanese tradition. In particular they decry the new freedoms granted women under the postwar Constitution, saying that women's new right to initiate divorce tends to destroy the family, as well as increase the divorce rate. These and other reactionary ideas common at the Eighth Branch show that its style of leadership is much like Kotani's. Although an irreparable rift between the headquarters and the Eighth Branch is unlikely at present, one senses a widening gap.

Reiyukai seems now to be at a turning point in its history, and its course must ultimately be steered by its president. Kubo Tsugunari's nonauthoritarian leadership differs greatly from Kotani's and from surviving first-generation branch leaders. He differs from them also in his youth (born 1936) and in his high level of education, factors that may not be viewed with unmixed enthusiasm by his senior colleagues in the leadership hierarchy. His innovations seem to have the serious intent of assigning subordinate status to more ecstatic forms of religious experience in favor of formulating a new, broader message, and this is appropriate to a leader who is generally perceived as less charismatic than his predecessor. To the extent that he succeeds in transforming the character of the group in this way, it is likely to follow the course of other groups' second generations, and we may see significant "routinization of charisma," widespread replacement of female leaders by men, and the creation of a wider appeal through systematization of the group's thought. At the same time, Reiyukai's continuing patronage of more conservative politicians will bear on the group's future as the nation as a whole moves toward the Right. The group's prewar history suggests that if it continues to espouse such rightist causes as renewed state patronage of the Yasukuni Shrine, and revision of the Constitutional renunciation of war for example, it will become more readily associated with extreme conservative politics than with an independent religious message, thus reducing the possibility of completing the transformation Kubo has initiated. The future promises to try and temper this able leader.

At present Reiyukai is a vital, dynamic group that commands the loyalties of nearly three million Japanese. It is dedicated to the reworking of tradition to fashion a viable lay Buddhist practice. The next chapter shows how the group performs in contemporary society.

Chapter Two

Contemporary Activities and Organization

For its description of the contemporary activities and organization of Reiyukai, this chapter relies, in addition to primary and secondary literature, on information collected in 1976 – 1977 through field work among members of the Eighth Branch in Osaka and on the results of a questionnaire distributed to 2,000 members in 1977. Thus, my attempt to produce a coherent portrait of Reiyukai members and their activities rests on a variety of sources of information. Following an outline of organizational structure, I present basic statistical data on such matters as members' occupations, income, ages, and educational levels and then discuss important group activities for the purpose of determining what they can tell us about the way members perceive themselves, their organization, and their place in the society of Japan. The chapter ends with a discussion of the lives of female employees of the Eighth Branch, where young women live in a manner that more closely approximates the ideal of the group than any other. Their lives are closely regulated, and in this they are not typical of the membership as a whole. However, there is value in discussing their situation since it allows us to glimpse what a world operated along Reiyukai ideals would resemble.

Part 1: The Branch System and Hōza

Reiyukai is organized according to the personal connection established by proselytization. These links are conceived of in familistic terms; the person who proselytizes is the "parent" (*michibiki no oya* 導きの親), and the convert is the "child" (*michibiki no ko* 導きの子). This relationship is the individual's most basic tie to the group as a whole. He will attend meetings (*hōza* 法座) held by the "parent," and he cannot ordinarily change his membership to another hoza. If the convert needs advice about some problem, it is to the parent that he will turn. In case the parent is not the actual leader of the hoza, the convert joins the hoza of which his parent is a member.

Groups of hoza formed by these parent-child links comprise a *shibu* 支部, or "branch," led by a *shibuchō* 支部長, a "branch leader." Most often, a branch is headed by a husband and wife, both addressed by the title branch leader. A branch is established when a leader has collected 500 members. From this minimum number the branch grows through proselytization until it receives the designation flag branch (*mihata shibu* 御旗支部), referring to the flag conferred to mark it as a strong and eminent unit of Reiyukai. The organization hopes eventually to establish twenty-eight flag branches, corresponding to the number of chapters in the Lotus Sutra.

A persistent problem for the continued growth of Reiyukai is its lack of a territorial base. If a hoza leader moves from the immediate vicinity of his converts, they will be left leaderless. Even if another hoza is meeting nearby, they will not ordinarily join its meetings, because they have no proselytization tie to it. This makes it very difficult to maintain close contact between the organization and all its members. Leaders in Reiyukai are well aware of this problem and recognize that separate organizational forms based on proselytization on the one hand and territory on the other have allowed groups like Risshokoseikai and Sōka Gakkai 創価学会 to surpass it in size, but so far there has been no consistent policy to establish similar units in Reiyukai. Leaders, especially men employed by the group, may be residing in Tokyo and working at the headquarters while their converts remain in the countryside. Some leaders try to commute once a month to those locales to hold hoza, or they may delegate this responsibility to their wives, who in any case may be the ones who actually performed the original proselytization. This problem is particularly acute in the case of young adults, since in the early years of working life young men are quite commonly transferred around Japan, and in this case their affiliation with the group as well as their family's may easily become tenuous.

During field work it became apparent that this problem is in fact leading to the decline of hoza in Reiyukai. In the dormitory where I lived, there were two younger women office workers, an older man working in the Eighth Branch office, and an older woman housekeeper. The two younger women both had converts in their home towns but during their three-year term of employment in Osaka were rarely able to hold hoza for them. They said that as time went on, more and more of their converts lost interest, and it was almost impossible to maintain contact with them. The older man was a hoza leader also, and his group was also in the countryside. Although hoza are supposed to meet monthly, he held meetings only occasionally. The housekeeper did not attend her hoza at all. This situation seemed to be quite common for those employed at the Eighth Branch.

A brief comparison of the situation in Reiyukai with that of Risshokoseikai, which originated as a schismatic movement from it, may clarify the problem. Risshokoseikai also employs the hoza, but its management is different. First of all, the organization has branch churches which are open daily for hoza meetings, and any person residing within the territory of the church may attend its meetings, at which a leader is always present. It does not matter whether that leader is the one who originally proselytized the people who appear for hoza. In addition, the headquarters is open daily for hoza and has meeting areas in the main building assigned to larger territories than those covered by the branch churches (a whole ward or an entire city), and anyone who chooses to attend these meetings instead of his local church may do so. These also are staffed daily by leaders.

In Reiyukai, however, not only is there no possibility of readily changing group affiliation regardless of proselytization, but the headquarters provides no facilities constantly open for hoza, and neither do the branch offices. Thus, hoza are held in private homes, or not at all, and increasingly the latter is the case. In fact, although Reiyukai originated the hoza system, it is more common nowadays for members to consult a leader on an individual basis than to present their problems before a hoza group.

Hoza that I observed in Osaka were held on an ad hoc basis and seemed on the whole to be rather ineffective. Meetings were sometimes scheduled to be led by several young hoza leaders together. In the case of the young office workers, there would be frantic telephone calls during the day to exact a promise of attendance from acquaintances or fellow members. It was desirable that members outnumber first-timers, and that all members make a concerted effort to persuade the newcomers to join Reiyukai. In this case hoza became the occasion for proselytization rather than an assembly of those already enrolled. These meetings opened with an address by one of the leaders, proclaiming the benefits of group membership, with emphasis on the possibility of finding friends and moral support. No promises of healing were made. Following this address came recitation of the sutra. Most of the nonmembers became visibly alarmed at that point and refused to participate, turning their backs and reading magazines. After the sutra recitation, members directly confronted the nonmembers and pleaded with them to join Reiyukai. On all occasions which I observed, they refused. Clearly the techniques in use are not entirely effective.

In contrast to the old hoza pattern of dealing with the personal problems of group members, the current pattern is for members to visit their branch leader on an individual basis for counseling. Sixty-three percent of questionnaire respondents, when asked if they had ever consulted their branch leader about some personal problem, replied that they had. Of those, 49 percent had consulted a woman branch leader, while 26 percent had consulted a man, and 25 percent had consulted a husband–wife pair of leaders. From this it is clear that female leaders assume a major responsibility for maintaining the tie between the group and individual members.

Women branch leaders whom I interviewed reported that their main contact with members comes not from hoza but from, in effect, holding open house for their members daily. They described a daily routine of rising early and completing housework chores by mid-morning, by which time numerous women members were assembled, waiting to speak to the leader privately. Leaders counseled these women until late afternoon and then again after the evening meal. When they hold hoza, leaders may borrow sound or videotapes of testimonies and the machines for showing them. However, it seems that personal consultation rather than hoza has become the most important means of binding members to Reiyukai. It is also clear that such a pattern of consultation is a realistic possibility only for women past the age when young children are in the home all day, and who do not work in the labor force. Few male leaders can conform to this pattern before retirement.

Part 2: Sociological Characteristics of Reiyukai Members

Let us turn to a discussion of the social attributes of the Reiyukai membership. The following information is based on a questionnaire distributed to 2,000 members in 1977 and on consultation with Reiyukai's statistics bureau. The total membership of the organization as of 1983 was 2,962,880. This figure is computed on the basis of monthly dues received and thus can be regarded as fairly accurate.[1] Of those, 55 percent are female, and 45 percent are male. Seventy percent reside in urban areas, while 30 percent reside in rural areas. However, since 58 percent reported that they were born in rural areas, we may tentatively conclude that at least 12 percent have moved to urban from rural areas.

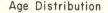

Age Distribution

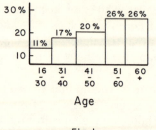

Age

Fig. I

[1] Some possibility of inflation exists in that leaders sometimes pay the dues of their own delinquent converts long after the convert has dropped out of the group, but the influence of this practice is probably negligible.

Table 3. Breakdown of Membership by Occupation

Occupation	Small-Scale Enterprise	Medium-Scale Enterprise	Large-Scale Enterprise
Owner-operator	13.4% (88)	2.0% (13)	0.3% (2)
Management	3.4 (23)	3.2 (21)	1.4 (9)
Skilled worker	3.3 (22)	2.7 (18)	1.5 (10)
Office, sales, service	6.1 (40)	5.3 (35)	4.0 (26)
Shop supervisor	1.2 (8)	0.6 (4)	1.4 (9)
General labor	4.4 (29)	4.4 (29)	1.7 (11)
Total	31.8 (210)	18.2 (120)	10.3 (67)

Small-/medium-scale agriculture, fishing, forestry general labor	2.4% (16)
Large-scale agriculture, fishing, forestry general labor	0.0 (0)
Owner-operator in agriculture, fishing, forestry	3.3 (22)
Family labor in agriculture, fishing, forestry	1.2 (8)
Self-employed	7.0 (45)
Day labor	1.1 (7)
Police, military	0.3 (2)
Civil service	9.7 (64)
Retired	5.0 (33)
Unemployed	1.8 (12)
Other	4.4 (29)
Total	36.2 (238)

Figure 1 shows a breakdown of the membership by age groups. Over 50 percent of the members are over fifty years old. The problems and interests of the higher age brackets are reflected in the group's social attitudes, treated in the final chapter.

Table 3 shows an occupational breakdown of the membership. Since an individual's social attitudes in Japan vary greatly by the size of the enterprise in which he is engaged, the categories small, medium, and large were introduced in the following classification, referring respectively to enterprises employing 29 people or less, 30 to 999 employees, and more than 1,000 employees. Fifty percent are employed in small or medium-sized enterprises, and the largest single occupational category was owner of a small business (13.4 percent). In addition, 7 percent are self-employed, a category which in many cases is not distinguishable from owning a small business, bringing the total involved in small- or medium-sized businesses or self-employment to 57 percent.

By contrast, those involved in large-scale enterprise in any capacity accounted for only 10.3 percent. Of those the greater proportion was performing white-collar jobs in sales, service, or clerical work. Only about 3 percent were blue-collar workers in large-scale enterprise. Of the remainder, 10 percent were civil servants, and 7 percent were employed in agriculture, fishing, or forestry. Five percent were retired, and 1.8 percent were unemployed.

The average number of persons per household is roughly 4.4, well above the national average of 3.35. This reflects the preference in Reiyukai for large families and for aged parents to live with their married children. Among those who are married, 69 percent had arranged marriages, and 31 percent had "love matches." Five percent had been divorced, more than the national average of 1.07 percent in 1975.[2] The average number of children each married couple had is 2.8, also somewhat above the national average.[3]

In terms of education, all but 1 percent had completed primary education, and this number (6) is probably from the prewar generation. Sixteen percent completed high school, which represents three years beyond the compulsory nine years, while roughly 15 percent have completed some form of higher education, whether junior college, technical college, university, or graduate school.

Household income proved to be higher than originally estimated, possibly reflecting the large proportion of persons managing small businesses, in which enterprise and household budgets often are not kept separately. Fifty-two percent reported annual household incomes of three million yen or more, U.S. $15,000 (U.S. $1 = 200 yen). Thus Reiyukai members belong to the middle class as regards income; few if any live in poverty. See Table 4 for more precise distributions.

---

[2] Wagatsuma Hiroshi, "Some Aspects of the Contemporary Japanese Family: Once Confucian, Now Fatherless," *Daedalus* 106, No. 2, (Spring, 1977), 184. Wagatsuma's figure of 3.35 as the national average household size is current for 1975. The 1975 rate of divorce was 1.07 percent. See Yuzawa Yasuhiko, "Kazoku mondai no sengoshi," in *Gendai no kazoku* (special issue of *Jurist*) (Spring, 1977), 43.

[3] See sources in note 2, above.

Table 4. *Distribution of Income*

Income	Individual Monthly	Individual Annual	Household Annual
Under ¥100,000	24.9% (149)		
¥100,000–¥150,000	22.9 (137)		
¥160,000–¥200,000	20.4 (122)		
¥210,000–¥250,000	12.5 (75)		
¥260,000–¥300,000	7.7 (46)		
¥310,000–¥400,000	5.5 (33)		
¥410,000–¥500,000	3.3 (20)		
Over ¥500,000	2.8 (17)		
Under ¥500,000		13.1% (74)	3.0% (14)
¥500,000–¥600,000		3.2 (18)	0.9 (4)
¥610,000–¥700,000		1.4 (8)	0.6 (3)
¥710,000–¥1,000,000		5.7 (32)	2.0 (9)
¥1,010,000–¥1,500,000		12.0 (68)	6.0 (28)
¥1,510,000–¥2,000,000		16.4 (93)	11.3 (53)
¥2,010,000–¥3,000,000		24.0 (136)	24.2 (113)
Over ¥3,000,000		24.2 (137)	52.0 (243)
N =	599	566	467

Let us consider the significance of the large proportion of Reiyukai membership being self-employed or involved in small- or medium-sized enterprises. In Japanese society as a whole, this sector of the labor force has distinctive social attitudes. Workers and management in these enterprises tend to work side by side and thus to see themselves in roughly identical positions, so there are few labor disputes. Also, both workers and management tend to accept the paternalistic notion that the employer–employee relation is analogous to that between parent and child; thus the level of union membership is very low. Among the management, especially, acceptance of paternalistic notions is characteristic, as is acceptance of the idea that social problems should be resolved through collective improvement rather than through political means. In social and political outlook they are conservative, supporting the Liberal Democratic Party.[4]

[4] Yasuda Saburō, *Gendai nihon no kaikyū ishiki* (Tokyo: Yūhikaku, 1973), p. 73 and chap. 3.

Table 5. *Contribution to Household Income*

Percentage Contributed	Wife	Children
0	52.1% (240)	42.6% (145)
1–10	18.0 (83)	10.6 (36)
11–20	7.8 (36)	7.6 (26)
21–30	9.1 (42)	12.6 (43)
31–50	8.9 (41)	11.0 (37)
Over 50	4.1 (19)	15.6 (53)
N =	461	340

Examples of small to medium enterprises that overlap with the self-employed are restaurants, small-scale wholesaling and construction, subcontracting manufacturing, and small shops attached to a residence selling such items as stationery, food, eyeglasses, photographic equipment, etc. Although outsiders may be employed, family labor is central. From this follows the tendency not to establish fixed salaries for labor performed by family members. Most often, knowledge necessary for carrying on the work of the enterprise is transmitted through an apprenticeship lasting several years. Nevertheless, these businesses have a great deal of trouble locating successors to carry on after the retirement of the head. Workers labor for long hours and cannot hope to receive extensive fringe benefits, to say nothing of long vacations. There are seldom established pension plans, and workers must be able to guarantee their own security in old age. Since family labor is so important, the enterprise as a whole depends heavily on the solidarity of family members. If family members are not willing to sacrifice individual desires to long hours of labor at little or no fixed wage, the enterprise suffers greatly. However, if the family is united, it is possible for such businesses to achieve considerable profits and thus achieve a comfortable income. It is especially important that the bond between husband and wife be strong.[5] These concerns are by no means irrelevant to Reiyukai members, and often econ-

[5] Kiyonari Tadao, "Toshi jieigyō no saiseisan," in *Gendai no kazoku*, pp. 122–27.

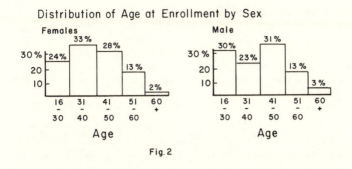

Distribution of Age at Enrollment by Sex

Fig. 2

omic issues underlie their religious concerns, as will be seen in the fifth chapter, on testimonies and witnessing.

Questionnaire respondents reported that they were persuaded to join the group by the following categories of persons in descending order of frequency: a spouse, parent, neighbor, relative, friend, and finally by a previously unknown person (an evangelist). This reflects the tendency, noticeable from other sources, for whole families to become affiliated after the wife joins. She usually joins on the occasion of some crisis in the family and later persuades other family members to join. This tendency may be seen also in the comparative distributions for men and women of age at joining the group. Some 33 percent of female members join between the ages of thirty-one and forty, while only 23 percent of men join in that age interval. By contrast 31 percent of male members join between the ages of forty-one and fifty. In many cases it takes the wife a number of years to persuade the husband to join Reiyukai, a theme often heard in testimonies. This is probably the reason for the differential age of enrollment for men and women. Figure 2 shows the distribution of age of enrollment by sex.

In Reiyukai there are five ranks, and the requirement for advancing from one to the next is proselytization. The ranks are "seeker" (the English word is used, and this rank is only for the Youth Group), *junhōzashu* 準法座主, *hōzashu* 法座主, *junshibuchō* 準支部長, and *shibuchō* 支部長. We might translate these ranks as vice-hoza leader, hoza leader, vice branch leader, and branch leader. These ranks correspond to proselytization of one, ten, fifty,

Table 6. *Proportion of Male and Female Leaders*

Rank	Male	Female
Branch Leader (shibucho)	55%	45%
Branch Vice Leader (junshibucho)	45%	55%
Hoza Leader (hozashu)	39%	61%

two hundred, and five hundred persons, respectively. The ratio of leaders to followers is low; the total number of branch leaders, vice branch leaders, and hoza leaders account for only 0.5 percent of the total membership. Women predominate in all ranks except the highest, the branch leaders, as Table 6 shows. Observation suggests that women are far more active in proselytization than men. However, there is the assumption that whole families will join and participate equally, and therefore, spouses of branch leaders are accorded equal rank, even if the proselytization required for attaining the rank was performed entirely by a single spouse. In practice this means that many husbands of women active in proselytization are accorded the rank of branch leader even though they themselves may not have brought in even a single convert. The branch leaders tend to be older than other members, and many widowed women achieve this rank, while men may become active in proselytization after retirement. The combination of these factors results in the disproportionate representation of men in the branch-leader rank and obscures the fact that women are the more active participants in this rank as well as others.

Figure 3 correlates leaders' rank, age, and sex. It can be seen that male leaders, especially, are concentrated in the higher age brackets. In the lower leadership ranks we see a more even distribution of age.

If we correlate rank, sex, and educational achievement, we find no significant variation from the overall distribution of educational achievement discussed above, except that somewhat more graduates of high school or higher forms of education are found in the lower ranks. This reflects the tendency in Japanese society as a whole for increasing numbers of high-school graduates.

Leaders Age by Sex and Rank

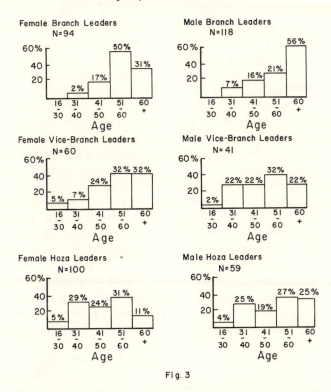

Fig. 3

Correlating rank and occupation we find that the higher ranks are dominated by those engaged in small- or medium-sized enterprises, and that those in lower ranks are somewhat more likely to be employed in large-scale enterprises or civil service. The predominance of those in the small- or medium-sized enterprises category in the higher ranks of leadership means that the attitudes and concerns of this group greatly influence other members' social attitudes.

Part 3: Who Are the Ancestors?

Reiyukai members usually begin compiling a death register, or Book of the Past (*kakochō* 過去帳) upon joining the group. In this book they register the death days of ancestors reckoned bilaterally, and there is a page for each day of the year, on which ancestors can be entered by their posthumous names. Once entered, special ritual is directed to them on the anniversary of their deaths. Four percent of questionnaire respondents indicated that they did not possess a death register, while 12 percent responded that they had registered between one and fifty ancestors. Fourteen percent indicated that they had registered between fifty and one hundred ancestors, and 70 percent indicated that they had entered over one hundred ancestors in their registers.

In Reiyukai ancestor worship becomes the central practice of a voluntary association. This is rare, if not unique, in the history of religions. Usually, ancestor worship is linked to kinship groups such as a lineage or extended family. In the Japanese case it has traditionally been linked to the *ie* 家, the joint-stem family system.[6] The possibility of a member of one ie worshipping the ancestors of another would be a mystery to most Japanese. Yet, in Reiyukai, precisely such a thing occurs, which means that the concept of "ancestor" itself is different from that found in the rest of Japanese society. However, it is difficult to give a clear picture of members' understanding of ancestors, because they themselves do not ordinarily consider the matter, and when asked give contradictory replies.

In the early part of my field work, I frequently asked people, "Who are the ancestors?" and received either blank looks or angry harangues on the failure of Americans to be filial and respect their parents and ancestors. Informants responding with blank looks had simply never thought about the ancestors as having any specific identity; to them ancestors are simply a category of deities on a par, roughly, with Buddhas and kami. Those who became angry were interested in ancestors as guardians of the values of the traditional family system. In calmer moments they spoke of a spirit world where countless ancestors are watching over their descendants and protecting them. The ancestors somehow retain their ie membership, and all the ancestors of a certain ie can act as a group. They can tell the ancestors of people who are not

---

[6] See pp. 99–102 below for fuller discussion of the ie.

Reiyukai members about all the good things that would come to them if their descendants would join Reiyukai, or they can punish their own descendants who are lax in ritual or in fulfilling their duties to the ie. Some members deny that the ancestors actually punish descendants, but this idea is heard in testimonies and interviews. In Reiyukai conception, the ancestors are no longer the deities of limited kinship groups, but take on an almost universal character.

Since it is believed that the ancestors can act in groups corresponding to affiliations among their descendants in the phenomenal world, members speak about all the ancestors of the Eighth Branch, for example, as if those spirits were capable of collective action. Eighth Branch members recite the sutra for the branch's ancestors when branch meetings are held, and branch members feel a responsibility to "save" those ancestors regardless of any kinship link to them. Also, they speak of the ancestors of Reiyukai as a whole, and when they meet at the headquarters in Tokyo, their sutra recitation there is directed to all ancestors of all members.

Another way to approach the question of who the ancestors are in Reiyukai is to consider the deceased persons recorded in the death register and their relation to the owner of that register. The basic principle is that ancestors are reckoned bilaterally, but members disagree among themselves on the question of the degree of collaterality to be included. Vertically, the reckoning should extend as far back in time as possible, including at least grandparents and great-grandparents as well as parents and their siblings of both sexes. However, in the second ascending (grandparents')

Collaterality in Reckoning Ancestors

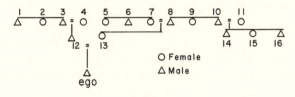

Fig. 4

Exclusion of Spouses of Collaterally
Reckoned Ancestors

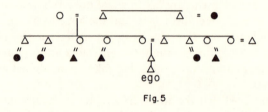

Fig. 5

generation, there is disagreement on the question of including female collaterals. Figure 4 is a diagram I prepared to elicit members' opinions as to who should properly be included in the Book of the Past. When this diagram was presented to a group of both male and female members, an interesting division of opinion emerged. Everyone agreed that male siblings of any grandparent, including 1, 6, and 10 should be registered in the Book of the Past. Male informants said that female siblings of grandparents, 2, 5, and 9 should be included if their names are known, but female informants said that 2 and 9 should not be included although 5 should be included. Thus, female informants seemed to accept as basic the idea that male collaterals should be included, but that female collaterals should not be, unless they were sisters of a grandmother, thence, a same-sex sibling of the individual to whom ego has a direct lineal tie. Everyone in this first group of informants, male and female, agreed that 11 should be recorded, thus accepting that spouses of grandparents' siblings should be considered ancestors. However, other informants disagreed and said that 11 should not be included, nor should any spouse of a grandparent's sibling of either sex, producing Figure 5, in which filled-in symbols represent individuals who are *not* included in the Book of the Past.

Returning to the first ascending generation in Figure 4, informants could not agree about 14, 15, and 16. All accepted that 14 and 16 should be included, but they were split over 15, whom female informants said should be left out. After some discussion among themselves, they decided that 15 should be excluded from the

Table 7. *Inclusion and Exclusion of Exceptional Cases in the Book of the Past*

Included	Excluded
Stillbirths	Abortions
Deformed births	Abandoned babies
The insane	
Children who die before their parents	
Ancestors of an adopted husband (mukoyōshi)	
Orphans' ancestors, when known	

Book of the Past unless ego had some personal feeling of wanting to include her.

Since on all occasions when I asked informants about the reckoning of ancestors there was considerable disagreement among them, it seems that the group has not entirely resolved the problems posed by the notion of reckoning ancestors bilaterally. They are unsure how far to extend the reckoning collaterally, and there is a tendency to revert in doubtful cases to a patrilateral skewing. In addition, there is sometimes the necessity to treat exceptional cases and make a judgment whether they should be considered ancestors. Table 7 shows which of these problematic cases are to be included in the Book of the Past.

Part 4: Ritual, Pilgrimage, and Branch Meetings

Reiyukai's most basic ritual is twice-daily recitation of an abridged version of the Lotus Sutra, called the *Aokyōkan*, the "Blue Sutra." If members recited it twice daily, they would average about sixty recitations per month, but in actuality, this ideal is not always attained. Only three questionnaire respondents said they did not recite it at all. Nine percent of the respondents indicated they recite it between one and twenty times per month. Forty percent recite it between twenty and forty times monthly; 27 percent, between forty-one and sixty times, and 24 percent, more than sixty times per month. There is some reason to suppose that the people who responded to the questionnaire are among the more active members of Reiyukai, and therefore, these figures may be somewhat higher than the actual, typical practice of members as a whole.

Reiyukai has three sites to which members make pilgrimages. That is to say, they go there to engage in religious training or to form a connection with a deity enshrined there. These sacred centers are Mirokusan, Shichimenzan 七面山, and Shakaden. Each in its own way is important in proselytization and training, and each illustrates a different aspect of Reiyukai's religious ideal.

In 1964 Reiyukai completed the building of the youth training center, Mirokusan, on a mountain renamed in the honor of the Future Buddha Maitreya, on the Izu Peninsula. The tomb of the founder Kotani is located on the mountaintop, suggesting a slight tendency to identify her with Maitreya. There are extensive facilities, including dormitories, cafeteria, lounges, meeting rooms, a large worship hall, and a pagoda housing a statue of Maitreya. Members of all ages attend three-day training sessions there, segregated by age (over or below thirty years), and the sessions run continuously from April to November. Mirokusan represents a major avenue of recruitment for youth, and young members try to persuade their friends to participate in a session as a preliminary to joining the group. Buses are chartered by local branches, and the cost for the whole excursion, including transportation, is only ¥7,000, or about U.S. $35. A journey there is considered a pilgrimage to undertake spiritual training and to form a special relation to the Future Buddha Maitreya.

I attended a Youth Group session at Mirokusan in November, 1976. Preparatory to setting out from Osaka on an overnight bus trip, the 540 persons from the Eighth Branch who were participating in that session assembled in the Youth Group Hall, Tengachaya 天茶屋, of the branch for sutra recitation, which was to be a "greeting" (*go-aisatsu* 御挨拶) to the ancestors of the Eighth Branch. Most people seem to have arrived in male–female pairs, and there was even one couple planning to spend their honeymoon at Mirokusan, in spite of sexually segregated dormitories. Leaders of the Eighth Branch Youth Group addressed the group, explaining that through spiritual training at Mirokusan it is possible to change karma and "open your destiny," *unmei o akeru* 運命を開ける. We were assigned to buses by groups of thirty-five or forty, and while on the bus we were to pass a prayer card from seat to seat, and each two seat-mates were to recite the daimoku for fifteen minutes before passing the card to the next seat. Thus prayers were said the entire time the bus was in motion. As we ascended Mirokusan itself the next morning, after ten or twelve hours on the bus, we donned group sashes and recited the daimoku in unison.

Arriving at the mountain dormitory, which can accommodate 600 people, the persons from each bus divided into male and female groups and were assigned to rooms in the dormitory. Each large room accommodates about forty people and is equipped with closed-circuit television. In charge of each room was a branch leader who explained the rules of the session and had us elect three leaders for the room. House rules forbid smoking in the sleeping rooms, frivolous conversation, and stretching out one's feet in the direction of the main worship hall. Particular emphasis was put on the importance of answering "Hai!" in a loud voice when addressed and coming quickly when called. The thirty-four women in my room were divided into four groups for introductions and mutual discussion of our first impressions of Mirokusan.

Soon the television came on and an announcer summoned us to the main worship hall (*haiden* 拝殿), where we recited the group's *Miroku kyō* 弥勒経 "Maitreya Sutra"[7] for about an hour and a half. Following the sleepless night on the bus, this recitation seemed to leave the participants quite weary. We returned then to the dormitory for discussion meetings and dinner. Then there was a choice of several events, including a folk-singing group, a movie on the life of the founder Kotani, a talk by a sumo wrestler, and talking with a branch leader. Most people chose the singing group.

Themes for group discussion are established in advance and circulated to participants in a pamphlet that everyone receives. Examples are, "In what situation do you most admire your parents?" "What does the Inner Trip mean to you?" "What new discoveries have you made in this religion?" "What do you do to

---

[7] Reiyukai's Maitreya sutra is a compilation of scriptural and noncanonical works relating to Maitreya. I have analyzed the composition of this work in "Maitreya and Modern Japan." (Paper presented at the Princeton Conference on Maitreya Studies, May 1983).

promote this religion at work or school?" and finally, "How do you feel when reciting the sutra?" In the small groups I observed, it was usually the last theme that was pursued. Leaders were obviously trained in how to handle negative reactions to the sutra and readily admitted that they had found it boring at first. However, when one participant said that except for the pain in his legs and feet caused by having to sit on his heels for a long time, he felt nothing, the young women leaders became quite emotional and upset, crying or praying silently. Another participant asked what the meaning of the sutra was, and the leaders were unable to respond. The situation was the same when they were asked what its main points are or why it is important in life. They seem to have been counting on a greater proportion of leaders being present, who, by their greater numbers could create a mood of enthusiasm for the group without becoming too specific about various practices. Here we see the price Reiyukai pays for having disavowed any form of doctrinal study. The collective task for this session was to formulate a vow to present before the whole group on the following day.

The next day at 5:30 a.m. the television came on and began broadcasting current American rock-and-roll hits to wake us up. After putting away the bedding, we recited the Blue Sutra against this somewhat incongruous musical background. The branch leader and the room leaders gave speeches admonishing us for lacking the proper spirit in shouting "Hai!" in group meetings; we were told to show more enthusiasm. Furthermore, we were scolded for lamentable laxity in lining up our slippers outside the sleeping room. They should be in straight rows at all times. We were drilled in shouting "Hai!" louder and louder while raising our arms and holding a rosary so that we would present a pleasing aspect in the main hall. We were being prepared for a meeting to give announcements of our determination to persevere in spiritual self-cultivation and proselytization. When the master of ceremonies, an official of the Youth Group, called for volunteers, everyone was to jump up on the benches with raised arms, calling "Hai!" Upon recognition from the podium, the chosen person could come forward and make his announcement to the group.

At the meeting, even those who had previously expressed distaste for crowd behavior clamored for the microphone, and the noise was truly deafening. The people went forward individually or in pairs, often struggling to fight back tears, and made vows to be more filial to their parents or to be more active in proselytization. Many announcements took the form of *zange* 懺悔, repentence, and speakers apologized to the group for having slighted their parents in various ways, not having been sufficiently meek (*sunao* 素直), having been too selfish, and so on. Obviously affected by the heightened atmosphere, many were too overcome with emotion to say anything at all at the microphone. Nevertheless, they returned to their seats and rejoined the thundrous roar of "Hai!" hoping to be called upon to speak once more. By far the greatest majority of those called upon were already group leaders, and only a tenth or so of the total were novices. Thus the more experienced were by their own behavior presenting models of preferred attitude and action.

After that meeting and a vegetarian dinner (all meals are vegetarian) there were two more group meetings—one for simply enjoyable activities such as singing, games, and disco dancing, and others for the members of each branch. The Eighth Branch is by far the largest, and in its meeting the only topic of discussion was the necessity of all Eighth Branch members joining together in the next morning's meeting to outshout all other branches and thereby show the great strength of the Eighth Branch.

The next morning the period after breakfast and sutra recitation was devoted to two meetings. One was a continuation of smaller groups formed from among the passengers of each bus. Each group was to announce its progress to the rest. The leaders of the group in which I participated said that the ratio of new to old members was too high, and that therefore there had been too much argument and contention. If leaders had outnumbered first-timers by an even greater majority, there might have been real progress, but as it was, nothing of any importance had been accomplished, in the view of the leaders. One of the leaders, a young man, sheepishly admitted that he did not really believe that karma could be changed by going to Mirokusan. His dubious outlook was seconded by two or three others. At that point, the young women leaders of our circle retreated into silent prayer and tears. Nevertheless, when the time to make an "announcement" before the group came, all members of our group, save two, eagerly stood on the benches in the hall and shouted loudly for recognition so that they could make a speech before the whole group. As the announcements progressed, it appeared that in many groups like ours, the proportion of leaders had been so small that novices' doubts had not been overcome, and "nothing was accomplished." This session continued for an hour and a half.

The final session was for announcements by each branch. Each branch was charged to show its enthusiasm by vocal volume, and without question the Eighth Branch outshouted all the rest. Again, upon recognition by the master of ceremonies, each branch's representative made an announcement in the form of a vow or repentence at the microphone.

Had the weather been fair, this session would have been followed by a worship service at the Maitreya pagoda, but as it was raining very hard, we went directly to the buses from the worship hall and returned to Osaka. The return bus ride was regulated in the same way as the original trip. When questionnaire respondents were asked whether they had ever gone to Mirokusan, 78 percent responded that they had participated in the three-day session more than ten times. Another 20 percent had gone one to ten times. Leaders estimate that at least half of the persons who join the group at Mirokusan drop out soon thereafter.

Active Youth Group members typically go to Mirokusan several times a year and are strongly urged to do so in order to make the meetings successful. Young members speak of Mirokusan as an enjoyable and personally meaningful experience with aspects of religious training and amusement, in the tradition of Japanese pilgrimages since the medieval period. They look forward to the opportunity to meet young people from other parts of the country and tell their friends about the new friendships, even the possibility of romance, to be had at Mirokusan.

While the symbolism of Mirokusan as a pilgrimage site remains largely implicit, important Buddhist ideas and symbols have been employed and transformed to suit the audience Reiyukai seeks to reach, in this case Japanese youth. Mirokusan was constructed following the founders' vow at Ise to construct a kaidan, or ordination platform, and the pilgrims are spoken of as lay Bodhisattvas; their clamorous "vows" are in imitation of the Bodhisattva Vow. Kotani's tomb on the mountain summit is clearly in the tradition of Kūkai's 空海 interment on Mt. Kōya 高野山 to await the advent of the Future Buddha Maitreya, then to come to life to be present when the new age is ushered in. Mirokusan pilgrims worship before her tomb, but the symbolism is never explained to them. Similarly, the pilgrims worship a statue of Maitreya and recite a sutra that foretells his reign on earth, but while the worship constitutes in traditional folk Buddhist understanding a *kechi-en* 結縁, or forming a personal relation to the Future Buddha, pilgrims receive no explanation or instructions on this point, and the sutra recitation does nothing to clarify the matter. Even when the Chinese original is rendered into Buddhological Japanese, it is recited at such a pace, after a sleepless night, that its meaning is conveyed to no one. The Mirokusan pilgrimage appropriates for Reiyukai a number of Maitreya-related symbols but presently does nothing to activate their latent meanings. That this new religion should take over the symbolism of the Future Buddha shows how Reiyukai selects elements from its Buddhist heritage, though at present it chooses not to explicate them but to keep them in reserve. At the schism of Risshokoseikai in 1938, Reiyukai made a choice to accord an absolute primacy to religious experience and to avoid an intellectual approach, and the result is that members are hard pressed to give any explanation of their beliefs. However, inasmuch as the president Kubo Tsugunari is a trained Buddhologist, we can expect him in the future to address the present inchoate state of affairs.

While a pilgrimage to Mirokusan is often a new member's first sustained contact with Reiyukai, there is another practice for the more experienced. Reiyukai's most arduous and sacred pilgrimage is that to Shichimenzan, a mountain in Yamanashi Prefecture long sacred to Nichiren Buddhism, and more recently to members of Nichiren-derived new religions, including Reiyukai.

Shichimenzan is near Minobusan 身延山, where Nichiren spent most of the last years of his life, and is the home of a major sect of the Nichiren school. It is thought that this mountain was a pilgrimage site long before its association with Nichiren, and it has been linked to the protective deities of the Nichiren school on the one hand and the question of the salvation of women on the other. Women were originally prohibited from climbing the mountain, but in 1619 and 1640 Oman no Kata お万の方, former concubine of Tokugawa Ieyasu 徳川家康, received special permission to ascend it. In modern times women are permitted to climb to the summit.[8]

Many legends are connected with Shichimenzan, but the following one is probably the most important to Reiyukai. As recounted in the *Minobu Kagami* 身延鏡 (1685), one day when Nichiren was reciting the sutra deep in the forest of the mountain, a beautiful woman came to listen. When Nichiren asked her name, she replied that she was none other than Itsukushima Benzaiten 厳島辯財天 (Sarasvati), and that she had come to hear the Dharma in fulfillment of a vow made lifetimes ago in the presence of Shakyamuni. Nichiren asked her to reveal her true form, and at that she changed into a great, red dragon and flew away to dwell in the pond on the top of Shichimenzan. Thereafter, she was known as Shichimen Daimyōjin 七面大明神. As she is pictured, the goddess holds a key in her right hand, and the wish-fulfillment jewel (*cintāmaṇi*) in her left. The key symbolizes alms-giving, and the gem, wisdom. Other legends portray the goddess of the mountain alternately as a tellurian snake- or naga-like figure who lives in the pond or as a heavenly dragon who flies through the air and lives on top of the mountain. The *Minobu Kagami* version seems to combine elements of both. Nichiren began to include the name of the deity in his calligraphic mandala in 1596.[9]

Close parallels exist between the Shimen Daimyojin legends and the incident in the Devadatta chapter of the Lotus Sutra which establishes a precedent for the salvation of women. In this story a female dragon or naga, daughter of the Sagara Dragon King, is brought before Shakyamuni by Mañjuśrī as one who has mastered the Dharma. However, her achievement is doubted by Śāriputra, who inquires how an eight-year-old female dragon could possibly have mastered the Buddha's teaching. She re-

[8] Satomi Saion, "Shichimen shinkō no keifu to tenkai," in *Kindai nihon no hokke bukkyō*, ed. Mochizuki Kankō (Kyoto: Heirakuji shoten, 1968), pp. 185–200.
[9] Ibid.

sponds by giving the Buddha the wish-fulfillment gem. When he accepts it, she says that her grasp of the Dharma was like Shakyamuni's receiving the jewel: complete and instantaneous. Śāriputra then agrees that she has indeed mastered the Law. The Dragon Girl then sat at the foot of a tree, and "exchanging the female root for the male," became a Bodhisattva and achieved supreme, perfect enlightenment. This incident established the precedent for women to attain salvation—having first changed into men. Subsequent commentarial literature expounds this theme, known as *henjō nanshi* 変成男子, and delineates courses of spiritual training whereby women may change their sex.[10]

In legends concerning Shichimen Daimyojin also we find the motifs of the jewel and magical physical transformation. The jewel is, in fact, characteristically associated both with the Indian naga and the rain-making dragon of Chinese and Japanese tradition. It has the power to grant all desires, and there are many legends telling how man tries to wrest it from the dragon, alternating failure and success. In the transformation motif, the legends and scriptural material pose an analogy between the passage from an unenlightened to an enlightened state, and the change from female to male gender. Simultaneously, the fact that the mountain's deity is female exalts the power of the female and juxtaposes this theme to the contrasting one of women's salvation lying in the casting off of sexuality. Thus, the mountain symbolically embodies the paradox, so important in Reiyukai, of power and pollution frequently attributed to female sexuality.[11]

In addition to this complex of symbols, Shichimenzan focuses the pilgrim's attention on the symbolism of Japan as a divine land. If one climbs to the top of Shichimenzan at dawn on the spring or autumn equinox and looks to the east, the sun appears to rise out of the crater of Mt. Fuji. Reiyukai especially reveres the

---

[10] Mochizuki Kankō, "Nyonin jōbutsu—henjō nanshi ni tsuite," *Seishin* (Minobusan), No. 36 (1962), 68–78; Mochizuki Kankō, "Debadattahon ni okeru nyonin jōbutsu ni tsuite," *Seishin* (Minobusan), No. 37 (1963), 44–57; pt. 2, No. 38, 26–28; pt. 3, No. 39, 23–42; Kasahara Kazuo, *Nyonin ōjō no keifu* (Tokyo: Yoshikawa kōbunkan, 1975), pp. 197–304.

[11] M. W. De Visser, *The Dragon in China and Japan* (1931; reprint ed., Wiesbaden: Martin Sanding, 1964), *passim*.

Shichimenzan pilgrimage undertaken on the equinox, and pilgrims worship the rising sun on these days. The equinoxes (*higan* 彼岸) are also sacred to the spirits of the ancestors, and traditionally special rites are performed for them on this day. Worshipping the ancestors in combination with the rising sun symbolizes the ancestors as founders and guardian deities of the Japanese nation.

In Reiyukai the Shichimenzan pilgrimage is undertaken in all-male or all-female groups. Pilgrims make a circuit of various holy sites on the way to the top, chanting the daimoku continuously. They wear traditional white garments to signify purity. No liquor or frivolous amusement is allowed, and only those certified by their leaders as having filial piety are permitted to participate. Menstruating women may not participate in the ritual of worshipping the morning sun. Eighty-seven percent of questionnaire respondents had participated in the Shichimenzan pilgrimage at least once.

The third Reiyukai pilgrimage site is the Tokyo headquarters building, Shakaden. By making the journey to worship the Shakyamuni statue enshrined there, it is possible to obtain the Buddha's protection and to borrow his strength in time of need. The group endeavors to make the individual's encounter with the deity a moving experience which will convince him that the group's teachings are true and meaningful in his life.

I participated in the Shakaden pilgrimage from the Eighth Branch in October, 1976, attended by about 350 people from Osaka as well as over 5,000 more from other parts of the country. From Osaka overnight buses were chartered for a trip of twelve hours, arriving at Tokyo at 7 a.m. Each bus was supervised by two monitors who addressed the passengers by microphone, explaining that at Shakaden they would personally encounter the Buddha; the statue there that appears to be made of wood is actually the Buddha, real and alive.

Ceremonies began at 9 a.m., and we were seated in the central hall for two hours to wait, while the overflow of the crowd was taken to a separate hall to view the ceremonies by closed-circuit television. Sutra recitation was the first activity and lasted almost exactly one hour, leaving everyone exhausted after a sleepless night on the bus. It was followed by a program called "Happy Together at Shakaden!" led by a troop of cheerleading girls of about twelve years of age, dressed in yellow bathing suits and carrying red pompons. They were accompanied by a brass band in blue uniforms, marching in formation around the stage in front of the altar while the audience clapped in time. Their act was followed by baton-twirlers and traditional Japanese dancing. The audience sang songs and did calisthenics in place, and then heard three testimonial speeches. Then we prepared to "meet the Buddha."

The side walls of the auditorium are paneled with very thin, streaked marble, lit from behind. At a signal from the mistress of ceremonies, the audience began to chant the daimoku. As we chanted, the overhead lights began to dim, leaving only the pale green light from behind the marble, and a blue ultraviolet light shining down on something behind the brass doors of the altar. After five minutes or so, eerie music of violins and falsetto voices began, and slowly, as the chanting continued, the great brass doors began to open. Parting, they revealed a huge unpainted wooden statue of Shakyamuni, the right hand raised in the *abhaya*, "fear not" mudra. Even from the back of the hall, the five-meter high statue evoked audible gasps of astonishment. Gradually the chanting ceased as the audience sat staring at the statue. Some people were crying or praying. Later, people I interviewed said that the statue was alive. A voice was heard, telling the audience to make a vow in the presence of the Buddha on how we would live our lives from that moment on. After an interval of perhaps five minutes more, we began chanting the daimoku again, and the doors closed.

Then came a period in which anyone could mount the stage and announce his vow to the audience. Fully half the audience ran to the stage and set up a great roar as they clamored for the microphone. To the many who were so overwrought that they broke into tears or were unable to speak at all, the audience shouted encouragement. Hundreds of people crowded the stage and gave their vows for half an hour. Most ended with apologies to their parents and ancestors, promising to show more filial piety in the future and to make many more converts. At 1 p.m. the meeting ended with singing the Reiyukai song, standing in the aisles with arms about each others' shoulders, swaying back and forth.

The Shakaden pilgrimage alternates phases of regimentation

and release and produces a most emotional experience in which individuals believe that they are participating in a sacred activity in a holy place. The long bus ride and the impossibility of sleep were quite punishing for the audience, but they endured that and an hour of sutra recitation before being allowed to relax their tension and attention for a brief period of purely secular amusement by the bands and entertainers. Following that, they returned to regimented activity in daimoku recitation and were rewarded with what they were told is the manifestation of a living deity. Emotions forcibly repressed during the foregoing portion of the pilgrimage are then directed to making a vow (as at Mirokusan, a "Bodhisattva Vow") before the deity, to prove oneself worthy of his protection. At last the pilgrims are allowed to release that emotion in proclaiming their resolution before the 5,000, and they responded without restraint, many dwelling upon their obligation and debt to Reiyukai for having given them such a moving experience and promising to repay by proselytization. Fifty-six percent of questionnaire respondents had made the pilgrimage to Shakaden more than ten times.

Let us turn now to an account of meetings held periodically in Reiyukai. Evening training meetings (*yakan shūyōkai* 夜間修養会) are held monthly or every six weeks by the male branch leader for the Youth Group members. These meetings, which last from two to three hours, begin with sutra recitation and speeches from Youth Group leaders encouraging the audience to be more active in proselytization, but the main event is an address by the branch leader. In the Eighth Branch these meetings are well attended, typically by 250 to 300 people. The branch leader first inquires how many of the audience have made new converts since the last meeting and invariably expresses disappointment at the result. Most of his remarks relate to the theme of the weaknesses of modern youth and imply that they are much in need of the guidance of their elders. After thus setting the stage, he responds to written questions handed to him, the inquirers remaining anonymous.

Typical questions concern proselytization. One questioner wrote, "No matter how hard I try, I can't seem to persuade anyone to join Reiyukai. What should I do?" The branch leader ridiculed the weakness of the questioner and recommended that he recite the sutra more often. Through sutra recitation, he said, it is possible to gain magical power, *jinriki* 神力 (Skt., *siddhi*). This will allow anyone to overcome potential converts' doubts. Variations on this question and the response were repeated many times. Another person inquired, "The person whom I recently persuaded to join, now hates Reiyukai. What should I do?" The answer was that *kuji* 九字 (exorcistic power; see Chapter 6) should be used to change the person's attitude. A young woman asked, "My convert refuses to practice hard. What should I do?" The response was that the meaning of the Inner Trip is to honor one's parents as one type of ancestor; the ancestors are the center. The woman should pray to her ancestors and respect her parents, and recite the sutra daily. She should also use jinriki and kuji. Another person said that when attempting to proselytize a young woman university student he had given her a Reiyukai pamphlet, but she had responded by handing him a pamphlet on the Communist Party, and told him to read that. How should he have reacted? This question provoked an angry tirade on the insolence of intellectuals who pretend to know so much but in fact are ignorant of the true power of the ancestors, the Buddhas, and the kami. One young man complained that no matter how hard he tried to be pleasant to his parents, they always seemed to be annoyed at him; what should he do? The branch leader told him that vigorous recitation of the daimoku should solve that problem. Someone inquired what he should do for his convert with a drinking problem, and he was told that he should pray and write posthumous names for the convert's ancestors. Once the ancestors were satisfied, it would be possible to break through this evil drinking karma.

The meeting closed with a talk on the subjects of democracy and the peoples of foreign nations. The branch leader stressed, for example, the idea that Koreans cannot obtain jinriki because they do not say the daimoku in Japanese. Democracy, he said, is equivalent to selfish egotism and runs counter to the finest traditions of Japan. It was ruthlessly imposed on the Japanese people during the Occupation, and since then has been carried to further extremes, so that now it is common even for first sons to abandon their aged parents who must then go off to the poorhouse to await a lonely death. People today do not realize that parents are one type of ancestor and should receive the appropriate treatment. Furthermore, the younger generation is weak and selfish because of having been inculcated with the ideals of democracy.

During the evening meetings the branch leader repeatedly promotes the idea that the young are weak and in need of their elders' guidance. The authority of the elders lies first in their unity with the ancestors. Even while they live, they must be considered "one type of ancestor." They should be revered if not worshipped, and youth should rely on them in all things. "Youth" in Reiyukai extends to the age of thirty, which means that the period of "guidance" is a long one. The branch leaders and their audience all seem to accept that Reiyukai's ideas are not popular in society and to take the attitude of a group unjustly deprived of respect and prestige. They see enemies in the forces of democracy, communism, and the educated elite. Also, members experience rejection far more often than acceptance in proselytization and thus come to think that society is hostile to them. This attitude is stronger among leaders than ordinary members and stronger in Osaka than in Tokyo.

Each flag branch holds layman's meetings (*zaike no tsudoi* 在家の集い), and at the Eighth Branch these are typically attended by 1,500 people, mostly women except when the meeting falls on a Sunday. Activities include sutra recitation and testimonies, but the main item of interest is a speech by the woman branch leader. Her speech sets forth the group's ideals for women and encourages them to adhere to the ideal. She dwells heavily on the necessity of fulfilling a woman's duty to persevere and endure the hardships of family life. By relying on the Buddha, praying to the ancestors, and believing in the power of the spirit world, all problems can be solved. Women must "protect" the home while men work. They must have children and raise them well, but whatever happens is because of their karma. Through proselytization and sutra recitation one can realize one's own desires. Members receive the mercy of the founder Kotani and must repay it with filial piety. Everyone must obey her senior in Reiyukai, and proselytization will lead to the ability to solve family problems. Reiyukai is creating the world of the *hotoke* 仏 (Buddhas and ancestors). The way to happiness is to practice the teachings of the Eighth Branch and to persuade husbands to join Reiyukai; this is a woman's duty. Believe in the power of the sutra and keep a copy of it in automobiles to avoid traffic accidents. Try to have religious experiences that can be presented as testimonies. Fulfill your duty and the ancestors will be satisfied. These are the major ideas of the branch leader's speeches, loosely strung together. She is revered as a living Buddha by many group members. The audience listens intently to her speech, occasionally nodding in agreement, praying silently, and applauding vigorously at the beginning and end.

Part 5: The Life of the Eighth Branch

The Eighth Branch of Reiyukai is located in Habikino City, Osaka Prefecture, at a distance of about ninety minutes by bus and train from the center of Osaka. The area is a distant suburb, composed mainly of single-family dwellings of two stories surrounding shops concentrated around two train stations. At a slight remove from the residential area is a tract of open land, in the center of which are located the worship hall, office building, and guest house of the Eighth Branch. The branch owns buses to take office workers and worshippers to and from the train stations. There are three dormitories for the branch's single employees—two for women and one for men. The men's dormitory and one of the women's are located in Osaka City, close to the Branch Youth Group Hall, Tengachaya. The new facilities at Habikino were built in 1961. On a site of 1,650 square meters, it is ten times the size of the former location at Tengachaya, built in 1951. There are presently about 600,000 members of the Eighth Branch according to its administrators. It is Reiyukai's largest. In the area immediately adjoining branch headquarters are a public hospital, a woman's junior college, an orphanage, and a home for the aged. Members visit all these places for proselytization. The Eighth Branch is headed by Masunaga Tadashi 増永忠, who is also a vice-president of Reiyukai, and his wife, Sadako 増永定子. Two of their sons and two sons-in-law are employed in the branch administration. Also employed full time in Habikino are twelve men doing administrative work, twelve young women doing clerical and miscellaneous office work, a male bus driver, one elderly man and one elderly woman doing gardening and maintenance work. In addition to this staff, one elderly woman is employed to supervise the Habikino dormitory.

All of the single men live in the Tengachaya dormitory, and five of the single women live in a dormitory, three in Tengachaya, where they share quarters with female employees of the Tengachaya facilities, and two in the Habikino dormitory. Actually, the women's housing in both cases is a single-family dwelling used by the group as a dormitory. In the Habikino case the house is a large, two-story dwelling formerly inhabited by one of the Masunaga daughters, her husband, and two children, all of whom are presently in the United States heading the Los Angeles office. During their absence the house is used as the Habikino dormitory.

The employees of the Eighth Branch receive four holidays per month. They must be present when there are meetings at the branch headquarters, and since these are often scheduled for Sunday, they seldom have a holiday on that day, nor are the holidays necessarily on the same days of the month for two months running. Thus, while the rest of Japanese society is accustomed to the five-day work week, this unit of time has little meaning in the lives of branch employees. A consequence is that it is difficult for employees to maintain contact with people outside Reiyukai because of problems of matching schedules. Especially in the case of young women whose school friends are most often employed by some city company on the normal system, the unpredictable work schedule of the Eighth Branch isolates them and forces them to rely on their acquaintances within Reiyukai almost exclusively for the three-year period of employment. During these years, it is expected that they will be at the service of their employers; thus, there are no stated conditions of labor or hours. Employees arrive at the office around 8 a.m. and routinely take only thirty minutes or so for lunch. They usually stop around 5 p.m., but if the branch leaders are present, employees leave only after the leaders, often as late as 7 p.m. Employees usually work fifty to sixty hours in a five-day period, but the pace of work is seldom intense. For this unmarried women receive a monthly base pay of ¥70,000, about half to three-quarters what a woman performing the same type of work at an ordinary small company would receive. The men's salary depends on age and seniority, but at a minimum is double that of the women.

Among the men employed at the Eighth Branch, the Masunaga sons have the highest positions—the elder as chief of the office, and the younger as general supervisor. Equal in position to the chief is the branch accountant, a Masunaga son-in-law. His house is located down the street from the Habikino dormitory, and he supervises its expenditures strictly, requiring a daily account of money spent for food and other items. He also prevails upon the dormitory housekeeper to act as maid in his home, without pay.

In many ways the Eighth Branch resembles an ordinary small-scale business in the paternalistic relation between employer and employee and in employment practices decreeing close supervision of employees even in nonworking hours. There are, however, significant differences in the lack of any necessity for employees to compete with each other, in the physical isolation of the location, and in the extreme deference shown the putative employers, the branch leaders. Also, certain religious practices set it apart.

Each day officially begins when everyone assembles in the worship hall for the morning "greeting" to the ancestors. Employees line up (women in the back), don sashes, and the chief or the oldest man present steps forward and leads the group in reciting the daimoku and a short prayer that the day's business be performed well and in the service of the ancestors. At the end everyone bows and disperses. The day ends with an identical "greeting" except for the omission of the prayer. The "greeting" is addressed to all the ancestors of all the members of the Eighth Branch and especially to those of the employees.

After work single employees are expected to participate in scheduled activities of the Youth Group. Women may participate in *ikebana* 生け花, flower arrangement classes, or in English conversation classes. Even those who enjoy studying English prefer to go only to the ikebana class, which is restricted to women, for they dislike situations in which they must compete with men. On the one hand, they are easily cowed by the brash attitude the young men frequently adopt with them, and on the other if their skills are better than men's, they feel a need to conceal their ability because it is considered unfeminine to be better at anything than the men.

The women are supervised in ikebana by a woman who re-enforces their ideas about male–female relations in addition to teaching them flower arrangement. The teacher is a perfect role model of Reiyukai's ideal woman. She dresses in a kimono almost all year round and speaks in an exceedingly high degree of honorific language. Upon entering the Tengachaya building, she goes to the room where the custodian is and greets him by going down on her knees and inclining her torso to the floor while making an elaborate speech of gratitude to him for "protecting" the building. She repeats this gesture when leaving and when any man comes into the room. This is far beyond the degree of deference that any Japanese woman outside Reiyukai would show in the same situation, but it is precisely this gesture that Reiyukai women are instructed to perform when sending off or receiving their husbands morning and night. She instructs the women to respect all men, to be grateful to them, to revere their parents, and to respect their employers as gracious benefactors. She instructs the young women to sit exactly eighteen tatami weaves from the edge of the mat and similar anachronistic items of traditional etiquette. The class members regard her as one to emulate.

Eighth Branch employees regard their branch leaders as living Buddhas, an attitude that is reflected in the extreme deference with which they are treated. When the branch leaders plan a visit to the office, an event that occurs once or twice a week, a phone call notifies the staff. Arriving in a chauffeured car, they are greeted by the entire staff, who stop working and assemble in the large workroom, women in the rear, and bow deeply as the leaders enter the room. After they proceed to the back of the room along a corridor separated from the work area by a counter, it is necessary to stop and change into slippers from outside shoes. At that point the staff does an about-face and bows deeply again. The leaders make a brief greeting or chat for a moment before retiring to their private office where they will be served tea and a son or son-in-law will administer a back rub. When the leaders depart, the staff again stop working, line up, and bow as the leaders change into outside shoes and proceed to the door. At the door the leaders bid the staff goodbye, and the staff turn 180° and bow again. They bow again when the leaders get into their car, assisted by the chauffeur. The car drives parallel to one side of the office building, and as it passes, the staff turns 90° again and bows, though their actions are invisible to the leaders. When the car is out of sight, they return to upright posture and disperse. None of the bows is of the perfunctory 10 to 20° variety, but more in the 75 to 90° range and held for as long as a minute. While the leaders are in the office, anyone who must move about does so at a trot. Women assume a posture in which arms are stiff at the sides, elbows turned in, eyes lowered.

Gestures of extreme deference plus attendance at various evening meetings in addition to long hours of work means that single employees' lives are almost entirely devoted to the Eighth Branch for the period of employment. Their working schedule is so out of synchronization with the rest of society that their personal relations are effectively limited to fellow Reiyukai members. Each day is spent in the company of fellow members so that contact with the rest of society, which does not necessarily subscribe to Reiyukai's values and world view, is minimized. Workers' time is so filled with Reiyukai activities that their movement in space is confined to the most direct routes between one Reiyukai facility and another. Deference accorded superiors in the group reenforces notions of the semi-divinity of these persons and the sacrality of the organization. Under these circumstances employees are not exposed to alternative views of life and society, and this lends the group's world view the appearance of being natural, inevitable, and desirable. The longer the employees live in these conditions, the stronger this attitude becomes.

The Habikino dormitory where I lived represents a living environment over which the branch has a great deal of control. A description of the organization of people and space there can bring out some of the principles by which, in Reiyukai thought, life is ideally regulated, and portraits of three of the people living there can perhaps contrast with these ideals, showing the ways in which individuals accept and internalize them.

The house itself is new, well-maintained, and by Japanese standards a rather luxurious dwelling with an attached garden. It is equipped with central heating and air-conditioning, as well as an automatic washing machine. However, none of these facilities is used by the residents because of the expense of electricity and gas. The women do their wash and that of the elderly man by hand, and all make do with a tiny refrigerator, though the house is fitted with a large one. Most of the bedrooms are closed off, so that three of the office women live in nine-by-twelve-foot room while many other rooms stand empty. All of these measures have as their purpose the inculcation of restraint and frugality.

An atmosphere of mutual supervision prevails by having the residents live at such close quarters, and three to a six-mat room is close even for Japan. It is impossible for failure to rise at 6 a.m. and recite the sutra to go unnoticed. Since dressers for clothes and personal belongings are kept in the altar room, one must often dress while another is reciting the sutra or praying before the altar. In such a case the subject matter of private prayers said aloud, and not infrequently ending in tears, is known to all, though everyone pretends not to hear. Similarly, each person unavoidably knows all the daily habits of the others and overhears their telephone conversations. The fact that the most intimate details of residents' habits and concerns are publicly observed pressures them to conform to unstated norms regarding the demeanor and aspirations considered appropriate to young women. They are supposed to regard their three-year period of employment, after which they will "retire" to get married, as "one thousand days of spiritual training," during which they are being prepared to "endure" and "persevere" in later life.

When I knew her in 1976–1977, Abe Yōko (the name is fictitious) was twenty-two, the ideal age for a woman to marry, according to Reiyukai thinking. She worked as a switchboard operator and had lived in the Habikino dormitory since starting her work there. She is shy, sensitive, and meek. She enjoys occasional breaks from the switchboard afforded by helping out with child care during meetings at the worship hall. She likes children and hopes to have several. She graduated from high school in Wakayama Prefecture, where she was born. She and I used to read Reiyukai literature together and discuss testimonies.

One night we were discussing a story of a woman who, while

feeling superior to him, converted her husband and began to spend much time proselytizing, doing her housework in a perfunctory manner. She was doing the absolute minimum amount of work possible, and that only with a grudging, self-righteous attitude. She repeatedly nagged her husband to recite the sutra and became angry when he refused.

Yoko defended the husband's refusal to recite the sutra, reasoning that when the wife could not even do her housework properly, she was hardly in a position to act as anyone's michibiki no oya. Yoko said that since a married woman's first and most important duty is housework, of course the husband was justified in rejecting his wife's claim to be above him in Reiyukai.

The woman in the story is selfish, Yoko said. She does things for others only to the extent that the deed presents her to good advantage. To Yoko she was a woman who does her husband's cooking and laundry only with the feeling that she is doing something praiseworthy, which may win the admiration of others. Such a woman does not accept her duty and fulfill it wholeheartedly. The woman in the story performs not only housework but proselytization and sutra recitation, too, in a self-serving manner. She fails to give herself to the service of others.

The couple's lives went on for a time in an ordinary way, but Yoko said that was a sign of trouble ahead. The woman fell ill with a fever. Yoko said that this illness was sent by the ancestors to awaken the woman to her duty. She was hurt and offended that her husband refused to recite the sutra for her even though she was ill. Probably, Yoko said, the husband sensed his wife's self-serving attitude and was rightfully refusing to validate it by acceding to her request.

For Yoko the turning point in the story came when the woman was unable to persuade a new convert to recite the sutra. Confronted with the convert's resistance, the woman realized that she also had been stubbornly blind to her own faults. Converts, said Yoko, are like mirrors the ancestors hold up to us to make us realize where we are lacking.

The testimony contained an image of the way in which women should live that Yoko cherishes as an ideal for herself. Women should be like the rice plant in full ear, bending back and forth in a summer breeze without resisting the will of others, but giving themselves instead to the service of those about them. Their passive, selfless service and sacrifice are beautiful, profound blessings in human life, like the abundant fertility of rice. Women should be meek and humble (*sunao*) to the point of having no will of their own. Yoko regrets that she falls short of this ideal and says that she is selfish.

In Yoko's view the problems of the woman in the story arose from trying to usurp her husband's prerogatives. Women should remain in the background while men put themselves forward and assume positions of leadership. Only women have the power to "endure"; men are not capable of such self-sacrifice.

At twenty-two Yoko has led a very sheltered life. She has been a member of Reiyukai since childhood, brought up in the faith by her parents. In 1976 she had twenty-two converts and thus held the rank of vice-hoza leader. Unfortunately, all the converts live in Wakayama, and thus she meets them only rarely. She cannot hold hoza for them on a regular basis and fears they will drop out without proper care.

Yoko rises daily to recite the Blue Sutra at 5:30 a.m. and when she is troubled, she recites the daimoku and other sutras as well. She says she does not understand the sutra's meaning, but that when she is chanting, the ancestors "teach" her and give her "strong power." While reciting, she feels "solemn," but her mind tends to wander if she does not concentrate on her parents and ancestors, as she has been instructed to do. Yoko says that she thinks of herself as a child and hesitates to make important decisions without consulting her parents, the branch leaders, and the ancestors in prayer. She occasionally spends the night at the house of the branch leaders in Osaka to seek advice.

Since Yoko is of marriageable age, many of her worries concern the marriage she will undoubtedly make soon. She has some doubts about marriage and wonders whether she can be happy, but she wants children and plans to have three so she will not be lonely. While I was living in the dormitory, her parents arranged a meeting with a prospective bridegroom of their choice, an *omiai* お見合い . Yoko's reaction to the man was completely negative as he was considerably older than she and quite unattractive.

However, since her parents found him suitable, she was reluctant to reject him. Not feeling capable of making a decision on her own, she consulted the branch leader and tried to divine the ancestors' will.

Yoko's divination consisted of setting out two glasses of water before the altar and designating one "yes" (she should marry the man) and the other "no" (she should not marry him). Bubbles would appear in one of the glasses, and this would indicate the ancestors' decision. In addition, she recited the sutra and prayed earnestly for several days, sobbing before the altar on her knees as she tried to reach a decision. During that time, the housekeeper and Itō Kyōko, the other office worker living in the dormitory, repeatedly expressed their concern. Kyoko said that Yoko is sometimes overly sensitive to the demands of others; she should relax and not take things so seriously. The housekeeper, on the other hand, was inclined to think definitely that Yoko should marry the man of her parents' choice: "Otherwise, she may not marry at all!" She was reminded of the story Branch Leader Masunaga Tadashi is fond of telling concerning his own marriage. His bride-to-be had never even met him, but meekly submitted to her parents' will when they told her that the man in a tattered photograph was to be her husband. Yoko preferred not to reveal the results of her divination of the ancestors' will or precisely what advice she had received from the branch leader, but in any event she decided not to marry that man.

During the summer of 1976 the Lockheed Scandal and the arrest of Tanaka Kakuei 田中角栄 occurred. Yoko said that for the most part she is not interested in politics, but that she could not forgive Tanaka for having betrayed the Japanese people. She asked whether Americans realize that it is a sin (*tsumi* 罪) for American companies to offer bribes abroad.

Yoko had made the pilgrimage to Shakaden, and she told me how she had cried when she "met the Buddha." Seeing the large, somewhat corpulent statue, she wondered whether the Buddha was a man or a woman. She was particularly struck by its thick, fleshy hands and feet. She found the feet especially poignant since they were bare, showing that the Buddha had walked barefoot all the way from India to Japan.

Yoko is considered by other women in the office to be a person who well represents Japanese tradition, in that by nature she is meek, respectful of her parents and superiors, and not particularly interested in foreign travel or fads for foreign things. They say of her that she is very *nihonteki* 日本的, "very Japanese."

The other woman living in the Habikino dormitory, Ito Kyoko, by contrast, is considered *gendaiteki* 現代的, "modern," meaning that she is more interested in foreign culture than Japanese tradition. Kyoko was born in a city near Hiroshima, where her mother is a stalwart Reiyukai member. Kyoko has been reciting the sutra since the age of ten, has seventy converts, and thus is a hoza leader. Twenty of her converts are Mexicans Kyoko proselytized when they came to Japan on an Inner Trip tour. Because she can speak a bit of Spanish and English, she was frequently asked to escort tour groups from Mexico and the United States. Her dream is to live for a time in the United States as a staff member of the branch office in Los Angeles. For that reason, she studies English as much as possible and prefers to attend that class instead of flower arranging, though the teacher and students of the ikebana class feel a bit miffed that she does not join in with all the other young women. Nevertheless, she is convinced that trying to learn to communicate the teachings of Reiyukai to foreigners is as important and worthwhile as traditional female accomplishments like ikebana. She would like to have an American boyfriend and possibly marry an American, an aspiration that is greatly disapproved by other Reiyukai members.

Since she has been a member since childhood, Kyoko knows the details of writing posthumous names well. She has her own interpretation of Reiyukai teaching which emphasizes the theme of blood. Since Reiyukai does not codify its doctrines or give systematic instruction in them, many members have their own interpretations of various elements, and thus Kyoko is not unique in this respect. From the ancestors, Kyoko believes, we have received many kinds of blood, some good, some bad. Karma is transmitted in the blood as propensities for certain types of action. For example, if a mother is a pickpocket, it is likely that her children will have the same vice. Likewise, the children of divorced parents are likely to experience divorce. Parents are "one type of ancestor," because both parents and ancestors bequeath blood to descendants. Kyoko says karma works like heredity, and that she learned that this is so in high school. Because we all have many different types of blood, we must purify it through spiritual training, by reciting the sutra, pilgrimage to Mirokusan, Shichimenzan, and Shakaden, and by winter austerities.

Winter austerities (*kangyō* 寒行) are performed in all-male or all-female groups. After midnight the groups gather outside by a well or water faucet, strip off their clothes, and pour icy water over their backs while reciting the daimoku. Not only do these austerities purify the blood, but also create spiritual power. Women have a special need to purify themselves not only because of the physical pollution of menstruation, but also because their inner nature (*konjō* 根性) is not as pure as men's. However, if women purify themselves through spiritual training, they can obtain more power than men can. Purification of the blood helps the ancestors attain salvation, which in concrete terms means being happy in the spirit world. Spirits that are not saved may become *ikiryō* 生霊 or *shiryō*, 死霊, "spirits of the living and dead." Kyoko once experienced unaccountable sluggishness and depression after passing an examination qualifying her to work at the Los Angeles office. She concluded that her mood was due to the work of a jealous ikiryo-shiryo. All these ideas are common in Reiyukai, though individuals choose to emphasize some in accordance with their individual personalities and concerns.

Kyoko is outgoing and straightforward, laughing often and generally enjoying her work. She likes to make others laugh, and she can be counted on to liven up an overly solemn assembly. She is thought to have a talent for dealing with foreigners, whom other members are reluctant to approach. Her life has not been as sheltered as Yoko's. In high school she had a boyfriend and would probably have had one at Habikino had supervision not been so strict. However, while the young men at the office enjoy her wit, they seem to consider her straightforward manner a sign that she has taken on too many foreign ways and may be too assertive to make a good wife. The male office supervisors frequently scold her for lacking grace and restraint, and tell her to be more refined and self-effacing. Kyoko doubts that they will allow her to travel to the

United States, and from what I could tell, she is probably right. This is a major disappointment, and Kyoko chafes at constraints on her ambitions.

Kyoko wants to delay marriage because "afterwards there is no freedom." However, when she does marry, she hopes to have an arranged marriage, because these matches are more stable than "love marriages." She will rely on her parents' judgment to a large extent because she regards herself as a child, although she is self-supporting, pays taxes, and votes. She is not interested in politics.

Other people in the Habikino office like both Yoko and Kyoko and consider them to be good members of Reiyukai. Their attitudes and behavior fall within the limits of acceptability, though they are vastly different in personality and aspiration. In contrast to these two, there was one person in the office who was regarded as something of a misfit, someone who others said, "doesn't understand the teachings of Reiyukai." They did not find fault with her for failing to understand any single point in ritual or doctrine, but because her attitudes and aspirations were not acceptable.

Nakamura Sanae was twenty-three in 1976. She was born in Okayama, where her father is a salesman and member of Reiyukai, as is her mother. Sanae was brought up in Reiyukai and since childhood has had the ambition to live abroad, preferably in England. She studied English in high school, and even after her graduation and employment in the Eighth Branch, she continued to take two lessons per week, one at a commercial language school. No one else at the Eighth Branch did such a thing, and Sanae was regarded somewhat suspiciously for this extramural activity. Everyone else wondered why Sanae would go outside the group for such a thing. Kyoko's guess was that Sanae is more interested in mastering the English language than she is in learning to explain Reiyukai ideas to foreigners. Sanae's outside English teacher said Sanae could not explain what Reiyukai's beliefs are and that Sanae stated she believed in them "only halfway." Nevertheless, Sanae recites the sutra every day and often goes to hospitals with other young women to make converts.

Sanae enjoys discussing ideas with others and does not shy away from disagreement and argument. Kyoko said she and Sanae used to talk about the existence of flying saucers and UFOs. Whereas Kyoko was willing to entertain the possibility that such things exist, Sanae had a strong opinion that the whole notion was nonsense. Kyoko was taken aback by Sanae's assertiveness. Having more practice than the others in English, Sanae was noticeably more fluent than they, including the men, and she had no qualms about demonstrating her ability.

In the autumn of 1976, Sanae began to make plans to go abroad. Apparently she never considered the idea of going to work for Reiyukai in its foreign offices. Instead, she wanted independence to explore foreign climes on her own. When this became known, others had a variety of reactions. Her parents were not pleased, but they resigned themselves since Sanae seemed determined to persevere in the face of their opposition. She had a boyfriend who was not a member of Reiyukai, and he was also opposed, preferring to marry right away and settle down. However, recognizing that he could not prevent her from carrying out her plan, he also was resigned. The branch leaders were much against the idea of Sanae traveling alone and repeatedly called her into their office to remonstrate with her. For the other office women, it was a foregone conclusion that Sanae would fall into a life of dissipation if she traveled without proper supervision. However, their attitude was that they had done for her all that could be expected.

Sanae often used to consult Yoko, whose judgment she trusted, about what she ought to do. Yoko would discuss with her the pros and cons of foreign travel, with emphasis on the latter. However, Yoko felt that her advice fell on deaf ears, because instead of listening meekly and following the advice of Yoko and others, Sanae seemed to have the attitude that she was fully capable of making her own decision after having weighed as many considerations as possible. A woman should be more humble. As Kyoko said, "Sanae goes straight ahead and makes up her own mind— just like a man." This remark was not intended as a compliment.

The Habikino housekeeper was particularly worried about Sanae. Previously Sanae had lived in the dormitory, and having lived under the same roof for some time, the housekeeper felt she had a number of reasons to be concerned. There was the question of Sanae's relationship with a man outside Reiyukai. Although there was no reason to suspect them of having carried things beyond the bounds of propriety, any relation with a person outside the group was automatically a matter of suspicion. Besides, the housekeeper had sometimes spoken to him when he called to talk to Sanae, and could tell by his telephone voice that he was not quite respectable. The housekeeper's conclusion was that "Sanae doesn't understand the teachings of Reiyukai. She doesn't understand anything at all!" In the face of Sanae's continued obstinacy, the housekeeper ended by feeling exasperated at Sanae's presumptuous self-reliance.

Over the course of a month or so, the atmosphere of the whole office was affected by Sanae's decision to leave before the end of the usual three years. For one thing, the rest of the staff was inconvenienced by the loss of her bookkeeping skills, and another woman had to be quickly trained to take over. By the time Sanae left, the other staff were rather negative to her, and said that unless she made a point of visiting them at the office, there would be no further contact between them.

Being thus ostracized, Sanae turned more and more to the one other person at the Eighth Branch office who obviously did not fit in, namely myself. It came out that, although she was seriously intending to leave for London within a month, having found herself a position as an *au pair* girl through her other English teacher, she had not the vaguest idea how to go about getting a passport, vaccinations, visa, etc. In other words, although her determination was strong, she had little idea how to operate outside the bounds of Reiyukai. She feared foreign cities, since her office-mates were quick to tell her of the dangers for a single woman. Caught by conflicting emotions, Sanae's conclusion was "I should have been born a man." On this if nothing else, other Eighth Branch members would have agreed with her.

In this chapter we have seen how Reiyukai has developed themes originally formulated by its founders and first-generation members. The second and third generations still find meaning in the ancestors, quite apart from any sense of "crisis," and they devote themselves to their religion with self-sacrifice and sincerity that does not pale by comparison with the founders. Problems that arose under Kotani's administration are still with her successors as the younger generations struggle to find an accommodation between a primacy of religious experience and a growing need for more systematic exposition of religious tenets. Kubo's and Kotani's attempt to establish the ancestors as universal deities succeeds well for contemporary members, symbolizing their traditionalism in social and religious matters. Social and religious concerns relating to women continue to occupy a central position in Reiyukai's continuing appropriation of Buddhist themes, and these define the parameters of personal aspiration as women both fail and succeed in remaining within the boundaries decreed by this Buddhist traditionalism.

Chapter Three

Reiyukai and the Family

This chapter examines the relation between Reiyukai and the family. Reiyukai members are greatly concerned about what they see as a "breakdown" of the family, and they hope to restore its values. Members have strong opinions as to how the family should be organized and regulated that differ from those of the general populace.

The family system has been undergoing radical change since 1945, but Reiyukai upholds the values of the family system as it was before 1945. Much of the thought and behavior of Reiyukai members is aimed at dealing with problems that arise within the family, and members believe that changes for the better in society and the world can result from proper adherence to the old system. Correct performance of one's role in the family is seen as having sacred meaning, and is linked to the service of the deities of the family system, the ancestors.[1] On the whole, members' social attitudes concerning the family system are somewhat more conservative and traditionalist than those of other Japanese, but not extremely so. That this is so can be seen from a comparison of

---

[1] There is some question whether all of the rites associated with ancestral spirits can be considered "worship" and thus whether it is appropriate either to speak of "ancestor worship" or to call the ancestral spirits "deities." Particularly in the case of those who have died in recent years, the term "memorialism" may be more appropriate than worship, and the term "deity" may be quite misleading. However, in general, the terms "deity" and "ancestor worship" are, as Robert J. Smith points out, correct descriptions of Japanese practice. *Ancestor Worship in Contemporary Japan* (Stanford: Stanford University Press, 1974), p. 146.

members' versus nonmembers' attitudes on selected issues related
to the family system.

Part 1: Changes in the Family System

Crucial to an understanding of Reiyukai attitudes is an examination of the Japanese ie 家, the household, since it is this that
members hope to establish as society's cornerstone. Reiyukai
members distinguish the ie from the nuclear family and hope to
revive the ethical ideals of the ie. The ie's members are traditionally engaged in a common economic enterprise such as agriculture
or merchandising. The ie includes a nucleus of consanguines
related through the paternal line but is not strictly patrilineal.
Collaterals or, in the past, retainers, might be set up as branch
houses (*bunke* 分家) subordinate to the main house, the *honke*
本家. In pre-Meiji times retainers and others not related by blood
were commonly adopted into the ie and resided with its other
members. The ie did not dissolve upon the death of the household
head and his wife but continued over generations. This clearly
differentiates the ie from the nuclear family. Properly speaking,
the term ie should not be translated as "family." Furthermore, the
ie could be perpetuated by adoption even if the actual bloodline
died out; actual patrilineal succession was not considered
essential.

The religious manifestation of genealogical continuity was
found in ancestor worship. The head of the household (kacho)
inherited ancestral tablets and ritual equipment upon the death of
his predecessor, and with his wife was the chief ritualist of the ie.
Only members of an ie could worship its ancestors, and participation in the rites of ancestor worship was obligatory for ie
members. It was not a matter of personal belief.

The ie typically performed multiple functions: economic production, education of children and youth, protection against unemployment (through absorbing excess manpower for labor-
intensive activities in times of economic distress), care of the aged,
and religious training through ancestor worship. The ie as a
system of integrating consanguines and nonconsanguines for

common enterprise has changed over time, and particularly important alterations occurred in the Meiji period.[2]

In the Meiji period changes in civil law drastically transformed the character of the ie. In the drafting of the Meiji Civil Code, European and American concepts of possession based on the individual were introduced. These conflicted with the Japanese concept of the wealth of the ie (*kasan* 家産), which belonged to no single member. However, since the ie was not a legal person, Meiji law specified the household head as the owner of its wealth, contrary to the former concept of the head being merely custodian of its wealth, not its owner. This gave the position of head more authority than in former times. Furthermore, the head was granted wide-ranging powers over lower-ranking ie members, especially regarding marriage.[3]

Meiji modes of marriage appropriated the former samurai pattern in which marriage was considered primarily a contract between two ie, not between the two principals. In other pre-Meiji classes, marriage was considered a contract between wife and husband. With the change to the samurai pattern, the status of women in marriage was lowered. Popular conception, powerfully molded by the national educational system, emphasized women's duty to bear children (as many and as soon as possible) and to perpetuate the husband's ie. Women who did not bear children could be summarily divorced; there was no recognition of male sterility.[4]

[2] On the ie see Nakano Tadashi, "Ie no kōzō to ishiki oyobi sono henyō" in *Shōka dōzokudan no kenkyū*, ed. Nakano Tadashi (Tokyo: Miraisha, 1974), pp. 106–193; Kawashima Takeyoshi, *Nihon shakai no kazokuteki kōsei* (Tokyo: Nihon Hyōronsha, 1965), pp. 77–141; Koyama Takashi, *Gendai kazoku no kenkyū* (Tokyo: Yoshikawa Kōbundō, 1960), pp. 291–374; Koyama Takashi, "Tokyo kinkōson no kazoku," *Sonraku shakai kenkyū nenpō* 10 (1960), 1–23; Nakano Tadashi, "Kazoku to shinzoku," in *Kōza shakaigaku*, ed. Fukutake Tadashi (Tokyo: Tokyo daigaku shuppansha, 1957), pp. 44–70; Kino Seiichi, "Ie o meguru ideorogii no kako to genzai," *Kagaku no shisō* 7 (January, 1973), 47–55.

[3] Nakano, "Ie no kōzō," pp. 155–59; Kawashima, *Nihon no kazokuteki kōsei*, pp. 86–103; Arichi Tōro, *Kindai nihon no kazokukan* (Tokyo: Kōbundō, 1977), pp. 1–5; Fukutake Ichirō, *Nihon kazoku seido shi gaisetsu* (Tokyo: Yoshikawa kōbunkan, 1972), pp. 199–205.

[4] Fukutake, *Nihon kazoku seido shi*, pp. 206, 218–22; Kawashima, *Nihon shakai no kazokuteki kōsei*, pp. 86–90.

Other provisions of the Meiji Civil Code tended to undermine the security of a woman's status in law. Although in-marrying wives attained the same status as other ie members, marriage itself depended on the approval of the household, often the husband's father. Marriage was made official by being registered in the census records, and only the household had the authority to enter this registration. It was not uncommon to delay registration until the birth of a child. In the interval the woman could be returned to her family in disgrace. Laws were made that recognized concubinage and made legal distinctions among adopted and natural children, legitimate and illegitimate children, and between recognized and unrecognized illegitimate children. Only those recognized by the father had legal claims upon him. Although official recognition of concubinage ended in 1882, the continued existence of the practice undermined the principle of monogamy and increased the vulnerability of the wife. If a family had no male children, then a daughter could succeed to the headship of the ie, but if she married, her husband automatically became kacho. A wife needed her husband's permission to engage in any economic activity; he had control over all her possessions. He could divorce her on grounds of adultery, but she could not do the same. Wives could initiate divorce only under very limited circumstances. Wives could inherit property only if there were neither children nor grandchildren in the paternal line. Thus the chances for women to inherit property or control economic enterprise were virtually nonexistent. This greatly went against traditional practice.[5]

Although ancestor worship within the ie has undergone various changes historically and also varies considerably from region to region, it is possible to generalize about its basic outline in relation to the family system. The ancestors are the founders and protective deities of an ie. For the most part they are worshipped collectively, without distinguishing separate personalities within the collectivity. Funerals and periodic memorial services are carried out by priests of the temple to which the particular ie is affiliated. Participation in various rites is a mark of relative status in the ie,

[5] Kawashima, *Nihon shakai no kazokuteki kōsei*, pp. 86–90.

and the scale on which they are held (the relative simplicity or extravagance of the rites) differentiates the relative wealth of various ie.[6]

Older Reiyukai members cherish the hope of reviving the ethical ideals of the ie system in combination with ancestor worship. For the most part, when they speak of the "old family system" (*mukashi no kazoku seido* 昔の家族制度), they refer to it as the group's oldest members knew it, as children and adults prior to 1945. This was the period when it was most heavily influenced by the state, which hoped to use the system to unify the people in support of its political goals, and when the status of women was at low ebb. Sacred meaning is attributed to the values of the old system. Obedience, loyalty, filial piety, and duty are the supreme ideals. These are connected with the principle of male dominance, female subordination, the authority of elders, and the notion of the nation as a single family. Although these ideals as interpreted in combination with state ideology from Meiji to 1945 had little relation to the customary practice of the people before that time, older Reiyukai members see in them the essence of timeless tradition, the core of Japan's pure and unique "beautiful customs" (*bifū* 美風). Older members feel nostalgia for a time of undivided loyalties, unclouded ideals, unambiguous roles and duties, and believe that many problems of modern society would be solved if people would return to the ways of the past.[7]

Under the postwar Constitution, the ie is no longer recognized

[6] Aruga Kizaemon, "Nihon ni okeru senzo no kannen," in *Aruga Kizaemon chosakushū*, 11 vols. (Tokyo: Miraisha, 1966–1971), 7:1–23; Abe Masatarō, "Senzo sūhai to sono shakaiteki kitei," *Nenpō shakaigaku kenkyū* 1 (1944), 134–61; Maeda Takashi, "Nihon sonraku ni okeru sosen sūhai to sōzoku no jittai," *Shakaigaku hyōron* 10, No. 2 (1960), 87–105; Takeda Chōshū, *Nihonjin no ie to shūkyō* (Tokyo: Hyōronsha, 1976), chaps. 1–4; Takeda, *Sosen sūhai* (Kyoto: Heirakuji shoten, 1957), pp. 203–208; Kazoku kenkyūbukai, "Sengo ni okeru kazoku no jittai," *Shakaigaku hyōron* 7, Nos. 27 and 28 (1957), 142.

[7] Jiyūtō kenpō chōsakai, "Nihon koku kenpō kaiseian yōkō," in *Nihon fujin mondai shiryō shūsei*, ed. Ichikawa Fusae, 10 vols. (Tokyo: Domesu shuppan, 1978–1980), 5:537–49; Tanabe Keiko, "Fukkatsu imi suru mono," *Sekai* 3 (1955), 21–67; Kawashima Takashi, "Kazoku seido no fukkatsu," in *Nihon fujin mondai shiryō shūsei*, vol. 5 pp. 569–78, and in the same volume, Wagatsuma Hiroshi, "Kenpō dai nijūyon an wa kaisei subeki ka?" pp. 579–83; Ishii Ryōsuke, *Japanese Legislation in the Meiji Era*, trans. W. J. Chambliss (Tokyo: Kosai Publishing Co., 1968), p. 379.

as the basic unit of society. In its stead the nuclear family, composed of a married couple and their children, has been so designated, and the ie now has no legal status. Even before 1945 the majority of families were in fact of the nuclear type but lacked a corresponding ethic. The proportion of nuclear families rose to 78 percent in 1965. At the same time the number of persons per household decreased from five to four from 1940 to 1965. The equivalent decrease took fifty years in the United States and Europe, showing that the speed of change has been very rapid in Japan. At present the proportion of nuclear families is around 96 percent.

Accompanying the trend to nuclear families as the social norm is a shift of the population from rural to urban areas. During the 1950s the balance shifted in favor of urban areas, and this urbanization has tended to weaken ancestor worship as a whole because the new urban families frequently lose contact with the temple and graves of the ancestors in the countryside. Fewer urban families include an old person who would in former times have been the natural one to see that the altar was cared for and daily ancestral rites properly carried out. Whereas the former ie was a multifunctional unit which both produced and consumed, the nuclear family is a consumption unit only, except in case of families managing a family business or farm. Now the general pattern is for the husband to work at a salaried job outside the home, while the wife occupies herself with child-rearing and housework, possibly returning to the labor force after the children enter school. Increased dependence on the labor market has decreased the family's ability to absorb unemployed members or to care for the aged. Nevertheless, there has not been a corresponding expansion of social welfare provisions capable of alleviating these pressures on the family. It is still expected for the most part that the family will perform the functions of the ie even though its resources have been drastically decreased. Concepts of duty and filial piety are invoked to assign these responsibilities, but it is clear that the old ethic is not entirely suited to the new unit, the nuclear family.[8]

[8] Yamamuro Kōhei, "Kaku kazokuron hihan ni taisuru gimon ni kotaete," *Shakaigaku hyōron* 16, No. 3 (1966), 121–29 and "Oyako kankei" in *Gendai kazoku no kenkyū*, ed. Koyama, pp. 93–121, and in the same volume, Aoi Kazuo,

A religious significance is attributed to marriage in Reiyukai, which is sometimes discussed in terms of yin and yang, but more frequently encountered is the idea that there exists some deep, hidden meaning (*en* 縁, *innen* 因縁) in the fact that these particular individuals married. It is not a question of then discovering what the meaning is or the reasons behind the union, but a matter of living out the connection that originated in ages past through their own karma and that of their ancestors. Marriage itself is considered a form of religious training (*shugyō* 修行) in which the couple must persevere together. It is taken for granted that marriage and raising children will require great sacrifice and endurance, and since this suffering cannot be meaningless, it must have a profound and sacred significance. The couple has a duty to serve their ancestors together and to produce children who will perpetuate the ancestors' will and ritual service. Members are insistent that children must be taught to perpetuate the ie, which has been handed down from the ancestors through the ages. For the most part they refer to the husband's ie, but if the wife was an only child or had female siblings only, the couple may have one of their sons take the wife's family name to perpetuate her ie. Thus the religious significance attributed to marriage is intimately linked to the worship of ancestors.

Older Reiyukai members were eager to explain their views on the family system to me at length. The post-1945 "breakdown" of the family and Reiyukai's relevance to the business of restoring it are subjects about which they hold strong opinions. Older members speak nostalgically about the days before the war when it was taken for granted that the first son would continue to live with his parents after marriage. In those days women "endured" more; they were humble and acquiescent in the face of the many burdens

"Fūfu kankei," pp. 121–206; Aoi and Masuda Kōkichi, eds., *Kazoku hendō no shakaigaku* (Tokyo: Baifūkan, 1973), pp. 53–69; Morioka Kiyomi, *Gendai shakai no minshū to shūkyō*, Nihonjin no kōdō to shisō, vol. 49 (Tokyo: Hyōronsha, 1973), pp. 92–112; Kawasaki Enshō, "Toshi ni okeru ie no shūkyō no henyō," *Ryūkoku daigaku bukkyō bunka kenkyūjo kiyō*, No. 13 (June, 1974), 70–84; Morioka Kiyomi, "Kakukazoku no gendai teki ishiki," special issue of *Jurist: Gendai no kazoku*, Spring, 1977, pp. 60–66; and in the same volume, Yamate Shigeru, "Mai hōmu shugi" pp. 136–42.

placed upon them. They willingly bore many children and obeyed their mothers-in-law. After 1945, however, the American Occupation introduced many insidious innovations. It declared that the sexes are equal, and this has given women the power to initiate divorce. Thus women no longer "endure," and they are not willing to fulfill their duties to their husbands and affines. They think only of themselves. In a materialistic quest for needless luxuries, some women continue working after they are married or try to go back to work after their children enter school, but this is unreasonable. Every job a married woman fills takes one away from a man who needs it more. Married women should "protect" the home instead of working. This is not a question of the equality of the sexes. Men and women are naturally endowed with differing abilities which are not directly comparable. They play different roles in society and do not naturally come into competition with each other, but if a married woman works, it upsets her household and her relation with her husband. Changes introduced by the Occupation have led to the virtual destruction of the family system, and these changes go against Japan's traditions and "beautiful customs." The youth of today must be taught by their elders what pure Japanese tradition is, and Reiyukai is helping in that endeavor. These ideas were repeated to me many times, and women are undoubtedly more vehement exponents of them than men.

There are a number of ways in which these and related ideas are promulgated within Reiyukai. In branch meetings, attended mainly by women, female branch leaders lecture the audience at length on problems between mothers- and daughters-in-law, with emphasis on the latter's duty to yield in case of conflict. They speak as if in fact all members were living in three-generation, ie-style domestic arrangements. It is taken for granted that such arrangements are most desirable. They tell their audiences that even if a family is in extreme financial difficulty, married women should not work. They should "protect" the home and devise ways to economize. Leaders often say that families would seldom find themselves in straitened circumstances if they did not aspire to possess inessential luxuries. It is better to adjust one's expectations to lower standards so that one experiences fewer disap-

pointments. In evening meetings led by male branch leaders, many
stories are told of the bad end inevitably met by unfilial, ungrateful
youth, particularly first sons who live separately from their parents after marriage. Female leaders who counsel women with
family problems recommend apology to husband and mother-in-
law as the sine qua non for a Reiyukai solution and in other ways
urge complete acquiescence in the role of wife. In these ways
Reiyukai works to instill in its members the values of the ie system
and to return to its organizational pattern for family life.

However, although Reiyukai members' ancestor worship is
consciously linked to the goal of establishing the values and organizational forms of the ie as the standard for Japanese society,
in fact the group's ritual seems paradoxically better suited to the
nuclear family. In the pattern of ancestor worship most typical of
the ie system, regardless of who actually performs the daily offerings of food and drink before the altar, the tablets and altar and
other ritual furnishings are inherited by the first son, and the
tablets may be collectively entrusted to a temple for permanent
ritual service. Thus, the patrilateral pattern is maintained over
generations. In Reiyukai, however, individual tablets are not used.
When an individual joins the group, a single tablet is made and
enshrined in an altar. If the member is single, it records the family
name of the person's mother and father. If married, the family
name of husband and wife are recorded, yielding a bilateral
pattern in either case. This tablet is burnt upon the cremation
of the spouse who lives longer. Thus, the cult is based upon the
conjugal pair and is not perpetuated beyond the demise of the
nuclear family formed by their marriage. When their children
marry, they will have new tablets recording the name of each
spouse, and therefore enshrining a different collection of ancestors. However, children may transfer names from the death register representing the collectivity of ancestors worshipped by
their parents to the new register they keep from the time of
marriage. In such a case, ancestors could be recorded and worshipped by more than one child. This would present no problem
from Reiyukai's point of view. The bilateral pattern of ancestor
worship in Reiyukai is more congruent with the nuclear family,
which members say has contributed to the breakdown of the ie

system, than with the patrilateral ie itself, which members would like to reinstate.

The following discussion attempts to locate the position of Reiyukai members in the larger spectrum of Japanese society's views on the family system. The family is expected to perform a variety of functions: raising children, caring for the aged, and perpetuating the cult of the ancestors. Reiyukai members believe that these functions can best be fulfilled by the ie, and that the nuclear family is inadequate. Thus Reiyukai members continue to be very concerned about the ie, though it has been disestablished and now has no legal status whatever.

This is not to say that in placing a high value on the family, Reiyukai members are unlike the rest of society. It is worth noting that in 1953, 1958, and 1973 the Japanese people as a whole ranked "family and children" (*kazoku, kodomo* 家族, 子供) as their first and greatest priority, ranking "life and health" next in importance. Thus it is not the case that the Japanese have become less interested in the family. They have, however, become less preoccupied with the prewar ie.[9]

As Reiyukai members continue to be concerned about the ie, the rest of society shows less and less concern for it and has accepted the nuclear family in its place. This is especially true of urban society. Rural Japan continues to be more concerned about the ie. This acceptance of the nuclear family occurred over the years 1945–1965. The change may be documented from opinion polls of the time. Thus there is a growing gap between Reiyukai and the rest of society on issues of the family. This discussion draws on the author's 1977 questionnaire to determine what family issues Reiyukai members are most concerned about. After identifying those problems, in Part 2 I attempt to show how they relate to the beliefs of the group and to the social position of its members.

A word of explanation about the surveys cited here is in order. After the establishment of the postwar Constitution, the Japanese government and the news media surveyed widely in order to

[9] Fukushima Tadao, ed., *Kazoku: seisaku to hō*, 7 vols. Vol. 3: *Sengo nihon kazoku no dōkō*, pp. 53–55 (Tokyo: Tokyo daigaku shuppan kai, 1977). Here the change in public opinion about the ie is documented over the period 1945–1965.

determine the extent to which the new laws were accepted. Even in 1947, when the first polls were taken, a majority of 58 percent supported the nuclear family over the ie, against a 37 percent rate of disapproval.[10] Of those approving the new system, women outnumbered men, the unmarried outnumbered the married, and persons engaged in farming or fishing tended to disapprove more than those in other occupational categories. Then in 1956 the Cabinet's statistics staff found that a majority expressed the desire to "preserve the traditional family system," seeming to reverse the findings of the 1947 survey. In the 1950s those approving the nuclear family were largely concentrated among the younger age groups, but by the 1960s approval had spread to all age groups. After 1960 those favoring the new system held the majority according to every major national survey.[11]

By 1966 the proportion of those approving the nuclear family was about two-thirds. This is shown by a 1966 survey in which respondents were asked to say whether they preferred the nuclear family or the ie with respect to these matters: husband-wife relations, the mother's role, the father's role, the strength of the family, and the discipline of children. On every issue except the last, 65 percent favored the nuclear family, as opposed to 12 percent in favor of the ie. Thus we can say with confidence that by about 1965 the nuclear family had firmly taken root in public opinion and had achieved acceptance.[12]

Because the nuclear family was found to be accepted in so many surveys, it ceased to be an issue for the poll-takers as well as for the general populace. Questions about acceptance of the ie ceased to be asked by surveyors, and Japanese society turned its attention to other matters.[13]

[10] Ibid.

[11] Ibid.

[12] Ibid.

[13] An examination of major public opinion surveys carried out over the 1970s shows that no major poll has asked questions about acceptance of the nuclear family. See Kokumin seikatsu kenkyūjo, *Nihonjin no seikatsu ishiki* (Tokyo: Chibundō, 1970); Nihon hōsō kyōkai seron chōsa jo, *Shōwa yonjū nendo kokumin seikatsu jikan chōsa* (Tokyo: Nihon hōsō shuppan kyōkai, 1966, 1971); Kōseishō ōkura kanbō tōkei jōhōbu, *Kokumin seikatsu jittai chōsa hōkokusho* (Tokyo: Kōsei tōkei kyōkai, 1980); see also the editions of all years from 1974–1979. In Nihon

However, Reiyukai continues to favor the ie and to disapprove of its disestablishment. This was clear to me from the experience of living with Reiyukai members, and it was on the basis of that experience that I designed the questionnaire as I did and attempted to guage the strength of Reiyukai members' views on family-centered questions and to compare them to the strength of those ideas as found among the general populace.

The ideal method of comparison would have been to compare my results to those of a national survey given in the same year on the same issues. But because these issues had ceased to be of urgent concern to the wider society nearly fifteen years earlier, there were no national surveys asking comparable questions. This meant that I could only compare Reiyukai in 1978 to the rest of Japanese society as it was several years prior to my survey, using whenever possible exactly the same wording as those surveys I used as a base of comparison. This inevitably produces the impression that the majority of Reiyukai members bears more resemblance to Japanese society as a whole in the 1950s than it does to Japanese society in the 1980s. This impression is not simply a distortion produced by the method employed here. In fact there is a general "lag" produced by the occupation of so many positions of leadership in Reiyukai by individuals now in their sixties, whose most

---

hōsō kyōkai, *Nihonjin no ishiki—NHK seron chōsa* (Tokyo: Chibundō, 1975), of 1975, the question was asked what type of family arrangement respondents hoped to live in after retirement, but nothing was asked regarding opinions on present family structure. No questions bearing on acceptance of the nuclear family were asked by the Keizai kikaku-chō kokumin seikatsu chōsa-ka, ed., *Kokumin no seikatsu to ishiki no dōkō* (Tokyo: Ōkurashō insatsu kyoku, 1976). In Keizai kikaku-chō, ed., *Shōwa gojū-roku nenban kokumin seikatsu hakusho* (Tokyo: Ōkurashō insatsu kyoku, 1981), pp. 79–80, it is documented that from 1970–1975, 97.2 percent of all families were of the nuclear type, while from 1975–1980 some 96.9 percent of all families in Japan were nuclear. The survey did not question respondents' attitudes toward the nuclear family. The same is true of all editions of this survey from 1973–1980. An interesting survey is Nihon chiiki kaihatsu sentā, ed. *Nihonjin no kachikan* (Tokyo: Chibundō, 1970); in questions 8–10 respondents were asked whether they believe the family is presently fulfilling its role as a place to raise children, and to state what they think the family's most important function is. Each of the survey's questions assumes that the subject in question is the nuclear family, not the ie. On page 73 the authors state that most people now think more often of the nuclear family than of the ie.

Table 8. *Do You Think the Japanese People Form a Great, Single Family?*

	Yes	No
Reiyukai	68.6%	31.4%
	(427)	(195)
Prime Minister's Survey, 1957	62%	25%

cherished beliefs on the good society were formed forty years ago, precisely when the state was busiest inculcating patriotic notions about the ie and its role in the preservation of a Japanese world order.

Two items pertaining to the persistence of the formerly state-sponsored ideas about the family system were asked in my 1977 questionnaire. The first was, "Do you think the Japanese people form a great, single family?" As noted in Chapter 1, the view that such is the case originated with State Shinto. This and the following question are linked to an image of society as a smoothly functioning hierarchy of complementary parts. Table 8 compares the results of the Reiyukai questionnaire with those of a 1957 Prime Minister's Survey.[14] While present-day Reiyukai members hold this view somewhat more frequently than the general population of 1957, the difference is not extreme. However, we may presume that in the twenty-odd-year period since the Prime Minister's survey, the percentage of the general population holding this view has declined, since the chief organ of its promulgation, the educational system, no longer actively promotes it. Thus, it is being spread to a smaller part of the population. The second question to be discussed in this regard concerns the perceived analogy between parent–child and employer–employee relations. The question was, "There is an opinion that the relation between a company and its employees is just like that betwe. parent and child—if the employee works hard for the company, the company will take a parental attitude and take care of its employees. Do you agree?" Table 9 compares results of the

[14] Naikaku sōridaijin kanbōgishitsu, *Kazoku seido ni tsuite no seron chōsa* (Tokyo: Prime Minister's Office, 1957), p. 615.

Table 9. *Employer: Employee: :Parent: Child*

	Agree	Disagree
Reiyukai	71.9%	28.1%
	(447)	(175)
1973 Survey	69%	31%

Table 10. *Should One Child Be Designated Solely Responsible for the Care of Parents in Old Age?*

	Yes	No
Reiyukai	43.1%	56.9%
	(274)	(361)
Prime Minister's Survey, 1969	48%	52%

Reiyukai questionnaire with a 1973 survey.[15] Reiyukai members support these notions, originating in part with State Shinto, somewhat more frequently than the rest of society, but without striking disparity. This indicates the continuing presence of these paternalistic ideals in society and suggests that Reiyukai is successful in perpetuating them, but does not set the group significantly apart from the rest of society.

The questionnaire included several items concerning the aged, who rely most heavily on the family system for their support. One item asked, "Recently, the number of elderly people who are in distress is increasing in Japan. Are you concerned about this problem?" Eighty-eight percent (555) of respondents replied that they felt considerably concerned, indicating that members are well aware of the problems of the aged. Respondents were also asked whether they thought one child should be designated as solely responsible for parents' support in old age; the present law calls for all children to share the responsibility equally. Table 10 compares

[15] Yasuda Saburō, *Gendai nihon no kaikyū ishiki* (Tokyo: Yūhikaku, 1973) p. 98. Yasuda notes that this idea is typically accepted by workers or owners of small- or medium-sized enterprises, and is typically rejected by blue-collar workers in large-scale industry.

Table 11. Should There Be a Legal Requirement That Children Act with Filial Piety toward Their Parents?

	Yes	No
Reiyukai	40.3%	59.7%
	(244)	(362)
Prime Minister's Survey, 1957	16%	84%

Table 12. Which of the Following Do You Think Is the Best Way to Live?

	Percent	Number
Alone	0.5	3
Married, with children, not living with parents	9.8	63
Married, with children, living with parents	85.5	547
Other	4.2	27

the results with those of a 1969 Prime Minister's survey.[16] Reiyukai members do not differ significantly from the rest of the population on this issue; this implies that they do not seek a return to the practice of holding the first son solely responsible for the parents. A related question asked, "Should there be a legally established requirement that children act with filial piety toward their parents?" It would be generally understood that financial support is included in the notion of filial piety. Table 11 compares the results with a 1957 Prime Minister's survey.[17] While the majority of Reiyukai respondents did not favor such a legal requirement, the 40 percent who did favor it greatly outnumber the corresponding 16 percent of the 1957 Prime Minister's survey. Furthermore, the same question put to the general population today would probably find even fewer supporters. A related item asked respondents to choose among several living arrangements for the purpose of determining what proportion favored the nu-

[16] Naikaku sōridaijin kanbō kōhōshitsu, *Kazoku hō ni kansuru seron chōsa* (Tokyo: Prime Minister's Office, 1969), p. 719; See also Kazoku Kenkyūbukai, "Sengo ni okeru kazoku," pp. 114–45.

[17] Naikaku sōridaijin kanbōgishitsu, *Kazoku seido*, p. 642.

Table 13. *Under the Present Civil Code, the Former Ie Has Been Abolished. Do You Approve of Its Abolition?*

	Approve	Disapprove
Reiyukai	29.4%	70.6%
	(179)	(430)
1947 Survey (*Mainichi Shimbun*)	58%	37%

clear family and the three-generation ie style. In Table 12 we see that Reiyukai respondents overwhelmingly favor the ie style of three generations residing together. It is taken for granted that the support of the aged is guaranteed under such an arrangement.

One item on which Reiyukai respondents differed significantly from the general population was the question of approving of the legal abolition of the ie system. Table 13 compares these results with those of a 1947 survey.[18] The *Mainichi* newspaper survey was carried out just as the new law was enacted, when public concern was at its height. Fifty-eight percent of respondents approved the abolition. In the thirty-odd-year interval interest in this issue has waned among the general populace, as demonstrated above, and most people are not concerned about it one way or the other now. Reiyukai's 71 percent rate of disapproval sets it apart from the rest of society.

A major provision of the old system required young people to obtain their parents' consent for marriage. I asked Reiyukai respondents whether they favored the old system or the new one in this regard and compared the results with a 1957 Prime Minister's Survey in Table 14.[19] We may assume that since 1957 those among the general population who favor the new system have increased, making the gap on this issue between Reiyukai and the rest of the population even greater than these figures suggest. This is a significant point of difference between Reiyukai and the rest of society.

A final point to be discussed concerning the family system is the

[18] *Mainichi Shimbun*, "Atarashii minpō kakuan no shōten," March 25, 1947, p. 595.

[19] Naikaku sōridaijin kanbōgishitsu, *Kazoku seido*, p. 615.

Table 14. Under the Present Legal Code, a Person Twenty Years Old May Marry without His Parents' Consent. However, under the Former Law Parental Consent Was Necessary. Which Do You Think Is Better, the Former System or the Present System?

	Present System	Former System
Reiyukai	46.2% (292)	53.6% (337)
Prime Minister's Survey, 1957	77%	33%

Table 15. If a Couple Is Childless, Do You Think They Should Adopt a Child?

	Yes	No	Other
Reiyukai	71% (452)	12% (75)	17% (111)
Prime Minister's Survey, 1957	69%	18%	13%
Prime Minister's Survey, 1969	35%	30%	31%

question of adoption. In the past a childless couple might adopt a child for the purpose of perpetuating the ie and to ensure its own support in old age. Adoption also has a religious significance in that it ensures the continuation of the cult of the ancestors. Table 15 compares results of the Reiyukai questionnaire with two Prime Minister's surveys.[20] While the Reiyukai respondents are fairly close to the rest of Japanese society as it was in 1957, they seem far more extreme in their attitudes when compared to the Prime Minister's 1969 survey. When asked their reasons for affirming the necessity of adoption, Reiyukai respondents cited first (most often) the need to perpetuate the cult of the ancestors, second, the need to perpetuate the ie, and third, the usefulness of children in ensuring parents' security in old age.

Reiyukai respondents differed significantly from the rest of the

[20] Naikaku sōridaijin kanbō kōhōshitsu, *Kazoku ni kansuru seron chōsa*, p. 727.

population on four items: the question of legally requiring parental consent for marriage, the question of legally requiring children to be filial, approval or disapproval of the legal abolition of the ie system, and the question of adoption. The tendency among Reiyukai members to hold the corresponding opinions increases with age and rank in the group, and decreases with educational achievement. Also, women hold them more frequently than men. Most of these items deal with matters of law. That members favor tightening present legal strictures and disapprove of the removal of earlier ones seems to indicate a fairly strong authoritarian tendency. Also, all four of these issues reflect on the tendency to look to children for support in old age.

All of these issues on which Reiyukai differs markedly from the rest of the Japanese population indirectly reflect either a felt need to have children (naturally or by adoption) or to be sure of being able to control children. These factors are related to financial dependence on children in old age. Surveys show that many Japanese hope to live with their grown children when they grow old. However, there is a growing desire among young people to live separately from their parents after marriage, deriving from a desire for independence on the one hand, and a wish to avoid the hoary "mother-in-law problem" and similar intergenerational conflicts on the other. Further, nuclear families dependent on a single salary, or somewhat more in the case of working wives, are increasingly less able to provide financial support for aged parents. Not only finances, but housing space as well is limited, especially among city-dwellers. In addition, there is a strong desire to devote savings to children's education, the costs of which continue to rise. All of these factors occur at a time when the population as a whole is aging; that is, the proportion of the population over sixty-five is increasing. This means that a rising proportion of the elderly is in distress. Nor do pension systems offer significant relief; Japanese pensions (private or state-sponsored) are among the lowest of the developed nations, and the government is reluctant to redress the situation. For example, the newly elected governor of Tokyo actually plans to cut back funds and services for the elderly, already at a low level. Unfortunately, there is little prospect for relief of these problems before the postwar baby-boom generation has died, around the year 2030.[21] Reflecting the growing level of distress among the aged is the rising level of suicide among them. Suicide is the ninth greatest cause of death among the elderly, and it is suspected that many deaths of aged persons actually result from suicide but are either not recognized or not reported as such. The rate of aged suicides in Japan is on the increase in both urban and rural areas, even tending to increase after the age of sixty-five. In Europe and the United States the rate tapers off after the age of sixty-five. For Japanese men over sixty-five, the suicide rate is ninth highest in the world, and for Japanese women it is actually the highest in the world (46 per 10,000).[22]

[21] "Rōjin to sumai," *Kenchiku to shakai* 50, No. 4 (April, 1969), 39–60; "Rōgo no seikatsu o yutaka ni suru tame," *Gekkan fukushi* 51, No. 9 (September, 1968), 10–34, 60–61; "Toshi to rōjin," *Toshi mondai kenkyū* 17, No. 6 (June, 1965), 3–98; Takenaga Chikao, "Gendai kazoku ni okeru rōrei jisatsu no ichikōsatsu *Tōhoku fukushi daigaku ronsō* 8 (March, 1969), 133–52; Takenaga Chikao, "Rōjin hōmu ni okeru oyako kankei no bunseki," *Tōhoku fukushi daigaku ronsō* 13 (March, 1974), 249–66; Tanaka Tadako, "Rōgo o kangaeru fujintachi no katsudō," *Gekkan shakai kyōiku* 16, No. 11 (November, 1972), 70–75; Okabayashi Shigeo, "Rōjin no kazoku kankei to kyojū keitai," *Shakai fukushi ronshū* 15 (December, 1971), 1–16; Ōkubo Sawako, "Fujin no rōgo hoshō—dokushin fujin o chūshin ni," *Gekkan fukushi* 51, No. 11 (November, 1974), 16–23; Saitō Masao, "Toshi no rōjin mondai: kazoku to rōjin no mondai o chūshin to shite," *Toshi mondai* 49, No. 3 (1958), 61–71; Saitō Masao and Satō Mamoru, "Tōhoku nōson mibōjin kazoku no jittai," *Shakaigaku kenkyū* 7 (1953), 41–55; Aruga Kizaemon, "Ie seido to shakai fukushi," *Shakai jigyō* 38, No. 9 (1955), 3–10; Nakano Michiko and Idenokami Masako, "Setai no raifu saikuru," *Jinkō mondai kenkyū* No. 133 (January, 1975), 30–42. On the comparatively low level of Japanese pension plans, see Kōsei tōkei kyōkai, "Hoken to nenkin no dōkō," *Kōsei no shihyō*, special issue (October, 1978), chap. 3. It is generally believed that most Japanese hope to live with and depend financially upon their children in old age, but some recent survey results suggest that a growing number hope to remain independent as long as possible. See Nase City, "Sumiyoi machizukuri no tame no shimin ishiki chōsa" (Nase City, October, 1977); Sōrifu rōjin taisaku shitsu, *Rōgo seikatsu e no tenbō ni kansuru chōsa* (Tokyo: Prime Minister's Office, 1977); Sōrifu seishōnen taisakuhombu, *Sekai seinen ishiki chōsa*, (Tokyo: Prime Minister's Office, 1977); Concerning the role of savings in supporting the aged, see Nihon ginkō, *Chochiku ni kansuru seron chōsa* (Tokyo: Bank of Japan, 1977).

[22] On suicide and other social problems of the aged, see Hasegawa Kazuo, "Shisetsu rōjin no shinri," in Kaneko Jirō and Arafuku Hisataka, eds., *Kōza nihon*

As far as Reiyukai members are concerned, the major safeguard against distress in old age is to raise filial children who will provide financial and emotional support. Given prevailing economic conditions and state reluctance to provide significant support, this is a highly realistic perception. Even acknowledging the family's decreasing ability to provide support, the family is in effect the only institution upon which the aged can rely in Japan. To the extent that Reiyukai membership helps a couple raise their children to accept an ethic of filial piety and the duty of supporting their parents in old age, it has a real instrumental effectiveness in their lives. That this effectiveness is recognized by members is clearly evident from data of testimonies, field work, and interviewing. This factor is an important one in accounting for the group's continued vitality.

Ancestor worship tends to strengthen the authority of elders wherever it is found. This is true of Japanese ancestor worship, which idealizes the wisdom of age, and the virtues of obedience and filial piety toward elders. These tendencies are stronger in Reiyukai than in ordinary Japanese ancestor worship since they are supported by a strong organization and systematic methods of spreading these values. In Reiyukai children are taught to be obedient, filial, and respectful, and to depend on their elders' judgment far into adult life concerning a range of matters including marriage, child-rearing, and business transactions. In a sense, ancestor worship is a symbolic manifestation of these attitudes.[23]

Survey results suggest that Reiyukai members are somewhat more conservative and authoritarian than Japanese society as a whole, but not so much so that they can be identified as extremely conservative, reactionary, or part of the right wing. Their interests

---

no rōjin, 4 vols., vol. 1: *Rōjin no seishin igaku to shinrigaku* (Tokyo: Kakiuchi shuppansha, 1972), pp. 204–242; in the same volume: Usui Jishō, "Rōjin no shūkyō," pp. 349–78; Ōhara Kenjirō, "Rōjin no jisatsu," pp. 320–48.

[23] Francis L. K. Hsu, "Variation in Ancestor Worship Beliefs and Their Relation to Kinship," *Southwest Journal of Anthropology* 25 (1971): 153–72; Meyer Fortes, *Oedipus and Job in West African Religion* (Cambridge: Cambridge University Press, 1959), p. 54; Meyer Fortes, "Pietas in Ancestor Worship," *Journal of the Royal Anthropological Institute*, No. 91 (1960), 187; Meyer Fortes, "Some Reflections on Ancestor Worship in Africa," in *African Systems of Thought* (Oxford: Oxford University Press, 1965), pp. 122–45.

are on the whole nonpolitical. This suggests that an attempt to account for the group's continued appeal with reference to its serving the interests of a distinct subgroup within Japanese society is not appropriate. An alternative is to examine the pattern of recruitment and individual motives for joining the group. Overwhelmingly that pattern is one in which a married woman joins the group on the occasion of some crisis of illness or domestic discord and later persuades her husband, children, parents, and affines to join.

Part 2: Women in the Family: Breaking Even against a Stacked Deck

Although the immediate occasion for enrollment in Reiyukai is most often illness or a family problem, these conditions are often rooted in a conflict between expectation and reality related to marriage. While the Japanese cultural ideal of a wife's position is a secure one not lacking in prestige, the reality is frequently quite different, and women not unnaturally seek to redress this imbalance.

One consequence of Japan's heritage of the ie system is the fact that the position of "wife" is widely considered in quasi-professional terms. Being a wife is regarded as serious business, a full-time occupation which is intrinsically worthwhile and necessary in society. This conception dates from an era in which women's work in the home often produced durable or salable items, and in which they spent proportionately more of their lives bearing and raising a greater number of children; they died younger. Under these conditions a woman's existence from cradle to grave was circumscribed by the family system, and being a wife occupied her fully from marriage to death. Now, however, the spheres of production and consumption have been separated, and nonemployed married women are not among the producers. Most will live into their mid-seventies but will have ceased bearing an average of two children and seen the last enter school by the age of thirty-five. Those not living with a married son will not advance to the position of "mother-in-law" and have the satisfaction of training the daughter-in-law to take her place in some ongoing enterprise.

Whereas in earlier days women's prestige and self-esteem often derived from the successful performance of time-consuming, difficult work which ended in the production of some commodity, now much of a woman's prestige and self-esteem are vicariously drawn from the husband's position and professional advancement and the educational achievements of her children. The material basis of much of the prestige traditionally accorded the wife's position has simply vanished.[24]

In traditional ideas about marriage still held today there is the concept that women's happiness, duty, and fulfillment lie in marriage. Work is seen as opposed to marriage, and the fact that many women must work to help support their families is not widely recognized. It is assumed by most people, female and male, that a woman's main sphere of competence is the home, where she will occupy herself with cooking, housework, childbearing, and directing her children's education. Women are considered naturally endowed with the ability and desire to perform these tasks. A woman who rejects these notions is commonly regarded as somewhat deviant. These ideas are generally accepted in modern Japan and are more strongly held by people living in rural areas, with less education, and the tendency to accept them increases with age. Reiyukai members generally accept them and add Buddhist ideas about karma and pollution.[25]

While marriage is considered necessary for all women, divorce is regarded as a great failure, a lifelong shame. Divorced women

[24] See Sōrifu, *Fujin no genjō to shisaku* (Tokyo: Prime Minister's Office, 1968), pp. 45, 85, 107; Nihon fujin dantai rengōkai, ed., *Fujin hakusho* (Tokyo: Sōdo bunka, 1977), pp. 29–36; Fuse Akiko, "Fujin o meguru henka," in *Kazoku hendō*, ed. Aoi and Masuda pp. 70–92; Susanne Vogel, "Sengyō shufu," in *Kokusai josei gakkai hōkokusho* (Tokyo: published privately, 1978), pp. 109–112; Susan J. Pharr, "The Japanese Woman: Evolving Views of Life and Role," in *Japan: The Paradox of Progress*, ed. Lewis Austin (New Haven: Yale University Press, 1976), p. 305.

[25] Mochizuki Taka, "Onna ni totte no kekkon," in *Onna ga kangaete iru koto*, ed. Nihonjin kenkyūkai (Tokyo: Murōseidō, 1975), pp. 75–101; Sōrifu, *Fujin ni kansuru shomondai chōsa kaigi* (Tokyo: Prime Minister's Office, 1968); Naikaku sōridaijin kanbō kōhōshitsu, *Danjo byōdō ni kansuru seron chōsa* (Tokyo: Prime Minister's Office, 1975), chap. 2; Sōrifu seishōnen taisakuhombu, *Sekai seinen*; Fujin mondai tantō shitsu, *Fujin mondai ni kansuru yūshikisha chōsa* (Tokyo: Prime Minister's Office, 1978), chap. 2.

and their children are under a heavy stigma in contemporary Japanese society. Furthermore, divorced women with young children typically face dire economic problems, particularly if the former husband is unwilling to support them. Once a woman has left the labor force, it is extremely difficult to reenter it except on a part-time or take-home basis, in which case the pay, unless the woman has rare professional skills, will be extremely low. Thus, there is a great reluctance to divorce, even when there are strong grounds for doing so. According to court records, leading all other causes of divorce by a wide margin are violence, drunkenness (or alcoholism), and infidelity on the part of the husband. In Reiyukai members' opinion as well, this kind of behavior on the part of the man is the main thing a family must guard against. For them the burden is on the wife; it is she who must see to it that the husband does not become unmanageable because if he does, her own survival and that of her children will be greatly endangered.[26]

As Reiyukai members perceive the matter, a family must unify itself around a common religious practice, and this is made easier if the marriage is originally concluded as an arranged marriage rather than a "love match." Reiyukai informants whom I interviewed or knew over a period of time were unanimous in saying that arranged marriages are preferable because they are more reliable, forming a stronger bond. Love, on the other hand, has no power to hold people together in times of trouble and is easily extinguished if not based on a prior commitment. Furthermore, whereas the level of love tends to decrease over a lengthy period in a "love match," in an arranged marriage it increases and draws the couple together more strongly as time passes. These marriages are arranged by a go-between, and either spouse may consult this person when difficulties arise and prevail upon her or him to exert pressure on the other spouse to conform to accepted rules of behavior. Within Reiyukai the go-between is most frequently a fellow member who may be trusted to hold similar notions of correct behavior in marriage. This similarity in ethical ideals

[26] Renate Herold, "Nihon to ōbei ni okeru fujin rōdō no mondai," *Kokusai josei gakkai*, pp. 28–30; and in the same volume, Fuse Akiko, "Gendai nihon ni okeru shufu no shūrō," pp. 112–24; and Naoi Michiko and Sodei Takako, "Rishibetsu josei no seikatsu to rōgo."

between go-between and at least one spouse is an aid in preserving the marriage.

Changes in Japanese society have exerted strong pressure on traditional ideas about marriage, and women now find their role as wife and mother is overburdened with a host of extra expectations which are beyond the ability of nearly any one person to fulfill. At the same time relations between husbands and wives are changing, so is the father's role in the household. Since the end of the war, at least, there has been a trend for women to manage the family's income. While this strengthens their position economically, it is also a task that most women are not formally trained to undertake. Particularly in the case of family businesses where household and enterprise budgets are often not kept separate, financial management is a heavy burden.

In addition, wives are routinely expected to take nearly all the responsibility for children's discipline and education. It is not expected that the father will play a primary role in these matters, and in a nuclear family there is less often a grandparent to whom the wife can turn for support and guidance. She is under great pressure concerning the child's education, since it is widely recognized that success or failure in the educational system exerts an influence over the child's future that lasts for a lifetime. The mother shares the child's success or failure and can be held responsible in the latter case. Thus, women in Reiyukai routinely consult local leaders for guidance in discipline and education, and leaders may make introductions for them to tutors or tutoring schools. It is well-acknowledged that the mother-child relationship in Japan is overburdened and unnaturally strained by too high expectations, and that this is a source of many pathological developments, including the alarming rate of juvenile suicide and mother–child suicide. Reiyukai mothers and leaders try to emphasize the healthy development of the child's personality more than high marks in school.

Accompanying growing pressures on the wife's role is the increasing peripherality of the husband. Several years ago this was a topic of considerable public discussion, and the father's weakness as a disciplinarian was linked to the fact that men working at salaried jobs typically spend very little time with their children except on weekends. The decreased presence and influence of the father in the family increases the burden upon the wife.[27]

Women who join Reiyukai as adults and become active leaders are respected and admired by their followers for having faced, endured, and successfully solved some great crisis in their lives. Typically the crisis occurs within the family and involves relationships with the husband and/or his parents. Most frequent causes of complaint are again violence, drunkenness, and infidelity by the husband, followed by lack of money and problems with affines. Often an illness escalates a long-term problem of this nature into a crisis. "Successful" solution of these problems within Reiyukai inevitably requires the wife to "repent" to the husband. Repentence is the beginning of a new relationship with the husband, which ideally entails reorienting family life around membership in Reiyukai. In addition to bringing husband and children increasingly under the influence of fellow members, active membership entails sustained contact with proponents of the values of the ie system. One of the pillars of that system is the ideal of male dominance, but at the same time the ideal position of the wife within the home, while subordinate, is strong, secure, and respected, especially after she has attained middle age. Membership in Reiyukai facilitates a woman's attempt to have her husband accept this ideal of a wife's position and act accordingly. For a woman who enters the group on the occasion of a crisis with her husband, Reiyukai membership enables her to bring her ideals of marriage and the reality more nearly in line. In so doing Reiyukai fulfills the promise made in so many testimonies that novices hear—that by joining the group a woman can recover the secure, respected position a wife ought to enjoy.

The position of Reiyukai women leaders for the most part is

[27] Wagatsuma Hiroshi, "Some Aspects of the Contemporary Japanese Family: Once Confucian, Now Fatherless," *Daedalus* 2, No. 2 (Spring, 1977), 181–210; Nihon Hōsō Kyōkai, *Oyaji: Chichi naki jidai no kazoku* (Tokyo: NHK, 1974), pp. 186–93; Nakane Chie, "Bunka ni okeru oyako kankei no sōi," in *Kōza oya to ko* (Tokyo: Tokyo daigaku shuppankai 1973), pp. 3–22; Takiuchi Daizō, "Saikin no oyako shinjū o tōshite mita nihonjin no kodomokan ni tsuite," *Kyōiku* 23, No. 6 (June, 1973), 26–37; Morioka Kiyomi, *Ie to gendai kazoku* (Tokyo: Baifūkan, 1976), pp. 74–98; Fukumoto Hiroshi, "Kazoku hendō to sono ijō," in *Kazoku hendō*, ed. Aoi and Masuda, pp. 115–32; and in the same volume, Fuse, "Fujin o meguru," pp. 70–92.

that married women should not work. That is, they should not be employed in salaried jobs; women in family businesses or agriculture are recognized exceptions to the general rule. They have no source of income entirely separate from the husband's, and in many cases the workplace is not separate from the residence. Thus at the same time that they are "protecting" the home, there is no possibility of their having a greater cash income than their husbands, a situation known to be threatening to the male ego.

Problem situations envisioned include the case of young children being left untended in the house or returning from school to an empty dwelling with no one to "protect" it. It is assumed that business calls, bill collections, and social calls will be made to the dwelling, and that the wife should be there to take care of these matters. Here members seem to think of a merchant's style of life, managing a small shop attached to the residence, as standard. This reflects the large proportion of small-scale merchants in the membership.

In fact, however, most Japanese families are not living in three-generational units where a business is managed by all adult members. Most depend on the husband's salary. The wife is liable to be working at the time of marriage and to stop working at marriage or the birth of a child. This means a decrease of income at a time when living costs are increasing. An employer may raise the man's salary at that time, but many couples still experience extreme financial difficulty.[28]

The question arises for many couples whether the wife should return to work. What are the implications for her as an individual and the family as a whole of a choice to return to work while she has young children? In considering this matter it is essential to bear in mind two "givens" of the situation for Reiyukai women. One is that day-care facilities are limited and priced out of reach of many families, and the other is that it is unlikely that the division of labor within the home can be altered so as to relieve the woman of the duties of housework and cooking significantly.

---

[28] Fuse, "Fujin o meguru," pp. 80–92; and "Chingin rōdōsha no rōdō," *Shakaigaku hyōron* 27, No. 1 (1976), 18–55; Fujin ni kansuru shomondai chōsa kaigi, *Fujin ni kansuru shomondai no sōgō chōsa hōkokusho* (Ministry of Finance 1974), pp. 729–31; Fuse Akiko, "Kazoku to shokugyō," in *Kōza shakaigaku*, ed. Fukutake Takashi (Tokyo: Tokyo daigaku shuppankai, 1976), pp. 182–204.

Let us assume that the woman does not possess special training or professional qualifications, and that she is a graduate of high school or middle school, as is the case with most Reiyukai women. Her choice of work will be extremely limited, the major possibilities being part-time clerical, factory, or piecework. "Part-time" in Japan means up to thirty-five hours per week. The salary will likely be very low, as even women employed full-time earn on an average only 56 percent of the amount earned by men doing the same work.[29] In the case of part-time work, the rate is even less advantageous. Being part-time, the work will not be accompanied by fringe benefits that go with full-time employment in a large company. In fact, most of the jobs women are hired to do are boring, repetitive, and carry little responsibility or chance for advancement. Japanese management has a tendency to consider all female employees as temporary, and hence expendable, replaceable with a younger, cheaper worker, no matter how many years a woman has in fact been working. Many women work overtime without pay and then return home to housekeeping, cooking, and child care. The burden is very great.[30]

Thus, in a limited sense, as long as it is marginally possible to depend on a man's salary, women who consider child-rearing and housework their primary interests and responsibilities do better to stay out of the work force. This course of action is limited in that it leaves aside the question of the degrading, insecure nature of a position of economic dependence. It assumes that the man on whom the woman elects to depend will remain able-bodied and loyal to her and her children. It takes for granted that the individual holds a world view in which all distress results from one's own moral lapses, and that therefore one is not justified in trying to bring about social change.

[29] Nihon fujin dantai rengōkai, ed., *Fujin hakusho 1980*, (Tokyo: Sōdōbunka, 1981), table 1–10, p. 37. See also Rōdōshō Fujin-shōnen kyoku, ed., *Fujin rōdō no jitsujō* (Tokyo: Ministry of Finance, 1978), tables 31–34.

[30] Fuse, "Fujin o meguru," pp. 80–84; and "Chingin rōdōsha," pp. 29–40; Rōdōshō Fujin-shōnen kyoku, ed., *Fujin rōdō no jittai*, pp. 16–20 and table 28, p. 66; Fujin ni kansuru shomondai chōsa kaigi, *Gendai nihon josei no ishiki to kōdō*, Ministry of Finance, 1974, pp. 183–90, 260–79; Sōrifu, *Fujin no genjō*, chap. 3; Nihon fujin dantai rengōkai, ed., *Fujin hakusho*, chap. 3.

The point concerning the essential insecurity of economic dependence is especially important. Major illness or permanent alienation of the male breadwinner can precipitate a dependent woman and her children into a situation in which she—and possibly the rest of her family—may have to depend upon her return to the labor force alone, and therefore on a salary only half or less than a man would earn. In short, Japanese women's economic situation in or out of the labor force is precarious.

Once inside a world of thought where women's economic dependence is considered natural, Reiyukai is realistic in suggesting that it is better for women to devise ways to economize, even if it means significant cutbacks in the family's standard of living, than to reenter the work force under present market conditions. The kind of work women do, in the circumstances and conditions under which it is done, is seldom sufficiently remunerative in any sense to offset the accompanying disruption of personal and family life. Although Reiyukai leaders who counsel women to accept the status quo are in effect supporting a system profoundly discriminatory to women, their advice represents a realistic, if limited, way of coping with it.

Reiyukai members attempt to cope with problems surrounding the family system that are particularly acute for women and the aged by trying to socialize children and husbands in the ethic of the former ie system. This ethic of frugality, filial piety, male dominance, and the rule of elders requires that children assume financial responsibility for the care of aged parents and that there be an unbreakable bond between husband and wife, based on a common goal of perpetuating the ie which they have "received from the ancestors" and passing it on, it is hoped with increased financial assets, to the next generation. Fulfilling these obligations has a religious meaning because the ie is considered a sacred entity protected by the ancestors in the spirit world. The ancestors require that women and men give themselves over to their respective roles within the system and renounce personal aspirations that conflict with duty. A person who has been less than totally committed to his role in the ie must repent and begin again, resolving to give his all. To perform the duties of wife, mother, mother-in-law, and so on with unqualified dedication and self-sacrifice is to lead a holy life. The person who does so acquires spiritual power and the authority to lead others.

However, it is clear that Reiyukai members find themselves in circumstances in which their attempts to reinstate the ie as the foundation for society are more and more at odds with the trends of the rest of Japanese society. The proportion of nuclear families is nearing 100 percent, and at the same time the resources of these families that can be devoted to supporting the aged and having large numbers of children are decreasing. Economic pressure on these families makes it necessary for many married women to work, and in many cases this economic imperative for the wife's cash income is too great to be compensated for by household frugality. Whenever possible, however, Reiyukai women find that a position of economic dependence upon the husband is preferable to working in the labor force.

In ideal cases Reiyukai women are able to surround their husbands and children with Reiyukai members who will teach them the ethic of the ie system. Women can raise their children to be filial and to practice Reiyukai ritual. The more the life of the household can be made to revolve around Reiyukai membership, the greater the probability that the husband will join her in ritual and other group activities. The greater his contact with group members, the greater his exposure to the ie ethic, and probably, the greater his commitment to solidarity with wife and children. At a time of crisis in which for some reason he is unwilling to support her, the Reiyukai wife has on the one hand the force of group opinion and solidarity with her children to sway him, but on the other she lacks the kind of economic power he has over her. In the end she can rarely answer any threat of loss of economic support. However, neither can most Japanese women hope to enjoy economic independence and live on the same scale as when supported by a man. Reiyukai women try to cope with their situation by strengthening their bonds with husbands and children through securing their commitment to ie values and stressing the religious meaning of that commitment by linking it to the service of the ancestors. To the extent that they succeed in this, Reiyukai has a genuine instrumental effectiveness in their lives.

Chapter Four

Reiyukai Ritual

Reiyukai's ritual of ancestor worship, senzo kuyo, symbolically expresses the major tenets of the group's world view. These include the power of the ancestors and of the Lotus Sutra to affect human life, and the ideal of harmony and reciprocity between ancestor and descendant, macrocosm and microcosm. Unlike other Buddhist schools of thought, Reiyukai insists on a direct ritual relation between ancestor and descendant, countenancing no priestly intervention. In its claim for direct reciprocity, Reiyukai takes sides in a debate concerning the nature of karma, merit transfer, and the status of the clergy that has a long history. Only by setting Reiyukai's rite in the context of this debate can we appreciate both its historical significance and its purposeful adaptation of traditional ideas to contemporary circumstances. The first part of the chapter attempts to clarify the history of debates about karma and the relation of these to ancestor worship. The second part concentrates on Japanese development of these themes, including Reiyukai's views. The third part describes Reiyukai's rite of ancestor worship and analyzes the composition of its abridged version of the Lotus Sutra in order to link the principles of its composition to the themes introduced in the first two parts.

Part 1: Karma, Merit Transfer, and Repentence

Karma has provided the subject of major doctrinal debate throughout Buddhist history. The central idea is that actions (*karman*) have consequences, either good or bad. These consequences accumulate over numberless lifetimes, building up propensities for more good or bad. The burden of karma determines the next rebirth; one who has sinned deeply may be born among the animals, the hungry ghosts, or in a hell. However, the scheme is not entirely mechanistic, because the consequences of an unintended sin are lighter than the same act committed with premeditation and malice. Moreover, the idea that sincere repentence can erase the effect of an evil act mitigates the dominant emphasis on individual responsibility. The questions raised by the problem of intention and the difficulties surrounding repentence are foci of much ethical reflection. In addition, the importance of ancestor worship in Buddhist societies is probably responsible in part for the incorporation of a minor theme holding that karma is not restricted to an individual but also may be inherited.[1]

The idea that karma can be inherited was present in Indian philosophy from early times and may be found in the Ṛg Veda (RV 5, 7, 86), the Braçmanas (Aita Br. 7, 29); Satapatha Br. 1, 2, 3, 21, the Laws of Manu (iv 74, 172; vii 28, 111) and is conspicuous in the Mahābhārata (i, 80, 2f; xii 22, 139; xiii 48, 42–43). In Chinese thought the idea of karma was influenced by Confucian thinking, in which the results of action may be transmitted by blood from parent to child.[2]

Another concept diluting the karma theory's insistence on individual responsibility is the idea that merit from virtuous acts can be transferred to someone else, to lighten that person's karmic burden. The idea of merit transfer is called variously *pariṇāma*, *pariṇāmana*, *paraṇāmanā*, and while these terms are not found in the Pali canon, the basic idea appears in *Udāna* 89, the *Mahavagga*, and the *Petavatthu*. Here it is held, for example, that by performing obeisance at the Buddha's feet it is possible to direct merit to another. Prominent also is the idea that when a devotee wishes to transfer merit to an object he is unable to contact directly, such as a deity or an ancestor, he should give alms to the

---

[1] Bhikkhu Sangharakshita, *A Survey of Buddhism* (Boulder, Colo.: Shambala, 1980), pp. 91–101.

[2] Mizuno Kōgen, "Gō setsu ni tsuite," *IBK* 2, No. 2 (1954), 115.

sangha, who in turn transfer the merit of that act of charity.[3] In the case of transferring merit to ancestors, once the balance tips in favor of merit rather than bad karma, the dead suffering an unfavorable rebirth in hell may be released from their torment. Problems arise concerning the nature of karma and merit and the qualifications for transferring merit to the dead. Must a priest, who accumulates merit through observance of the precepts, act as an intermediary between laymen and their ancestors, or is the nature of karma such that *no* intermediary can rightfully enter into the transfer of merit by descendants to their ancestors?

The text setting an important precedent for the view that only the sangha can transfer merit is the *Avalambana sutra*. Maudgalyāyana, the most gifted of the Buddha's disciples in the exercise of supernatural powers, experienced a vision of his dead mother suffering in hell among the hungry ghosts. Her skin and bones had shriveled, her hair had fallen out, and her gaping mouth was immense. He tried to feed her, but the food burst into flame and became charcoal; he could do nothing to help her. After the vision, he asked the Buddha how he might come to her aid. The reply was that she had sinned deeply, and thus all of her son's powers would be of no avail. Even if he were to gather all the deities of heaven and earth, they too could do nothing. Instead, he should assemble all the Buddhist priests from the ten directions on the fifteenth day of the seventh month, the last day of the rainy season retreat, and offer to them the *pravāraṇā* meal, a splendid feast of one hundred kinds of food and drink, the five grains, incense, and aromatic oils. The merit of the assembly would then be transferred through the priests' recitation of a litany for parents and ancestors of seven generations, and Maudgalyayana's mother would be released. Following these intructions, Maudgalyayana was able to bring about his mother's liberation through this transfer of merit.[4]

[3] Sakurabe Hajime, "Kudoku o kaisen suru to iu kangaekata," in *Gō shisō no kenkyū*, ed. Ōtani daigaku bukkyō gakkai (Kyoto: Bun'ei dō shoten, 1975), pp. 94–98; John Holt, "Merit for the 'Departed': The Living and the Dead in Early Buddhist Tradition" (Paper presented at the 1980 meeting of the International Academy of the History of Religions, Toronto, August 1980).

[4] This sutra is located in Taishō 16, 799, translated between 265–290. The

In this sutra karma and merit are complementary terms; karma is the negative effects of past misdeeds which consign one to rebirth in hell, while merit is the counterbalancing, positive effect of good deeds which mitigates karma and can lead to a good rebirth. If Maudgalyayana's mother's karma can be outweighed by merit, she can be released from the hell of hungry ghosts, but this can occur only if someone else transfers merit to her. Maudgalyayana, acting not as a priest, but as his mother's descendant, must secure the mediation of the priesthood in order to have the merit transferred. The Buddha's answer makes it clear that he can do nothing by acting alone, in spite of his great magical power. Karma cannot be transformed to merit without an assembly of the priesthood.

The priest accumulates merit through observing the precepts, which require renunciation, notably of marriage. Renunciation is a source of power linked to the nonhuman worlds of existence. Through this link their merit may be transferred to the unfortunate inhabitants of subhuman realms. This is the priests' qualification for mediating between ancestor and descendant. The layman's life is dedicated to the things of this world; he does not observe the strict precepts requiring renunciation of marriage, but he too can accumulate merit, by giving to the priests. To give with no expectation of return is *dāna*, first of the "perfections" (*pāramitā*), and such an act produces merit. Such a gift is understood to be a form of repentence for wrongdoing, which itself has the potential to undo the effects of karma.[5]

The laymen make a gift of a special meal to the priests, and the

---

Sanskrit text is no longer extant, and no Tibetan version is known. There were three Chinese versions, of which two very similar versions are presently extant. The second is located in Taisho 49, 780. The first mention of the Maudgalyayana legend in Japan occurred in 984 in the *Sambō ekotoba* 三宝絵詞. See Iwamoto Yutaka, *Mokuren densetsu to urabon*, Bukkyō setsuwa kenkyū, vol. 3 (Kyoto: Hōzōkan, 1968), pp. 9–10, 50. The story related here appears to be a type; the identical story, substituting Sariputra for Maudgalyayana, is found in the *Petavatthu*; see Sakurabe, "Kudoku o kaisen suru," p. 98.

[5] M. De Visser, *Ancient Buddhism in Japan*, 2 vols. (Paris: Librairie Orientaliste, Paul Guenther, 1928), 1:76–77 quotes this story from the *Bussetsu kyūmenzen gaki darani jinrikigyō*, trans. Sikshananda, 695–700.

priests transfer the merit of this act of charity to the donor's parents and ancestors, according to the litany recited in accepting the food. The layman must depend upon the priests for the transfer. This priestly model of merit transfer might be diagrammed as in Figure 11.

In the *Avalambana sutra* the privileged position of the clergy regarding merit transfer rests on their renunciation and observance of the precepts, but in Japan, the status of priestly renunciation is very different. Since ancient times, part of the clergy, particularly the priests of Shugendō 修験道, and since the fourteenth century those of Jōdo Shinshū 浄土真宗, have married. Further, since 1872 civil law has formally sanctioned clerical marriage and meat-eating.[6] Presently the great majority of the Buddhist clergy marries. Seen from the point of view of Buddhism as a whole, it is not surprising to find that relations between clergy and laity vary accordingly, and that the matter of transferring merit would take a different form.

If one consults a compilation of ritual texts to be used by the laymen of each Buddhist sect in its morning and evening rituals for worship of the Buddhas and ancestors, the following sects include a passage for the transfer of merit: Tendai 天台, Shingon 真言 (Kōyasan 高野山派, Chizan 智山派, and Toyama 豊山派 subsects), Sōtō Zen 曹洞禅, Jōdo Shū 浄土宗, Jōdo Shinshū, Jishū 時宗, and Nichirenshū 日蓮宗. The only major exception is Rinzai Zen 臨済禅, whose lay texts include no *ekō mon* 廻向文, as the passages for the transfer of merit are called. Thus it seems that Japanese Buddhism as a whole perceives no difficulty in the idea of laymen transferring merit.[7]

Outside the Tantric tradition, a married Buddhist clergy is unique to Japan, and thus the clergy's relation to the laity necessarily differs from that relation in other Buddhist countries. If in Japan the clergy does not renounce marriage, then its position must depend on other qualifications, most importantly its special training in ritual. If there is no obstacle to laymen transferring

---

[6] Tomomatsu Entai, "Zaike bukkyō no katsudō," in *Kōza kindai bukkyō*, ed. Hōzōkan henshūbu. 6 vols. (Kyoto: Hōzōkan, 1961–1963), 2:217–19.

[7] Fujii Masao, *Bukkyō girei jiten* (Tokyo: Tokyodō shuppansha, 1977), pp. 231–66.

merit, then the question of merit can be reversed in a way that calls the clergy to account: what unique qualification does the clergy possess that justifies its monopoly on funerals and rituals for the dead, including composition of posthumous names and periodic memorial services? This is essentially the question Reiyukai has raised.

Besides merit transfer as a device to allay the effects of an individual's karma, it is also possible to lessen or remove karmic burdens through repentence. Repentence has been an important element in Buddhism from early times. In early Indian Buddhism confession of sins, *kṣama*, *deśanā* (Jap. *zange*, *sange* 懺悔), was an essential part of the *uposatha* rite, which also included recitation of the original monastic code of rules, the *prātimokṣa*. Early texts guarantee absolution of misdeeds through confession, for example Cullavagga v 20, 5: "... he who realizes his lapse to be such and remedies it according to law, obtains absolution at once." Eventually confession became the central duty of monastic life.[8] The offering of the *pravārana* meal to the priests is mentioned as a type of repentence in that it is offered with no expectation of return. In Japan both Tendai and Shingon developed rites of five repentences (zange), paralleling the closing passages of a much-used Japanese translation of the Lotus Sutra (*Hokke sambukyō* 法華三部経).[9] Repentence is thought not only to destroy evil karma but also to create merit; thus these rites are accompanied by litanies for transfer of merit. In addition, other beneficial results are attributed to repentence: time spent in hell will be shortened; defiling passions (*kleśa*) are destroyed; rebirth in the heavens is granted; life is prolonged; there is escape from desire, lust, and greed; and *maṇi* jewels will rain down.[10] Laymen's liturgical handbooks of most sects include *zange mon* 懺悔文, passages

[8] N. Dutt, *Early Buddhist Monachism* (London: Kegan, Paul, Trench, Trubner & Co., 1924), pp. 90–106.

[9] *Kokuyaku daizōkyō, kyō-bu daiichi.*

[10] De Visser, *Ancient Buddhism in Japan*, 1:271–79; Shakusha Kōki, "Zange metsuzai ni tsuite," *Bukkyōgaku kenkyū* 30 (1973), 22–42; Kawamura Kōshō, "Zaishō shōmetsu ni tsuite," *Seishin* (Minobusan), No. 29 (1953), 154–56; Kōchi Michigaku, "Metsuzai sei ni tsuite," *IBK* 17, No. 2 (1969), 540–41; Uemura Shinkei, "Ha-gōshō no shisō to hokekyōgaku," *IBK* 11, No. 1 (1963), 20–26.

expressing repentence. Further, the idea of repentence is extremely important in the new religions in general: not only in the Buddhist groups, expecially Reiyukai and its schisms, but others as well, for example, Ittōen 一燈園, whose founder Nishida Tenkō 西田天香 entitled his autobiography *A Life of Repentence* (*Zange no seikatsu* 懺悔の生活).[11]

The Lotus Sutra as used in Japan has been particularly associated with repentence on the one hand and with improving the lot of the dead on the other. Ennin 円仁 brought rites of repentence through reading the Lotus Sutra from China to Japan in 847. In later times these rites were performed for the dead, *hokkedō* 法華堂 (halls of worship for the Lotus Sutra) were erected in various spots, and these became places of masses for the dead. The Court led the way in this use of the sutra. Repentence ceremonies using the sutra, *hokke sembō* 法華懺法, for the repose of souls of imperial ancestors were held at Court until the Meiji period.[12] In Reiyukai's ritual as well, the main significance of the use of the Lotus Sutra is as a device of repentence and merit transfer.

Part 2: Japanese Doctrinal and Ritual Developments

In Japan ancestor worship is almost exclusively a Buddhist observance. One of the most common terms for ancestor, *hotoke* 仏, ほとけ, has unmistakably Buddhist roots. Much argument surrounds the question of the "original" pre-Buddhist conception of ancestors, and it seems that there were observances directed to ancestral spirits prior to the coming of Buddhism to Japan.[13] Now, however, the word hotoke is written with the same character as the word for Buddha, and the two meanings are no longer distinguished by most people, since in speech the word hotoke also refers to Buddhas. The word hotoke is thought by some writers to originate in the word Buddha but to differ from it by including the

[11] Nishida Tenkō, *Zange no seikatsu* (Tokyo: Shumbunsha, 1967).

[12] De Visser, *Ancient Buddhism in Japan*, 1:355–66.

[13] Takeda Chōshū, *Sosen sūhai* (Kyoto: Heirakuji shoten, 1957), pp. 22–23. On contemporary Japanese ancestor worship, see Robert J. Smith, *Ancestor Worship in Contemporary Japan* (Stanford: Stanford University Press, 1974), *passim.*

meaning of protecting the ie. This component of meaning is thought to predate the Buddhist overlay of concepts.[14]

Japanese scholars have tried to discover the pre-Buddhist meaning, if any, of the word hotoke etymologically. Yanagida Kunio's is the best known of these studies and it holds that the term originated in the medieval word *hotogi* 缶 or 瓮, meaning a ritual vessel into which food offerings for the dead were placed.[15] People subsequently began calling all the dead hotoke, and the entry of Buddhism further obscured the term's original meaning. Aruga holds, in contrast, the view that the overlay of Buddhist concepts occurred not in the medieval period as Yanagida supposed, but as early as the Nara period. In Aruga's view, since Buddhism was first accepted through various clans in connection with their separate cults of clan ancestors, the *ujigami* 氏神, Buddhist statues were believed to protect the clan just as ancestors did, and so the Buddhas were originally conceived of as a type of ancestor. Thus the Buddhist associations of the term hotoke may be much earlier and more pervasively inextricable from the "original" idea than Yanagida realized.[16]

Inseparable from the Buddhist connotations of the concept of ancestors are ethical values surrounding ancestor worship, namely filial piety. When the story of Maudgalyayana (Jap. Mokuren 目蓮) came to Japan, it was embellished with many elaborations shifting the emphasis to the relation between suffering mother and filial son. In a Muromachi literary adaptation,[17] the setting is given typically Japanese literary flourishes with remarks on the four seasons and a stress on the pathos of separation of mother and child and their teary reunion.[18] Here Mokuren meets his mother after his own death and journeys to hell to meet her there. After seven days he is reborn and performs rites to save

[14] Aruga Kizaemon, "Nihon ni okeru senzo no kannen," in *Aruga Kizaemon cho sakushū* Ashita, 11 vols. (Tokyo: Miraisha, 1966–1971), 7:325–56.

[15] Yanagida Kunio, *About Our Ancestors*, trans. Fanny H. Mayer and Ishiwara Yasuyo (Kyoto: UNESCO, 1970), p. 107.

[16] Aruga Kizaemon, "Hotoke to iu kotoba ni tsuite," *Kokoro* 27, No. 10 (1974), 10–13.

[17] *Mokuren sōshi*, author unknown. See Iwamoto, *Mokuren densetsu*, p. 81.

[18] Iwamoto, *Mokuren densetsu*, p. 134.

her. The motif of a journey to hell is thought to have entered the story through the influence of Chinese popular literature.[19] In the Tokugawa period the Mokuren story became the theme of popular sermons, in which Mokuren is said to be the son of a king who joins the priesthood and makes a journey to hell not after his death but with the aid of supernatural powers.[20]

A text which circulated until the beginning of the Meiji period, *Mokuren sonsha jigoku meguri* 目蓮尊者地獄巡り (Saint Mokuren's journey to hell) is particularly vivid in cosmological detail. It is well known as a filial piety piece, and it incorporates popular notions about women's evil karma.[21] In the scene in which Mokuren meets his mother in hell, he arrives at the gate of hell and addresses Enma 閻摩 (Skt. Yama), judge of hell, who has his eight-faced henchman Hachimen 八面 take Mokuren to meet his mother. This hell has the shape of a huge cauldron, so Hachimen flies to the edge and lifts the lid. With a golden pole he dips into the pot's foul contents and stirs about, finally drawing out a charred, blackened cinder on the end of the pole. Mokuren at first fails to grasp that this dessicated shred of matter is his mother. Gazing at the unlikely object before him, at first he can neither speak nor cry.

Hachimen transforms her into her human shape by speaking magical words into her mouth. Once she is restored to human form, Mokuren clutches his mother and cries, "Of what sins is this the result, that you should fall into hell and be ceaselessly tortured? Truly, it is wretched!" Next, his mother inquires how it is that he happens to be in hell, and learning that he has come to rescue her through the Buddha's mercy, she rejoices that her son grieved so much that he would come to her even in hell. Thereupon they clasped each other's hands and wept insensibly, as the great drum from the realm of the *asuras* began to sound. Their reunion is interrupted by the ghoulish Hachimen who informs them that their time is up, and that Mokuren must take his leave. Mokuren stood helplessly by as Hachimen threw his mother back into the cauldron to resume her suffering.

Hurrying to the Buddha, Mokuren reported these events and

[19] Ibid.
[20] Ibid., p. 135.
[21] Ibid., p. 170.

begged to be allowed to descend once more to hell. His wish was granted, and when he approached the lid of the great cauldron, he lifted the lid and threw in a copy of the Lotus Sutra, whereupon the cauldron broke into eight pieces, each one changing into an eight-petaled lotus. His mother floated in upon a lotus and thanked Mokuren. Appearing in majesty, the Buddha attributed the mother's release to the power of the sutra, but said also that since her karma was not yet exhausted she must return to hell. When Mokuren implored the Buddha to be allowed to suffer in his mother's place, the Buddha praised him for his filial piety. It was arranged for his mother to be released to a certain temple as an aid to the merciful Bodhisattva Kannon 観音 (Skt. Avalokiteśvara).[22]

From its canonical version in the *Avalambana sutra* to the later Japanese text *Mokuren sonsha jigoku meguri*, we can see that the Mokuren story has been subjected to important adaptations. In the sutra the mother is saved through the merit transfer of an assembly of priests. In contrast, there is no mention of an assembly of the clergy in the later work. The release is set in the context of a pathetic reunion of mother and son, and the fact that Mokuren has become a priest and a disciple of the Buddha highly skilled in supernatural powers remains in the background. Mokuren here is the filial son come to rescue his mother. This he does by two means: the power of the Lotus Sutra and the inherent virtue of filial piety. On the one hand, he marshals the magical power of the sutra and destroys the cauldron-hell where his mother is forced to suffer. Nevertheless, this is insufficient; the mother still bears evil karma and must return to her suffering. Only when Mokuren pleads with the Buddha, exhibiting his filial piety, is she released. Thus in the end it is filial piety that prevails over karma.

In this story the Buddha can overturn the supposedly inexorable force of karma. He chooses to do so in response to a devoted son's filial piety. Thus the "merit" of filial piety is placed above that of priestly ritual. Instead of the canonical device of release through transfer of priestly merit, we find a more simple tale of virtue rewarded. There is here a contrast between clerical transfer of merit and the virtue of filial piety that is important for an under-

---

[22] Ibid., pp. 162–69.

standing of the conceptual inspiration of Japanese layman's Buddhism.

The idea of merit transfer in the Nichiren school is difficult to clarify. The founder Nichiren held that in the "Latter Days of the Dharma" (*mappō* 末法), merit transfer is null and void. That is to say that while he recognized its efficacy in earlier epochs, he denied it under the conditions of mappo. He seems to have focused his denial on the clergy; their greater corruption in mappo rendered them incapable of transferring merit.[23] Nevertheless, in his writings he seems to assume that a mechanism very like merit transfer still operates. He says in the *Hōon shō* 報恩抄 that the merit of his own deeds will be received by his teacher.[24] In letters to his devotees he refers to the idea of descendants making offerings to transfer merit to the ancestors (*tsuizen kuyō* 追善供養) as a natural expectation.[25] The practice of rites of merit transfer continued to influence the Nichiren school after its founder's death. The founder of the Fujufuse 不受不施派 sect, Nichiō 日奥 (1565–1630), refused to participate in 1595 in Hideyoshi's "Thousand-Priest Kuyo," a national-scale ritual commemorating the "opening of the eyes" of a huge Buddha statue. The thousand priests received a ceremonial meal, and the merit of these acts of charity was to be transferred to Hideyoshi's ancestors. Other sects of the Nichiren school decided to participate, initiating a lasting division in the school.[26] Tokugawa Mitsukuni 徳川光国 (1628–1700) built a great Nichiren temple complex and seminary at Mito to commemorate the thirteenth anniversary in 1673 of the death of his mother, a firm believer in the Lotus Sutra. This was intended to transfer merit to her, as was his sponsorship of copying the Lotus

[23] Murakami Shigeyoshi, *Butsuryū kaidō Nagamatsu Nissen*, (Tokyo: Kōdansha, 1976), p. 52.

[24] *Hōon shō*, in Risshō daigaku Nichiren kyōgaku kenkyūjo, ed., *Shōwa teihon Nichiren shōnin ibun* (hereinafter, *Shōwa teihon*), 4 vols. (Minobu: Sōhonzan Minobu Kuonji, 1965); 3:1249.

[25] *Ueno dono gohenji*, in *Shōwa teihon*, vol. 3, p. 836; *Kōnichi shōnin gohenji, Shōwa teihon*, vol. 2, pp. 1879–80.

[26] Kasahara Kazuo, ed., *Nihon shūkyō shi* (Tokyo: Yamakawa shuppansha, 1977), 2:92–98. The reason Nichiō refused was that he upheld Nichiren's view that one should neither give nor receive from one who was not a believer of the Lotus Sutra, and Hideyoshi was of the Pure Land school.

Sutra seven times. He took the precepts from Nichiren priests no less than four times, though this had to be concealed from public knowledge. He also sponsored lavish rites of repentence, practicing repentence severely himself in preparation for the Kyoto ceremonial. Through his many acts of charity to the Nichiren school, all for the purpose of transferring the merit to his mother, its priests acted as his close advisors and administered the precepts to many members of Mitsukuni's entourage.[27] Thus, while Nichiren questionned the special status of priestly transfer of merit, his school nevertheless participated in ritual for this purpose, finding some of its most powerful patrons through this means.

The question of merit transfer was hotly debated in the schools' Honmon hokke shū 本門法華宗 at the end of the Edo era and the beginning of Meiji. At that time calls for reform were heard both inside and outside monastery walls, and these demanded that the clergy be peopled by men of true vocation rather than those intent on self-aggrandizement at the expense of parishioners forced under Tokugawa law to maintain temple affiliation and support the priesthood. In the Happon 八品 branch of the Honmon hokke shū, reformist clergy denied that beings in the lowest three realms, that is, the animals, hungry ghosts, and hell, could be saved by clerical transfer of merit. It was an assumption of the sect that beings in these three realms (*sanzu* 三途) depended on merit transfer for their salvation (*jōbutsu* 成仏). The debate over *sanzujōbutsu* 三途成仏 concealed an attack on the privileged status of the clergy, denying their power to bring about the salvation of beings in these three realms. A zealous proponent of the idea that the priesthood did not have such an ability was Nagamatsu Nissen 長松日扇 (also known as Seifū 清風) (1817–1890), founder of the laymen's group Butsuryūkō 仏立講. In this group there was little distinction between priest and layman, and eventually Nissen took up an entirely lay life, marrying a member of the group. In its priority on the concerns of the layman and its according important religious roles to women, Butsuryuko is a distant ancestor of such twentieth-century groups as Reiyukai.[28]

[27] Kageyama Gyōo, *Nichirenshū fukyō no kenkyū* (Kyoto: Heirakuji shoten, 1975), pp. 300–341.

[28] Murakami, *Nagamatsu Nissen*, pp. 52–55.

Centuries of state patronage had ill prepared institutional Buddhism to assume a place at the forefront of changing thought on social issues in Japanese society in the late nineteenth and early twentieth centuries. Leadership of Buddhist thought passed largely out of the hands of its clergy and into those of its laymen, whether the intellectual elite or lay reformers such as Tanaka Chigaku, Nishida Toshizo, and Kubo Kakutaro. We saw in Chapter 1 how Kubo's anticlericalism focused on the inappropriate intervention of the clergy in the relation between ancestor and descendant, again questioning clerical prerogatives in matters of karma and merit transfer.

The theme of zange metsuzai (destruction of sin through repentence) has received sustained attention in Japanese Buddhism. Hōnen asserted in the *Senchaku hongan nembutsu shū* 選択 本願念仏集 that chanting the nembutsu 念仏 undoes the effect of evil karma. A later commentator, Shōgei 聖冏 (1341–1420) reiterated this point and said further that it was not necessary for the devotee to have the intention of repentence for nembutsu chanting to have this effect. Kantsū 関通 (1696–1770) in a *mondō* 問答 identified reliance on Amida as the sine qua non. Since all power flows from Amida, the devotee's repentence is impotent in itself. Hōjū 法洲 (1765–1839) questioned whether repentence was necessary at all, and concluded that it was an aid to zange metsuzai, but by no means an absolute requisite. He opined further that the proof whether sin had been destroyed was to be seen at the moment of death.[29]

Nichiren knew of Honen's claims for the nembutsu to bring about zange metsuzai, and seemingly in imitation thereof, he made similar claims for the daimoku in the *Hokke daimoku shō* 法華題目抄.[30] In other works, especially letters to warrior followers, he recommends sincere repentence for the sin of killing and affirms the idea that repentence can erase the karmic effect of even so great a sin.[31] Proselytizers of the school took up the idea of

[29] Kasahara Kazuo, ed., *Tsumi to batsu.* Kyōikusha rekishi shinsho, Nihonshi, vol. 80, (Tokyo: Kyōikusha, 1980), pp. 192–94.

[30] Kageyama, *Nichirenshū fukyō*, pp. 130–31; *Shōwa teihon*, vol. 1, p. 393.

[31] Tokoro Shigemoto, *Nichiren no shisō to Kamakura bukkyō* (Tokyo: Fuzanbō, 1965), pp. 507–515; *Shōwa teihon*, vol. 1, p. 255.

the usefulness of the daimoku in zange metsuzai, developing a mandala to be written upon the shroud of the dead (*rinjū mandara* 臨終曼陀羅) which included the names of Enma, the King of Hell, and five Judges of Hell (*godō meikan* 五道冥官). Inclusion of these figures among the other protective deities of the school was to imply that they would actually protect the devotee in the other world. The moment of death was of special importance, and it was recommended that devotees chant the daimoku to the end.[32]

In the Meiji and Taisho periods interest in the zange metsuzai theme reemerged. Clerical reformers such as Shaku Unshō 釈雲照 (1827–1909) tried to revive lay interest in the precepts and asserted that repentence cancels the effect of breaking them.[33] Nagamatsu Nissen rendered some Tendai writings on zange metsuzai into quasi-vernacular, and these were recited by Butsuryuko believers as the core of lay ritual, setting an important precedent for the centrality of zange in modern lay ritual such as Reiyukai's.[34] The Sōtō Zen writer Ōuchi Seiran 大内青巒 (1845–1918) took as his central theme Dōgen's interpretation of zange metsuzai in an attempt to reorient Buddhism to achieve a meaningful ethic for the layman, emphasizing the need for repentence.[35] Kotani Kimi wrote that repentence destroys social evils as well as individual karmic burdens.[36] All these writers identified repentence as a necessary practice for laymen, and in so doing they sought to shift attention to individual responsibility for one's own fate, and for the quality of social life. To do so was to pass over as unworthy of serious consideration the notion that the priesthood had significant influence in these matters.

[32] Matsumura Jūgon, "Nichirenshū 'Rinjū mandara' no seiritsu to tenkai," in *Nichiren kyōgaku no shomondai*, ed. Miyazaki Eishū (Kyoto: Heirakuji shoten, 1974), pp. 415–26. The earliest extant such mandala is from 1592.

[33] Kasahara, *Nihon shūkyō shi*, vol. 2, pp. 338–40. On the movement to revive the precepts, see Ikeda Eishun, *Meiji no bukkyō—sono kōdō to shisō*, Nihonjin no kōdō to shisō, vol. 31 (Tokyo: Hyōronsha, 1976), pp. 2–35.

[34] Nishino Nichien, "Nagamatsu Seifū to honmon butsuryūkō," *Asoka*, (special issue 2: Kindai shūkyō, hyakunen no shōgen, 1968) p. 41.

[35] Kasahara, *Nihon shūkyōshi*, vol. 2, pp. 341ff.

[36] Kotani Kimi, *Watakushi no shugyō seikatsu, sanjūgo nen* (Tokyo: Reiyukai, 1958), pp. 198–204.

Part 3: Reiyukai's Senzo Kuyo

Reiyukai began as a group whose members perform a ritual called senzo kuyo, ancestor veneration or worship. Because there is no systematic doctrine, the group's unity lies mainly in this common ritual, which is also its most important link to Buddhist tradition. Through examining the ritual we can see how Reiyukai attempts to resolve conflicting conceptions of priest and layman, karma and merit. The final significance of the ritual, of resolving these conflicts in the context of ancestor worship, is the maintenance of harmony between macrocosm and microcosm.

Let us begin with an outline of the actions the ritual entails.

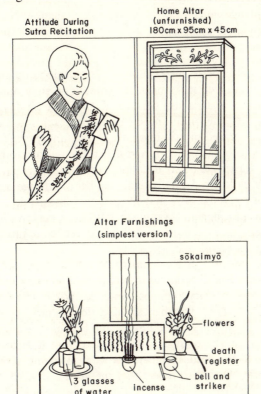

Fig. 6. Ritual Posture and Altar Furnishings

Preparation:

Place a fresh glass of water in the altar. (Flowers and incense may also be used.)
Turn the page of the death register to the day's date.
Put on the sash and hold the rosary in the right hand.
Assume kneeling position before the opened altar.

Sutra recitation:

Bow.
Ring the bell.
Recite the daimoku three times.
Recite the Blue Sutra by reading the book as written, or reciting the text from memory.
Bow.

Individual prayers: (optional).

The ritual is performed in the home morning and evening or when there is a meeting of branch members, hoza, or other assembly of members. It is also performed on the death days of both founders, i.e., the ninth and eighteenth of each month. It may also be performed in meeting halls, at the family grave, and the gravesites of both founders, and it is recited at group members' funerals. Ideally, a married couple performs the ritual together with their children. An individual member of any age old enough to read or recite the sutra may recite it any time in addition to the prescribed morning and evening recitations. A person who feels in need of guidance from the ancestors may recite the sutra in order to receive that guidance.

The significance of Reiyukai ritual is best explained by presenting members' views on its meaning while pointing out where it differs from ordinary Japanese practice. When asked why this ritual is carried out, members say they do it in order to make the ancestors in the spirit world happy, and because it enables ancestors to be saved (jobutsu). When asked what it means for the ancestors to be saved, members say it means being happy in the spirit world. They also report that the ancestors need the ritual much as the living require food; thus it provides a kind of sustenance for them. Ancestors who do not receive descendants' ritual

1. Kubo Kakutarō, Kotani Kimi, and Kubo Tsugunari, First, Second, and Third Presidents of Reiyukai

2. Shakaden, the Tokyo Headquarters

3. Members Assembling at the Entrance to Shakaden for a New Year's Visit

4. Interior of Shakaden

5. The Statue of Shakyamuni Revealed

6. The Shakyamuni Statue at Shakaden

7. Youth Members Getting Acquainted at Shakaden Services

8. Mother and Child Reciting the Sutra Together

9. Reiyukai Sash and Rosary Beads

10. Branch Leader Preaching at Mirokusan

11. Mirokusan Worship Hall Complex

13. *Women's Group Members Listening to Testimonies at Mirokusan*

12. *Mirokusan Pagoda*

14. Testimony at Shakaden Mother-Daughter Meeting

15. Testimony at Mirokusan

service will suffer and become wandering spirits. If people neglect their ancestors, social disruption and natural disasters may occur. If, on the other hand, descendants bestow on the ancestors the ritual service they require, the ancestors will protect and bless them. Ideally the two should be in a relation of reciprocity.

These various statements contain both positive and negative sanctions regarding performance of the ritual, and can be summarized by saying that the ritual is believed to establish and maintain the correct relationship between the microcosm and the macrocosm. This understanding of the ritual depends on unstated cosmological principles. Most basic is the idea that the universe is divided into two parts: *shaba* 娑婆 (Skt. *sahā*), "this disgraceful world," as Reiyukai's preferred English translation has it, the human world, the microcosm, and the *reikai* 霊界, the spirit world, the macrocosm. The sutra mentions other realms of existence, but for the most part members envision a bipartite universe in which the two halves are relatively undifferentiated within each bounded realm. When asked to describe the spirit world, members stress the suffering of its inhabitants and their need for human aid through ritual; the spirit world is an unhappy place for those spirits not receiving ritual. Spirits suffer because of accumulated bad karma, which in their present existence can be improved only by living descendants' ritual. Some spirits may be reborn as humans, animals, or hungry ghosts. Coexisting uneasily with the idea of rebirth is the idea that the soul is eternal.[37]

The society of the spirit world resembles that of the human world. Just as the living are grouped into households, the spirits' ie membership is maintained. Though the ancestors of a certain ie may not be conceptualized as having separate identities, their connection somehow continues, and they can act as a group. Ancestors of various ie are in contact with one another, and the ancestors of Reiyukai members may notify other ancestors of the benefits of Reiyukai ritual, thus leading those spirits to influence their descendants to join Reiyukai too.

The world view of Japanese folk belief posits parallel life cycles

[37] Takeda, *Sosen sūhai*, pp. 230 ff. Takeda notes that the idea that the soul is eternal is commonly found among even those people who also recognize the idea of rebirth. Thus this phenomenon is not limited to Reiyukai.

of living and dead. In human life it is desirable that individuals pass through certain experiences: birth, marriage, parenthood, and death. Likewise in the spirit world, a spirit experiences a traumatic transition from the microcosm to the macrocosm, and thus death in the former leads to a kind of "birth" in the latter, assisted by funeral ritual to comfort it and a new name, the posthumous name. Then for a time its status is somewhat uncertain until it merges into the larger community of spirits, this passage being marked by memorial services in the human world. The spirits' progress in the macrocosm, their happiness and well-being, depend on those rites. If the rites are not forthcoming, the spirit loses its place and may roam about the universe causing all manner of misfortune to the living as a wandering spirit. If, however, descendants faithfully perform the necessary ritual, the spirits will bless and protect them. Continued reciprocity allows ancestors and descendants to pursue their separate but parallel courses of development.[38]

Reiyukai members view senzo kuyo as absolutely essential for the salvation of their ancestors. They say that the rite is the ancestors' food, and that reciting the sutra is also an expression of filial piety. Further, the sutra begins with an extensive passage transferring merit. Thus the ideas of nurturance, virtue, and merit are all merged, so that one can say that virtue and merit themselves are types of sustenance upon which the ancestors feed and without which they will suffer.

The treatment of posthumous names clearly separates Reiyukai's ancestral ritual from traditional practice. The posthumous name is necessary to ensure that the benefit of ritual reaches the ancestors for whom it is intended. A popular notion holds that without the name the spirit cannot attain Buddhahood, implying that it is a prerequisite for salvation.[39] The custom of inscribing posthumous names on the gravestones of ordinary people or en-

---

[38] In addition to the works by Takeda and Yanagida cited above, the best contemporary study of Japanese ancestor worship is Smith, *Ancestor Worship in Contemporary Japan*.

[39] Popular ideas about posthumous names are treated in Morioka Kiyomi, *Gendai shakai no minshū to shūkyō*, vol. 49: Nihonjin no kōdō to shisō, (Tokyo: Hyōronsha, 1973), pp. 114–16.

tering them in death registers began in the early modern period.[40]
In Japanese society generally there is a certain resentment against
the clergy's rather exorbitant fees charged for composing posthumous names as a part of funeral ritual. A roughly standard
amount is ¥10,000 (U.S. $50.) per character used in the name,
with at least eight or ten characters each. The idea is that a longer
name benefits the spirit in some way. That this benefit should be
bestowed or withheld according to financial means, with no consideration of the character of the person's life, is galling to many,
Reiyukai members among them.

Reiyukai has developed a system for laymen to write posthumous names, called *hōmyō* 法名, based on the ideas of Nishida
Toshizo. Reiyukai does not recognize the authority of the clergy
to compose these names; instead it teaches that composing the
name is one of the duties of descendants to their ancestors.[41] The
system is known as the *sei-in-toku* 生院徳 system. The character *in*
院 stands for the household in which Buddhist spiritual training
was carried out, i.e., the person's ie name of birth. If that character
is used in the name, the spirit cannot be reborn as an animal. If
the character *toku* 徳, "virtue," is used, the spirit will surely receive "life," *sei* 生. Thus all posthumous names must include these
three characters. They form the basis of all Reiyukai posthumous
names.[42]

There are three types of homyo. The first is the sokaimyo, enshrined in a married couple's altar, representing all their ancestors,
known and unknown, traced bilaterally. On the tablet is written a
single posthumous name for all those ancestors, and that name is
the sokaimyo. The sokaimyo is inscribed on the tablet as shown in
Figure 7. The interpretative reading of the name is "Ancestors,
may you be filled with virtue and goodness and aspire to Buddhahood." The lacunae would be filled on the left with the husband's
name, and the right with the wife's maiden name. This tablet
(which itself may be referred to as the sokaimyo), becomes the
central object of worship in the domestic altar.

[40] Ibid.
[41] See also Nawata Sanae, "Reiyukai," In *Reiyukai, Risshōkōseikai, Sōka
Gakkai*, pp. 23–26 on this system of writing posthumous names.
[42] Ibid.

FIG. 7.	FIG. 8.		FIG. 9.
諦生院法道慈善施先祖 ∘∘ ∘∘ 家家 德起菩提心	眞生院法成清德信士	禪生院妙讚孝德信女	馬一匹大悲生所善義起菩提心
	MALE CHILD	FEMALE CHILD	HORSE

Fig. 7. Posthumous Names on the Sōkaimyō

Fig. 8. Posthumous Names of Children

Fig. 9. Posthumous Names for an Animal

The second type of homyo is for individuals; in these too the characters sei, in, and toku must appear. They are differentiated by sex, age, and type of death. Individual homyo should have nine characters and are not recorded on tablets but in the death register. There are special endings for male or female children, and other endings to indicate abortions, stillbirths, and miscarriages. Samples for female (right) and male (left) appear in Figure 8.

The third type of homyo is for animals. These may be composed for pets or other domestic animals, since some of one's ancestors may have suffered birth as animals. There are also miscellaneous reasons that may arise, calling for the composition of animal homyo, as the following example illustrates. During the summer of 1976, the Reiyukai women's dormitory at the Eighth Branch in

Habikino City was suddenly infested with ants. When ordinary methods failed to daunt them, it was decided that their ancestors were suffering in the spirit world and were actually hoping that posthumous names would be composed for them. The names were duly composed, and a lethal dose of insecticide applied. Following that treatment, their visitations ceased, and it was concluded that their ancestors had now found peace in the spirit world. Figure 9. shows a homyo for a horse.

Reiyukai's conception of ancestral spirits draws upon ideas about the dead found commonly in Japan, but departs from them in important ways. In Reiyukai the ancestors are seen against the background of the spirit world, protecting their descendants as long as the latter perform ritual service. If they fail in that, harmful results such as sickness and material decline may be expected as ancestors become wandering spirits and harm the living. Some members say the ancestors' distress is "reflected" back to the human world, and others interpret misfortune as punishment by the ancestors. Descendants' ritual creates merit which can override the ancestors' karma, the cause of their suffering, thus relieving that suffering and enabling them to bless descendants with benefits and protection. In addition, descendants' repentence before the altar destroys evil karma and accumulates merit. A basic presupposition of this conceptual mechanism is the idea that descendants and ancestors are linked by shared karma, which is believed to be inherited in the blood. Ritual performed by a person lacking shared karma, for example, a Buddhist priest performing for a fee, cannot improve spirits' karma or lighten their misery.

In contrast to Reiyukai's conceptions, contemporary ideas commonly found in Japanese society simply describe ancestral spirits for whose salvation descendants hope, with no provisions about what will happen if ritual is not performed, nor with any very clearly defined idea of spirits' manner of existence, nor with any specific reference to karma, merit transfer, or repentence. However, people who perform ancestral rites as prescribed in the handbooks of a Buddhist sect would be familiar with those ideas.[43]

---

[43] See Yanagida, *About Our Ancestors*, Takeda, *Sosen sūhai*, and Smith, *Ancestor Worship in Contemporary Japan*, cited above.

Let us turn to an examination of the Blue Sutra recited in Reiyukai's senzo kuyo. The arrangement of its passages highlights the ideas of merit transfer, the power of the Lotus Sutra, and zange metsuzai. It opens with an invocation, followed by a merit transfer section, a passage hailing the Lotus Sutra's power, and an extended repentence piece. These four passages are introductory in nature, leading up to a group of selections encapsulating the major tenets of the Lotus Sutra. These passages are followed by another repentence piece and a final invocation that repeats much of the substance of the opening invocation.

The invocation calls on numerous Buddhas, Bodhisattvas, devas, saints such as Nichiren, and the Daughter of the Sagara Dragon King to "wash away all the sins and mistakes which I have unintentionally committed," and protect the devotee. This sets the stage for the merit transfer section.

The merit transfer passage is a prayer composed by Reiyukai, and thus not appearing in the Lotus Sutra. This passage is given a special priority, so as to transfer the merit of the entire recitation that follows to the ancestors. This feature distinguishes Reiyukai's senzo kuyo from lay rites of sectarian Buddhism in that there the merit transfer section, the eko mon, typically comes last, as the closing passage. Reiyukai's merit transfer section is:

May Merit be Transferred!

Forgive all the spirits of my ancestors, all the spirits whose memorial day is today, and all the spirits with any sort of relationship with those for whom I pray. Forgive them and all my family for their erring hearts and misleading thoughts and for the sins and mistakes which they have unintentionally committed.

Not through my own power do I reverently read this holy sutra but through the merits of Buddhas and devas. Now I pray that you hear me read this sutra and cause all for whom I pray to aspire to enlightened wisdom.[44]

---

[44] In citing Reiyukai's Blue Sutra I have used the group's authorized English version and the Japanese original. In cases where the two differ, I have interpolated the Japanese into the English. The Reiyukai, *The Blue Sutra* (Tokyo: Reiyukai, 1975); Kotani Kimi and Kubo Tsugunari, eds., *Aokyōkan, Namu myōhō renge kyō, asa-ban no otsutome* (Tokyo: Ishiyama Kyōshindō, 1978).

The third of the introductory passages is taken from the Measureless Meaning Sutra (Amitārtha Sutra),[45] traditionally the opening passage of the Lotus Sutra as used in clerical liturgy. This passage hails the power and merit of the Lotus Sutra to change the nature of man, "... it shall make one who is without mercy be a man of mercy; it shall make one who is fond of killing direct his mind toward great compassion." Thus this passage calls for the power of the sutra to be directed to the salvation of those for whom it is recited, the ancestors in this case.

The fourth introductory piece is a passage from the Sutra of Practice by Meditation on Samantabhadra. The excerpt is a repentence piece, essentially like the zange mon of laymen's liturgies in sectarian Buddhism but much longer than they usually are, more than three pages, as opposed to the usual two or three lines. The passage expounds how to repent of all the sins of the "six roots" (*rokkon* 六根: eyes, nose, ears, tongue, body, and mind). By means of repentence these six are purified, and karma is destroyed, as the passage explains.

> These six practices are named
> the purification of the six sense organs.
> The ocean of karmic hindrance (*gōshō* 業障)
> is created by erroneous thought.
> If you really want to repent,
> Then think of Ultimate Reality,
> While sitting straight and properly.
> Then all kinds of sins will vanish
> Like dew before the morning sun.
> Therefore, with sincerity,
> Repent from the errors
> Of the six sense organs.[46]

Outside Reiyukai an excerpt from this sutra usually forms the closing passage of liturgy, expounded after the main text of the Lotus. Reiyukai's innovation in placing the passage at the beginning of the Blue Sutra accords an extra importance to repentence.

---

[45] Taisho 9, 276.

[46] *Bussetsu Kan Fugen bosatsu gōhō kyō*, trans. Dharmamitra, 424–41. This sutra is a counterpart to the twenty-eighth chapter of the Lotus Sutra. Taisho 9, 227.

Following the four introductory passages described above is a group of excerpts from the main body of the Lotus Sutra, explaining its major doctrines. An excerpt from the chapter on skill and means expounds the wisdom and spiritual accomplishments of the Buddha. Then a passage from the Devadatta chapter assures the believer that one who relies on the sutra "shall not fall so low as to be born into a hellish existence, or be born among hungry spirits or beasts, but shall be born before the face of the Buddha...." Here the believer is assured of not being born in the sanzu. A passage from Chapter 6, "The Endless Duration of the Life of a Tathagata," proclaims that the Buddha only seemed to disappear from the world as an expedient device; actually he is eternally preaching the Dharma atop Vulture Peak. The semblance of extinction was intended to quicken backsliders. An excerpt from Chapter 20, "Jofukyo Bodhisattva" prophesies the ultimate enlightenment of all sentient beings through the work of this bodhisattva who appears in the last days to preach Dharma. Nichiren believed himself to be a reincarnation of this figure, and Kubo Kakutaro, who regarded himself as an incarnation of Nichiren, believed that he incarnated the virtue of this bodhisattva as well. A passage from Chapter 21, "Mysterious Power of Tathagatas," announces the limitless powers (siddhi) of the Buddhas. Verses from Chapter 23, "Ancient Devotion of Yakuo Bodhisattva (Skt. Bhaiṣajyaguru)," tell of the sutra's healing powers: "... this sutra is like good medicine for the diseases of the people of the world. When such a one listens to this sutra he will be rid of his disease, not become old, and never die." Lines from Chapter 25, the sutra on the Bodhisattva Avalokiteśvara, describe the infinite mercy and compassion of this bodhisattva, proclaiming its ability to come to the aid of devotees in whatever form (male, female, monk, nun, deity, etc.) is best suited to the believer's need. The rewards accruing to faith in the Lotus Sutra and the terrible fate of unbelievers are set out in Chapter 28, "Encouragement by Fugen Bodhisattva." Fugen is the Japanese rendering of Samantabhadra, the figure of the introductory repentence piece.

One who scoffs and hoots at those devotees, in future existences will have broken and separated teeth, ugly lips, a flat nose, contorted hands and feet, squinty eyes, a flithy body, and also he will have an abcess with pus and blood, his belly will swell with water, he will be short of breath and have all sorts of serious and malignant diseases.

These passages outline the Lotus Sutra's fundamental doctrinal claims, and are collected in such a way as to encapsulate the sutra's doctrines and power in miniature. This abridgment of the sutra is not, as some writers have asserted, compiled in such a way as to emphasize ancestral spirits.[47]

This doctrinal outline of the Lotus Sutra is followed by a second excerpt from the Sutra of Practice by Meditation on Samantabhadra, in effect a second repentence piece. Here five kinds of repentence are expounded, naming various meritorious deeds expressive of repentence: "To develop a true mind ... to support, serve, and respect the keeper of the Law of the Mahayana ... to act filially toward ... parents and support them, and to show reverence to ... teachers and elders." Those who practice these "ways of repentence" will be protected by the Buddhas and will surely attain supreme, perfect enlightenment. By the device of quoting twice from this scripture, Reiyukai's Blue Sutra frames the basic doctrines of the Lotus Sutra with repentence pieces, the purpose of which is to focus the power and merit of the Lotus Sutra on the destruction of evil karma.

The Blue Sutra closes with an invocation paralleling the opening invocation passage and repeating part of it verbatim. It calls upon the Buddhas, Bodhisattvas, and devas invoked to "cleanse the stains of the six organs of karmic hindrance of all my family."

Reiyukai's senzo kuyo is completed by recitation of the daimoku and a bow. Members who wish to add individual prayers do so at the conclusion of sutra recitation. These prayers are addressed to the ancestors, and the penitent not uncommonly prostrates the entire torso to the floor, arms extended, crying in repentence to the ancestors. At the conclusion of private prayers, sash, rosary, and sutra volume are replaced in the altar drawer, and the glass doors closed.

---

[47] This is the view of the *Mainichi shimbun* editors in *Shūkyō o gendai ni tou*, 5 vols. (Tokyo: Mainichi shimbunsha, 1976), 2:167–70.

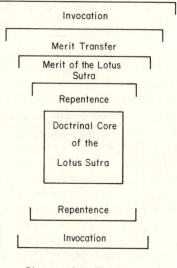

Diagram of the <u>Blue Sutra</u>

Fig. 10

We may diagram the structure of the Blue Sutra as shown in Figure 10 for the purpose of summarizing our discussion. The ritual purpose of the Blue Sutra is to encapsulate the Lotus Sutra and to unlock the power its doctrines proclaim by surrounding the core with merit transfer and repentence pieces. These direct the power of the Lotus Sutra to the destruction of evil karma through repentence. The merit of repentence and the karma-destroying force of the ritual are trained upon the ancestors from the beginning by the merit transfer section.

Adding this understanding of the Blue Sutra to our other information about the significance of the senzo kuyo ritual, we can outline Reiyukai's model of the reciprocity between ancestor and descendant. In the previous discussion of the priestly model of merit transfer, we saw that the process was one-way; the descendant/donor gives to the priests, and the priest transfers the merit of the gift given without expectation of return to the descendant's ancestors. There the ritual action ends. No exchange

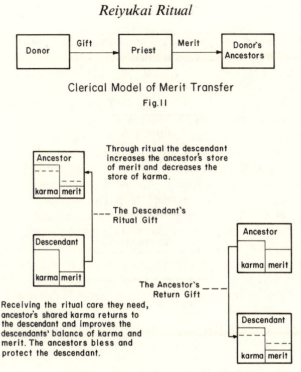

Clerical Model of Merit Transfer

Fig. I I

Reiyukai Model of Merit Transfer

Fig. 12

between ancestor and descendant takes place. In Reiyukai the ritual is one of reciprocity.

Ritual reciprocity occurs through shared karma. The descendant's meritorious ritual improves the ancestors' karma and thus the balance of karma and merit. The benefit of this filial piety comes back to the descendant in subsequent sharing of his karma; when the ancestors' karma is improved, his own is also. The ancestors gain jobutsu, which in the interpretation of Reiyukai members means happiness in the other world, so that they can protect and bless their descendants. The reciprocal exchange is perpetuated by daily ritual. These rituals, if carried out universally, could in members' view prevent the catastrophes attendant on neglect of ancestral spirits, thus ensuring cosmic har-

mony, maintenance of which is accordingly the ultimate significance of Reiyukai's ancestral ritual.

In this conception of mutual dependence of ancestors and
descendants, Reiyukai ritual draws the two closer together and
proposes that cosmic harmony results from correct maintenance
of the relationship. The ritual is set in the home and draws together
husband, wife, and their children to worship ancestors collectively. The notion that the salvation of all concerned depends on
performance of these rites creates a positive religious significance
for marriage and the family. This is the direct opposite of the
Buddhist concept that women, marriage, and the cares of a
householder's life are the greatest hindrances to male salvation.
Thus Reiyukai ritual represents a significant departure from the
sectarian ideal and creates a lay Buddhist practice in which marriage and family are viewed positively, and in which women have
an authentic part, no longer relegated to the status of representa-
tives of men's illegitimate attachment to things of this world. Thus
the microcosm–macrocosm thought of the traditional Japanese
world view is significantly recast while retaining the central values
of reciprocity between ancestor and descendant.

Chapter Five

Witnessing and Healing

This chapter introduces the phenomena of witnessing and healing in Reiyukai. Witnessing is an important practice in teaching the novice the group's ideas and in developing a newcomer into a potential leader of others. Furthermore, it is in testimonial texts that we can best see how members make religious ideas an integral part of their lives. The texts reveal the major religious themes that actively come into play when a member is faced with a real problem. Testimonies show how traditional Buddhist ideas are reinterpreted and applied to contemporary situations.

Reiyukai testimonies, called *taiken* 体験, "experiences," are among the most valuable available documents. They are the products of individuals' reflections upon their own experiences within Reiyukai. Testimonies are not raw data, but carefully considered retellings of events, shaped by prior exposure to the testimonies of others. Members are taught that certain norms and values apply to human experience, and that there are certain rewards and sanctions that accompany adherence or nonadherence to them. These norms, values, rewards, and sanctions are linked to ideas about the basic structure and principles of the universe. Thus testimonies show the group's world view put into practice.[1]

Witnessing is central to the process of binding the individual to

[1] The word *taiken*, "experience," is commonly used outside Reiyukai for discussing any experience, religious or secular; its use is not restricted to a religious context. When Reiyukai members describe religious experience, they say *taiken o eru* 体験を得る or *taiken o itadaku* 体験を頂く, "receive an experience."

the group. When members convert a new person, he signs a membership card and thus becomes a member of the group upon paying monthly dues. However, it is assumed that he will not immediately understand why, for example, he should recite the sutra daily. The michibiki no oya does not ordinarily explain the directive to recite the sutra in terms of its benefits for ancestral spirits. Usually no explanation is given at all. Instead, the new member is expected to go through a period of uncomprehending performance. Leaders say that the new member is like a child who must obey his parents' commands whether he understands or not. If he does not learn the habit of obedience, he might endanger himself, just as a disobedient child might dash into traffic, heedless of a parental command to stop. So for a longer or shorter period following enrollment, the new member is encouraged to keep reciting the sutra, and in general to adhere to the leader's advice even though he may find the sutra tiresome or the advice unwelcome. During this time, the senior member (*senpai* 先輩) tries to draw the novice (*kohai* 後輩) into as many Reiyukai activities as possible. At the same time, the new member meets a variety of other members. Those of longstanding membership make an effort to include new members in special-interest groups or proselytization expeditions. However, it is especially important that the new member be exposed to *taikendan* 体験談 meetings at which members present testimonies. Hearing men and women of varied backgrounds and circumstances, the new member begins to sense the possibilities open to him in religious experience, and he also perceives the limits of acceptability of those possibilities. He learns ethical rules that ideally pertain to conduct in domestic roles, and he is taught that certain rewards and sanctions apply to better or worse performance in those roles. He comes to understand the role of the leaders in bringing members' problems to solutions that are acceptable in terms of those norms and roles which the group recognizes as paradigmatic for conduct in any circumstances—norms and roles patterned on those of the domestic group.

While the new member is undergoing this period of more-or-less uncomprehending ritual practice and group activity, the senior members hope to impress upon him the idea that Reiyukai can be of central significance in his life. The key is to move him to a point at which he experiences a taiken. What that means is that the novice brings a personal problem to a senior member or leader and negotiates the situation in a way compatible with group norms. If he does so, his problem is "solved" in the sense of being properly handled. Ideally, the individual will also experience a sense of satisfaction in the resolution, a sense of gratitude to Reiyukai for its role in the solution, and a sense of confirmation at a personal level of the truth of those notions that underlie the insistence on daily ancestral ritual (i.e., the existence of an unseen spirit world, the power of the ancestors to influence events in the human world, the power of the sutra itself). It is to this sense of personal confirmation that members refer when they say after experiencing taiken that they are coming to understand the teaching of Reiyukai. The individual who experiences taiken incurs obligation to Reiyukai, part of which may be repaid by witnessing before a group, thus encouraging others. It is customary to conclude one's testimony with a public vow to persevere. The vow signals the individual's recognition of the obligation he now owes to the group and, indirectly, the legitimacy of the authority its leaders and his seniors exercise over him in requesting that he allocate an increasing portion of his time to its activities, especially proselytization, and that he continue performing ritual.

From the point of view of the novice, witnessing is an experience that confirms his commitment to Reiyukai. Often the experience related is one in which he solved a personal or familial crisis—perhaps precipitated by sickness, economic misfortune, or domestic discord—with the help or support of Reiyukai, its members, leaders, and ideas. Testimonies are related orally before groups in order to encourage others to persevere in solving their own problems and are also taped and printed in Reiyukai's books and periodicals. At meetings at the Tokyo headquarters, they are given live before audiences of five thousand in the main hall, and the presentations are simultaneously broadcast by closed-circuit television to distant parts of the complex. One of the slogans Reiyukai currently uses for itself is "taiken Buddhism," indicating that witnessing is at the heart of the group. A new member is said not to understand Reiyukai ideas until he has had a personal experience of them and has testified to the experience. Witnessing strengthens the individual's grasp of semi-doctrinal notions, and also his commitment to continued group participation and to the assumption of some measure of responsibility for proselytization.

For the occasion of the opening ceremonies at Shakaden, in November, 1976, the staff of the headquarters solicited testimonies from the entire membership. Members with especially impressive ones made audio tapes of them, and those were sent to a panel which selected 183 to be presented at the opening ceremonies. Later the staff of the group's publishing company, Hotoke no Sekaisha, transcribed and edited tapes of those live presentations and printed them in a two-volume paperback edition for sale to the membership and the general public. Each separate text is accompanied by the speaker's name, age, occupation, and present household composition. Although there are some cases of omissions of this information, they provide an invaluable source of information. While one might collect testimonies by other means, such as taping live presentations, interviewing, sampling those printed in other Reiyukai publications, the two-volume *Shakaden kara no shuppatsu* (Setting out from Shakaden 釈迦殿からの出発) provides a collection that is unified in regard to time, place, and purpose of the presentation, a unity which no sporadic sampling of other available sources could hope to match.[2]

Although this collection has the advantages just mentioned, it has limitations as well. First, the texts have been edited, and it is inevitable that their printed versions cannot replicate the situation of the original delivery. Testimonies are usually delivered with a great deal of emotion, and there is much repetition of key words and phrases. Shouting at intervals, breaking into tears, and subsequently having to pause to regain enough calm to proceed are quite common for both men and women. The speaker's delivery is responsive to the audience, who will clap and shout encouragement if the speaker seems to falter. Especially for women, dress, posture, and tone of voice are very powerful vehicles of expres-

[2] The process of selection of taiken for inclusion in this work was described to me by officials of the Overseas Department of Reiyukai headquarters. Okazaki Toshimasa, ed., *Shakaden kara no shuppatsu*, 2 vols. (Tokyo: Hotoke no sekaisha, 1976).

sion. Women of middle age or older most often wear kimono
rather than Western dress to testify, and they adopt a stiff, stern
posture which increases the impression of the gravity of their
words. Women who wear kimono show that they believe they are
doing something both serious and specifically Japanese—
untainted by any frivolous taste for foreign things. Obviously this
sort of thing eludes a printed rendition, even before it is further
diluted by translation. Furthermore, any editing to meet spatial
limitations is bound at times to ride roughshod over crucial points
in a speaker's presentation.

In addition to the editing, the original choice of those testimonies which were given at the Shakaden ceremonies represents
a prior selection by a special committee. Thus there are very few in
the resulting publication that fail to have happy endings. Also,
those which appear there are somewhat more dramatic than what
one hears at an average monthly meeting.

However, despite the drawbacks inherent in any attempt to use
this publication as representative of testimonies in general, there
are definite advantages. There is no readily available principle of
closure in selecting testimonies. They are presented daily all over
Japan both orally and in print, on a variety of different occasions,
before larger and smaller audiences of greater or lesser responsive-
ness. On the basis of hearing and reading taiken for four years in
several regions of Japan, I believe that the *Shakaden kara no
shuppatsu* collection is representative of the themes that members
most often report. This collection has the advantage of representing all regions of Japan, a mixture of leaders as well as the general
membership, and the inclusion of at least a minimum of sociological or demographic information about each individual. From this
it can be established that the collection represents a wide range of
age and occupational groups, and further, all the testimonies
collected were given in the same place for the same occasion. For
these reasons it is maintained here that the advantages of this
collection outweigh the disadvantages, and that the likelihood of
collecting a better sample is remote.

The translations are the present writer's; they are complete, and
no material has knowingly been omitted. Material in brackets has
been added. The original texts occasionally contain ellipses (. . .);

these are reproduced here; none have been added. In many cases in which a speaker's original delivery was colloquial and informal, I have tried to retain those features. Informal, colloquial style, not to mention frequent usage of regional dialect, which it is impossible to render into English, are part of a speaker's efforts to gain rapport with the audience and occasionally reveal important nuances. I have tried to convey these nuances in English.

Testimonies differ widely in tone, degree of emotional involvement, and technique for attracting and holding the audience's attention. One must bear in mind that the testimonies are in effect performed. The speaker presents himself as he wants others to know him, which presupposes the existence of some common ground between speaker and hearer. It is the speaker's job to create that common ground, a task that must be performed as quickly and as skillfully as possible. Thus the speaker must develop a keen sense of his audience's background and present mood. He may fill out the bare bones of his story in any number of different ways, emphasizing now this, now that aspect or event in his tale, adopting a very reserved or a very relaxed manner, using standard Japanese or a dialect as the occasion seems to demand. There are so many techniques open to the individual that the sense in which we can speak of the "same story" being told over and over again becomes elusive. No matter what else testimonies may be, they are performances. The impact they have when reduced first to print and then to translation is far different from their effect in live performance.

I have selected testimonies to illustrate themes commonly heard in testimonial presentation. In that a text may touch upon more than a single theme, this division is artificial, introduced only for the convenience of discussing a single theme in isolation. First we examine the theme of the benefits to be enjoyed by the stalwart member, the rewards of the True Law. Second we examine how the zange metsuzai theme so important in ritual is activated in daily life, the theme of apology and repentence. Third is the theme of undoing karma, breaking away from the paths toward a bad end, resolving karma. Last is the theme of healing, the most complicated of all.

Part 1: The Rewards of the True Law

In one sense we can say that all testimonies address the theme of the rewards, "favors" (*okage* 御陰) of membership in Reiyukai and of adherence to its ideas and practices. There is no notion that one should be in any way ashamed of expecting a reward for faith and perseverance. Members say that the basic aim of ancestral rites is to serve the ancestors and that it is wrong to do so in the expectation of reward. One's first concern should be for the ancestors' welfare, but on the other hand, if one is truly devoted to their happiness, it is natural to think that devotion will be rewarded in some way with health, happiness, long life, or resolution of domestic discord—the most common forms of reward or blessing members mention. Furthermore, longtime adherence to the group is thought to be a source of spiritual power, itself a form of reward. The idea of reward for faithful execution of daily ritual and other requirements of group membership is closely tied to the orientation of the individual in his social nexus.[3]

The following text relates various rewards of the True Law. The speaker Miyahara is forty-four and is married to a construction worker. She is childless.

I have numbered each of the 183 texts of the *Shakaden kara no Shuppatsu* collection, and they are referred to herein by that number plus volume and page numbers.

Text 9, 1:60–65

It was the autumn of 1974. I live in Nagano City and help out with the Youth Group. With Family Day of Proselytization Month coming up, and hoping to notify as many people as possible about this religion, even if only one, I set out by car with a group of girls from the Youth Group.

---

[3] The idea that true faith will bring material reward is included in the theme of *gense riyaku* 現世利益, "this-wordly benefits." The most important works on this topic are Nihon bukkyō kenkyūkai, ed., *Nihon shūkyō no gense riyaku* (Tokyo: Daizō shuppan, 1970); Miyata Noboru, "Nihonjin no shūkyō seikatsu to gense riyaku," *Nihon bukkyō*, No. 34 (1972), 43–57; Fujii Masao, "Gense riyaku," in *Girei no kōzō*, ed. Tamaru Noriyoshi. *Nihonjin no shūkyō*, 4 vols., vol. 2 (Tokyo: Kōsei shuppan, 1972).

Heading west along the Susobana River, in less than an hour we reached the Kinasa Village, where there is the Susobana-gawa Park, and the Mizubashō Forest, famous for the story about the female devil. We stopped at the house of an old couple in Kinasa.

"The teaching of Reiyukai is to recite the sutra for the ancestors with your own hands." We spoke earnestly and were able to persuade them. When I was copying the posthumous names of their ancestors, I noticed the photograph and spirit tablet of a young woman. When I asked if it might be a dead daughter, the old couple seemed about to cry.

"That's the first wife of our eldest son. She was pregnant with her first child, and we were overjoyed with the thought of seeing our first grandchild, but in her last month, when she was about to go down the mountain to stay with her parents, she suddenly said she wasn't felling well. . . . Maybe it was because the path was so steep. When we got her to the hospital, it was too late. She died right there."

Hearing this sad tale of the loss of a bride and the first grandchild all at once, we were choked with emotion and invited them to recite the sutra before the photograph. Facing the tablet, all of us recited the sutra as one.

A month later we visited them again. They looked so happy that they seemed like different people. "Well, to tell you the truth," they explained, "our first son married again after the death of his first wife, but relations with the daughter-in-law were bad, and we were plagued with family discontent for ten years. Then for some reason you all happened to come here and set up an altar for us, and when we all recited the sutra together, her attitude suddenly changed, and she started being nice to us. It's just like a dream."

The old man chuckled as he told his story. When we inquired more closely, it came out that relations with the daughter-in-law up until then had gone so far wrong that things had seemed really hopeless. She wouldn't listen to them or work in the fields, and it looked like the marriage would end in divorce. She wanted a lot of alimony, and the son and the old couple had even resolved to sell some forest land to get it for her, and had been on the verge of concluding the sale. That was just at the time when we had come and had urged them to join Reiyukai. The month before, when we were all reciting the sutra together, the daughter-in-law who was on the verge of divorce had come and listened at the door. Hearing our words she had felt her heart completely cleansed, with a profound emotion such as she had never experienced before, and her whole body began to tremble. It caused her to reflect deeply on herself, to see that she had defied her father- and mother-in-law.

When the daughter-in-law's attitude changed, the old couple relented, and they stopped talking about divorce. And of course there was no more talk about selling the ancestral forest. Now the whole family has joined their hands together before the altar and are building a new life.

Obviously thoroughly pleased, the old man added, "I'm glad not just because we didn't sell the land, but because family peace and tranquillity, which money can't buy, have returned. That makes me happier than anything else could." I understood the old couple's feelings. I also understood, as if it were myself, how the daughter-in-law who opposed her husband's parents, upon hearing our voices reciting the sutra, could feel that her heart was cleansed. The reason is that I had a similar experience in my youth.

I lived in Tokyo as a little girl with my parents who ran a fruit store and raised me tenderly. However, they weren't my real parents. When the war got really violent and I was to be evacuated to escape the air raids, I went to the ward office to get a copy of my registration papers so I could enter another school. Discovering in the space for my parents' names two entirely unknown names, I turned pale.

Where was my real mother—the one who had given me birth? What kind of man was my father? I hated the parents who had concealed the truth and had toyed with me, saying nothing. I opposed everything they did and said to myself, "I just want to die."

The couple who had raised me were actually the brother- and sister-in-law of my real parents. My real parents had separated without ever having married and had entered me in the census as the child of complete strangers. The shock of this discovery was very great, and I began to distrust everyone and to hate living. I truly thought I wanted to die. But about that time I tried reciting the sutra on the memorial day of my grandfather, who had been kinder to me than anyone else. I really didn't know what religion was all about; I just knew it reminded me of my grandfather, and that I felt as if I were depending on him again while I was reciting the sutra. My heart which had been so choked up and anxious felt washed and cleansed, and I noticed that my headaches, which formerly just would not quit, had been relieved; and actually, wasn't I feeling exhilarated and refreshed? From that day on I became fonder of reciting the sutra than anything else.

Up on the mountain in such a lonely farm house, that daughter-in-law came as a second wife to her husband and her father- and mother-in-law, who probably were constantly reminiscing about their dead daughter-in-law and forever pointing out the faults of the new one. So then wouldn't she naturally become temperamental and grow to hate her parents-in-law? Then, the flowing voice of the sutra echoed to the bottom of her heart in a single moment's emotion, just like the day my heart was washed by reciting the sutra for my grandfather.

In my case, I had six parents: the real ones, the ones of the census register, and the ones who had raised me. I really don't know if that's a happy or an unhappy thing. But nevertheless, it is due to the reward of the Law of Reiyukai that I have come to think that one must be grateful to all parents—of whatever kind. Just the fact that I have six parents in this world must mean that there is some very deep connection.

Learning the address of my real mother from my stepmother, I visited her natal house in Shizuoka Prefecture. As it happened, she had married and moved away from there long ago, borne and raised children, and was leading a housewife's life. I was afraid my visit would cause trouble, but the old couple who were my grandfather and grandmother were still living there. Meeting their granddaughter after thirty-odd years, they cried for joy. "Ah . . . now we have a reason for living. We never forgot you—even for a single day. We really have to apologize to you for having switched mothers on you that way. . . ."

As they bowed their heads and clasped their hands before me, I realized that I truly had been unfilial to my real mother. Then I wanted to pray for her sake. Both I and the daughter-in-law on the mountaintop were saved by being able to realize that our innermost natures are polluted. All human beings are weak and full of confusion, but through spiritual training one can find a new way of life and can wash the heart to the core.[4]

The girls of the Youth Group who had come to proselytize with me saw this for themselves and were deeply impressed. We vowed to encourage each other in our training and to notify as many people as possible about the Law. Here in Shakaden where we can have a heart-to-heart talk with Shakyamuni, I vow to make every effort to lead at least one new member into our midst.

Text 9 is divided into two parallel parts: one about the speaker herself, Miyahara, and the other about a family she has proselytized in a remote mountain village. She has not witnessed the crucial events of the first half, but is told about them when she and the young women of the Youth Group return for a second visit. Later Miyahara draws parallels between her experience and the daughter-in-law of the mountain family. The following diagram is included for convenience of comparison.

Text 9

The mountain daughter-in-law	*Miyahara*
1. Second wife; unfavorably compared to first wife	1. Deceived by "parents" about true identity
2. Grows "temperamental"	2. Shock

[4] "Watashi ni shite mo Kinasa-mura no oyomesan ni shite mo, jibun no konjō no yogore ni kizukasete itadaite sukuwareta no desu. Ningen wa dare de mo yowaku, mayoi ōi mono desu ga, shugyō ni yotte, kokoro no naimen made ga araware, atarashii ikikata o jibun de mitsukedasu koto ga dekimasu."

3. Hates affines; refuses field labor; demands large alimony
4. Hears sutra recited
5. Heart cleansed
6. Realizes she was wrong to defy affines
7. Starts being nice to affines

3. Hates stepparents; opposes them
4. Recites sutra
5. Heart cleansed; headaches relieved
6. Realizes she has been unfilial to real mother
7. Grateful to all six "parents"

Both saved by realizing own essential pollution

In each half of the story the main character's position in the domestic group is anomalous; the mountain daughter-in-law arrives as the second wife, and Miyahara is the illegitimate child of her guardians' brother- and sister-in-law. Miyahara is precipitated into a crisis during childhood when she discovers that the couple who have raised her are not her parents. In the mountain daughter-in-law's case, she grows temperamental and starts to hate her affines, Miyahara infers, as a result of the affines constantly reminiscing about their son's first wife and criticizing the newcomer. Then both experience hatred and stop fulfilling their respective roles as "child" and daughter-in-law. For both of them, their originally anomalous position in the domestic group has become even more so, and the point at which their ties may be completely severed, one contemplating divorce and the other suicide, seemed to be drawing near.

In both cases, sutra recitation turns the tide. In the case of the mountain-daughter-in-law, the sound of the sutra being recited cut through accumulated resentment and injured feelings. This seems identical to Miyahara to her own experience: "just like the day my heart was washed by reciting the sutra for my grandfather." This change of heart is a reward of the Law in that it attests to the power of the sutra itself to open the heart and show the way back to fulfilling role expectations properly.

Seeing the example of the mountain daughter-in-law, who becomes "nice" to her affines, Miyahara becomes aware of the significance of the "connection" with her parents—all six of them: the biological ones, the ones who raised her, and the unknown couple of the census register. Acting on this realization, she seeks out her mother, and unable to contact her, nevertheless has an emotional reunion with her grandparents.

Then, just as the mountain daughter-in-law realized that she had "defied" her father- and mother-in-law, Miyahara realized she had been unfilial. Miyahara's meaning is somewhat unclear at this point. Should she have sought out her mother long ere her contact with the mountain family; should she have prayed for her since childhood? Both? She simply is not clear. However, both Miyahara and the mountain daughter-in-law reach a realization of wrongdoing. They repent. This becomes the basis for the mountain daughter-in-law ceasing that activity which formerly jeopardized correct fulfillment of the obligations of her role. She becomes "nice" and avoids divorce, and presumably goes out to work in the fields. Thus the family is able to retain its forest land, and she becomes a worthy daughter-in-law.

Miyahara's concluding interpretation, saying that both she and the mountain daughter-in-law were "saved" by realizing that they are "polluted" (konjō no yogore ni kizukasete) presents considerable difficulties. From what were they "saved," and what is the source of the pollution, mentioned only in the story's closing lines? In Reiyukai one finds no philosophizing on the original nature of man, whether it is basically good, bad, or otherwise. However, the concepts of pollution and karma overlap considerably. This means that karma is seen as a kind of pollution that attaches to the innermost nature, the konjō 根性. Miyahara implies that the sutra has the power to purify. When this happens, all the pollution disappears, since the heart is "washed to the core." This "saves" the individual from failure to perform correctly his role in the family; the mountain daughter-in-law can become a better daughter-in-law, and Miyahara can become a better "child." They are saved from imminent failure in their roles in the family.

The rewards of the True Law come in many forms besides the healing of familial strife seen in this text. These include physical healing, recovery of lost articles, and many other experiences of blessing too numerous to name. They have in common the fact that through Reiyukai a member experiences happiness and satisfaction and a renewed sense of gratitude to the organization and fellow members.

Part 2: Apology and Repentence

In Reiyukai there is a great emphasis on repentence and apology. The significance of the act differs according to a variety of circumstances. In the context of a domestic problem, apology is felt to be a good way to clear the air and move from deadlock to some new approach to the problem. Leaders often tell their followers, especially young and female members, that it is a good idea to apologize every once in a while to their elders or male superiors, whether or not there is any special problem at the moment, or, if there is, regardless of whether they caused it. Particularly in the case of women, there seems to be the notion that the pollution inherent in being female causes various "nuisances" (*meiwaku* 迷惑) to the people around them, and that that is sufficient reason to apologize. Also, if a woman balks at the idea of apologizing, is that not evidence that she is insufficiently meek and should apologize for her lack? The answer to the question "Who apologizes to whom?" is that usually apology follows the hierarchy of the family: women apologize to men and affines; the young apologize to parents and elders. The reverse sometimes occurs, but when it does it most often follows a previous apology by the one in the subordinate position in the hierarchy. In this respect it is sometimes used by those in a subordinate position as a technique of manipulation: to elicit an apology from a superior as a prelude to reducing the social distance between them. Leaders not infrequently elicit an apology from a novice by shock techniques. This may be a first step in reenforcing the leader's authority or leading the member to a more subordinate status in the domestic group. This seems to be the case in the following text, presented by an unmarried man of twenty-six residing in a provincial city with his parents. He is a teacher of elementary school.

Text 16, 1:86

"I'm not a kid anymore! I'm going to live my own life. There's no way I'm going to run along the rails laid down by my parents like a toy train!"

I thought that was the privilege of youth, so I lived on this selfish feeling of freedom and thought nothing of staying out two or three nights in a row. Sometimes I didn't speak to my family for three or four days.

Mother is actually my second stepmother, and, caught between my grandmother and me, she had nothing but trouble, but I was indifferent to her. I felt that if she was unhappy it was because of her own whims, and I never once had apologized to her for the way I was acting.

Our household was well-off, so I had everything I wanted, but as long as I was just playing around, there could be no peace in the family. After suffering a long time, Mother joined Reiyukai. She was very serious about reciting the sutra and clung to what the branch leader told her: that if she would believe in the spirit world and recite the sutra, surely a way would be opened for her.

I used to sneer at her and say, "That's ridiculous, depending on some sort of gods that way...." But no matter what I said, Mother wanted to take me to see the branch leader. She cried and clung to me, so much that I finally went along.

That was in November of 1972. The first time he looked into my eyes, the Twenty-Seventh Branch leader bellowed at me: "Humph! Man, the lord of creation, can't be filial? Well, if that's how it is, are you even human?"

I was bowled over by his power. All at once the false bravado about the privilege of youth was stripped away from me, and I felt like a naked baby. I grabbed for Mother's hand and apologized to her. That was the first time I ever apologized to her. By reciting the sutra I came to understand the meaning of life. Now I'm really living.

Text 16 is the story of wayward youth brought back to a properly subordinate relation to his second stepmother through being shocked into apologizing to her by a branch leader. The speaker describes his stepmother's dilemma as the third wife and hence a somewhat anomalous position to being with, coupled with the ordeals of managing the grown children of her husband's previous marriages and his mother as well. Nevertheless, the speaker remained indifferent to her and selfishly asserted that he would do as he pleased now that he was no longer a child. This attitude he equated with freedom and "the privilege of youth." Furthermore, he ridiculed his stepmother's belief in Reiyukai and had to be dragged almost by main force to see the branch leader. For that leader, the failure to be filial is such a grave moral lapse that our speaker's very humanity is called into question. His reaction to the shock is instantaneously to abandon his former position of "privilege" and apologize immediately to his stepmother. He mentions that this was the first time he had ever done so, and seems to imply that subsequently he had other occasions to repeat the performance of apology. He also began to recite the sutra. One infers from this information that his relationship with his stepmother was radically altered, and that he took up a much more subordinate position in relation to her.

In previous chapters Reiyukai's concept of repentence was traced to traditional Buddhist ideas. It was shown that repentence and ritual are regarded as essential for increasing the ancestors' store of merit, by transforming karma to merit. As ancestors' merit increases, they bless their descendants, who consequently find life as a whole improved. These rewards of the True Law entail an obligation to Reiyukai, which the beneficiary repays through proselytization. Repentence in testimonial texts takes on a more concrete meaning. In the context of messy, personal, and intransigent problems that make up daily life, Reiyukai members use the concept of repentence to break out of, or at least make sense of the problems that face them. In this contemporary adaptation and application of the traditional concept of repentence, we can see how it continues to exercise an influence over the lives of women and men and how they continue to keep it vital by using it in daily life.

Part 3: Resolving Karma

In Reiyukai the idea of karma is reinterpreted in two ways, by linking it with notions of blood and inheritance, and by asserting that its fatalistic predispositions can be undone by spiritual training. As outlined in Chapter 4, in Reiyukai a part of karma is believed to be inherited. One inherits karma bilaterally, from both maternal and paternal ancestors, and this inheritance predisposes one toward the qualities and vices of the ancestors. Personality traits and artistic talents are also thought to be linked with blood and karma. Thus we can conclude that short-tempered persons have short-tempered ancestors. Inherited karma is linked to blood, which is also thought to be inherited. The exact connection is never made clear, but it seems that blood in the sense of a bloodline, a lineage, and the liquid substance itself are involved in the hereditary transmission of karma. Members speak sometimes as if blood and karma were interchangeable terms, and occasionally one hears stories of how a person's personality was entirely changed as the result of a transfusion. A change of blood can erase former personality traits such as a cheerful disposition, and artistic skills, such as a fine calligraphic hand. A chain of karma initiated in some unknown way in the remote past is destined to perpetuate itself and inflict itself on anyone who carries blood tainted with it. However, the chain can be halted and undone by spiritual training. This is called "resolving karma" (*innen o kaiketsu suru* 因縁を解決する) or "opening up destiny" (*un o hiraku* 運を開く). The following text shows how this idea works out in practice.

The speaker is Fujimoto Keiko, who is forty-eight years old and resides in a provincial city with her husband and son.

Text 14, 1:78–83

Two years after the end of the war, I married at the age of twenty-one. My husband was twenty-six at the time and worked for a seaman's union.

The Fujimoto household, which had fallen on hard times since a business failure in the previous generation, was living in a small rented house, and in the old, worn-out ancestral altar, there were many spirit tablets lined up, but if you looked carefully, you realized that there were two wives for each of the husbands represented there. To make a long story short, three generations of wives had died, leaving the husband to find a second wife.

Moreover, in the previous generation, children had died in infancy one after another, and in fact my husband had been adopted into the house at the age of five. He too was sickly, and about a year after we were married he was hospitalized with pulmonary tuberculosis and began a life of prolonged illness.

I thought to myself, "Well, this is quite a family I've married into," but once having married into it, I resolved to work singlehandedly to rebuild it.

My eldest daughter was born in 1949, and in 1950 my eldest son, but I left them with my mother-in-law and went to live all by myself in Nagoya, leaving our home in the town. I took a room in a boardinghouse and opened a street-stall bar and *worked*, oblivious of everything else.

To me, who had no experience of working around drunken people, this was a bitter experience. However, if I didn't work, I could never come up with the money for my husband's medical expenses, and there would be no support for the children and my mother-in-law.

My husband was operated on and had a lung removed, after which he slowly recovered at home for a year. In due course, his health returned, and he found work again. Nevertheless, I continued to work. Somehow or other the savings increased. Wanting to get out of life in a rented house, I wanted to buy our own house and land as soon as possible.

That is how it happened that after six years of hard work, I was able at last to stop. That was in 1957. It was around that time that my elder sister first spoke to me about Reiyukai.

She spoke very soberly: "Your household is a line in which for three generations the first wives have died young. If you have no desire to recite the sutra for your ancestors, you won't live long. In this religion, we laymen can recite the sutra for the ancestors, and we can truly resolve karma. You have married into the Fujimoto house because of some spiritual connection with them. First of all, pray to your ancestors. You must set your heart on creating family harmony. That is the most important thing of all."

My sister's words made me tremble. When I asked my husband's advice about it, all he said was, "If you feel like joining, I won't stand in your way. They say women have many karmic hindrances, so you ought to have religion."

I received a sokaimyo for my room in the Nagoya boardinghouse and energetically collected my ancestors' posthumous names, and never missed a day's recitation of the sutra. Maybe that's the reason that a year later my dream came true and we built a new house and realized the joy of being able to live together as a family again.

Then ten years passed. In 1968 my husband had an argument with his boss, and abruptly he turned in his resignation and found himself out of a job. He received no unemployment compensation. Having quit the company where he had worked for so long, he became neurotic and slept all day, his head under the blankets. I could hear him sobbing miserably under the covers.

With a feeling of helplessness, I kneeled before the altar and prayed to the ancestors to save him. Maybe the sound of my voice reciting the sutra with all my heart began to echo in his heart as well, but all at once he was unexpectedly saying, "I want to go and worship at Mirokusan," and began copying the Maitreya Sutra.

When the session was over and he returned, his features were so firm and resolute that he looked like a different person. Out of the blue on the first night of the pilgrimage, while lying asleep in the lodge in the dead of night, he had awaked when he heard a voice roaring like thunder in his ear saying, "It [the sutra] will make him who is without mercy become a man of mercy!" Wondering what it could mean, he opened the sutra and found the very same words.

Then the next morning when he heard Reverend Kotani's sermon in the main worship hall, he was shocked beyond belief. The voice he heard scolding him in the dream was the very same. In fact, the voice in his dream and that in the sermon were exactly alike.

He explained, "For the first time I felt that the eye of my heart had opened. I realized that the reason I had ended up quitting my job was that I lacked mercy. I thought only about how hard *I* was working, and in my pride and self-centeredness, I hated my boss for not sympathizing with me. That was because I had no mercy. When I was at Mirokusan, I understood the faults of my nature clearly."

After notifying our ancestors of this miraculous experience at Mirokusan, kneeling before our altar he hung his head and said to me, "When you were working so hard, I thought nothing of it, since as my wife, that much can be expected, and I forgot to thank you. I apologize."

My heart filled up and with trembling hands I apologized in return. "No, it wasn't you who was in the wrong. *I* was wrong. Please forgive me. . . ."

Actually, since my income was greater than his, I had begun to think, "What a shiftless excuse for a husband he is." Although I never said as much, I had been taking him for granted.

Then he sat up very straight and said, "Up until now I've always thought in terms of 'you' and 'me' or 'husband' and 'wife' but from now on I'll be 'the one who belongs to you' and you will be 'my wife.' From now on let's talk things over and work together to begin again, no longer relating superficially to each other, but changing so as to cherish the bond between us."

We vowed together to change our natures from that very day, and felt inspired to repay Maitreya's mercy by leading at least one more person into the Way, no matter what. We set out to make converts together, and while we were working wholeheartedly for the Law, there came news of a new job, and my husband entered a petroleum-related company in January of 1970. Since then he has received the recognition of his superiors and co-workers for his work and has been made a section chief and is still working hard. We are so grateful to the ancestors for all of this, and we are devoting ourselves to our faith with all our hearts.

Not only that, but thanks to this religion, I've been able to build true family harmony. I've realized the importance of true human fellowship, and I reflect every day on the joy of life that comes from treating people kindly. Particularly in June of 1971, when my mother-in-law returned to the spirit world at the age of eighty-one, I rejoiced from the bottom of my heart that I had faith in Reiyukai. What I mean is that for the three months of her final illness, while I nursed her and had to wash a mountain of diapers in the dead of winter day after day, I didn't feel it a hardship in the least. Right after she took to her bed, I had a dream in which I realized that in a former life we had been parent and child. I was the parent, and she was the child. For that reason, I felt it was only natural that I should change her diapers.

If I hadn't had faith, I wouldn't have had that dream, and even if I had had it, I wouldn't have believed it, and could never have had the experience of understanding the spiritual connection that led me to marry into the Fujimoto house. Also, faced with a senile, sick person, I would have complained about my hard lot, and undoubtedly would have burned with anger. Usually a light eater who never snacked between meals, my mother-in-law began demanding this or that special food to eat once she took to her bed. But no matter how unreasonable her request, I got it for her.

A week before she died, she called me to her side and said, "I have just one thing to ask you. Starting tonight, I want to have an evening drink. Please get me the top grade of Gekkeikan Sake. Please...."

My husband's answer when I asked him about it was, "She probably always was fond of sake but refrained from drinking because she is a woman. It's all right, so let her drink." I stocked up on sake, and by hand fed her that and side dishes by turns. Tears came to her eyes as she said, "Delicious, delicious" over and over again. I continued for six nights, and she died peacefully in her sleep.

The day before she died, she grasped my hand and murmured, "Mama, you've been so good to me for so long, and you've been so kind I can't thank you enough. When I die, I'll protect you...." [5]

Entering the Fujimoto house as a second wife, losing her children and having to adopt a sickly son like my husband, my mother-in-law endured much hardship in her life. And then she became just like a little girl as she grasped my hand and said, "Thank you, Mama, thank you." A lump rose in my throat as I replied, "Thank you, Granny." Thanks to joining this religion I was able to serve the ancestors *and* be filial. How joyful a thing! I was deeply grateful and clasped her hand.

If I hadn't had religion, I would have been stingy with food, and maybe Granny would have gone to the spirit world as a hungry ghost, a horrible prospect, if you think about it.

Three years ago my eldest daughter got married. Having been so fond of her grandmother, she married into a house with a grandfather and grandmother, converted them all, and built a happy home. She has already borne descendants.

My eldest son graduated from Meiji University and says he wants to work in Tokyo, but having come back to our town for his grandmother's funeral, he ended up taking a job at the local city office.

Presently the three of us: myself, my husband, and my son, are living together. Our ie is full of happiness. Having married in that topsy-turvy time right after the war, taking charge of a newborn child, a sickly husband and my mother-in-law, I used to wonder how in the world we could manage to get by, but all that seems like a bad dream now.

Slaving away at work, trying somehow to get out of that vale of tears,

[5] Although it is not uncommon for a mother-in-law to address her daughter-in-law teknonymically as *kaachan, okaachan* (母ちゃん，お母ちゃん), etc., with no implication of looking upon that person as her own mother, the sense of the word in this context is much altered, and the two have reversed positions, making the translation 'Mama' possible in both senses: "Kaachan, nagai koto, iroiro osewa ni narimashita. Hontō ni kaachan ni yō shite morōte, arigatō. Watashi ga shindara, kaachan o mamoru de na...."

my heart was so completely wretched that I only grumbled complaints at my mother-in-law. Not knowing the Law of Reiyukai, if I had continued to pile up days and months like that, what would have become of us?

Looking down on my husband, hating my mother-in-law, we would have had a life like the hell of ghosts, and by now we'd be tired and tattered in body and spirit. Having been able to change our destiny was unquestionably due to Reiyukai. I give thanks and will never forget my debt, and I vow to tell many people the true value of serving the ancestors.

In Text 14 we have two separate chains of karma to be resolved. The first is the tendency of Fujimoto brides to die young. This trend has continued for three generations, as is shown in the spirit tablets that have been placed in the altar. We are not told how this chain of fate originated, and the beginning is treated as irrelevant to the solution. An early death is likely to be the fate of our speaker, as her sister informs her, and that is the main point. Resolving this karma is inextricably linked to the idea of a connection that led Keiko to marry into the Fujimoto household, and the necessity of building family harmony. Thus the battle is to have two fronts: one is the ie, its lineage, and the other is within the domestic group. Keiko consults her husband about her sister's advice, and he concurs that she probably ought to join Reiyukai, given that women's karmic burdens are greater than men's and that therefore they have a special need for religion.

In terms of the Fujimoto hierarchy, Keiko enters as the "bride" (*yome* 嫁). Ideally, she should succeed to her mother-in-law's position when her son marries and brings in a new bride. Since no father-in-law is present, Keiko's major senior is the mother-in-law, and it is through her that Keiko is able to realize her spiritual connection with the household. In a former life they were mother and child, as Keiko learns in a dream, the reverse of their present relation. In this life the relationship is revived when Keiko assumes the parental role during the old woman's last illness, nursing her, feeding her, and changing diapers. "Realizing" the connection is an experiential matter of reliving it as it was in a former life. In so doing Keiko fulfills her duty as the daughter-in-law (this life) and as the mother to the old woman (a previous life) simultaneously. It is the fulfilling of duty that enables her to break the chain of fate which otherwise would have caused Keiko to die young. The day before the old woman died, she uttered the words which prove that the destiny of Fujimoto wives to die young has been changed: she promises to protect Keiko from the spirit world. In other words, when the mother-in-law becomes an ancestor, she will protect Keiko from dying an early death, as her predecessors in the Fujimoto household suffered. Thus the chain of fate has been broken.

Resolution of karma causing children to die in infancy will revolve around Keiko and her husband. Keiko's husband had been adopted after the family's natural children died, but the noxious tendency of children to die young carried over to him as well, and he was sickly as a child and later contracted tuberculosis. This endangers the possibility of his being able to fulfill his duty as the son by producing and raising healthy children. He also has a duty to increase the family's assets, but illness prevents him from working for a long time, and later he loses his job through a squabble with his employer. This plus the business failure in the previous generation reduce the Fujimotos to living in rental housing. The only solution was to send Keiko out to the streets of Nagoya to open a street-stall bar. She worked energetically for a full six years, joining Reiyukai through her sister's encouragement around the fifth year. When things were at the nadir, Keiko prayed to the ancestors and awakened a desire in her husband to do likewise.

Taking the pilgrimage to Mirokusan, the husband experienced a change of heart after hearing the voice of Kotani Kimi thundering the Maitreya Sutra at him. He realized that he had taken both his employer and his wife for granted, and he apologized to Keiko. This prompted Keiko to make a counter-apology to him for having looked down on him when his earning power was less than hers. The two of them vowed to reorient their relationship thoroughly, based on their Reiyukai membership.[6]

---

[6] This passage resists smooth translation, and it is doubtful whether English can reproduce the subtle distinctions Keiko's husband makes in the use of Japanese particles. The original is: "Ima made wa, ore *to* omae, otto *to* tsuma, to iu kankei datta ga, kore kara wa, omae *no* watashi de ari, watashi *no* tsuma de aru, to iu naka ni narō. *To* kara *no* no kankei e seikatsu o kirikaete, otagai no aratamerubeki ten wa aratame, hanashiatte ikō"; emphasis in original.

Later her husband took a new job and advanced himself, earning the respect of others. The prospect of an early death seems a thing of the past, and the fact that their son has graduated from a top-ranking university and is now living at home suggests that the tendency to physical weakness is absent in the son. We can expect him to take over from his father. The karma has been resolved by the husband's and wife's spiritual training, and the reorientation of their relationship to one in which the wife respects the husband as the major breadwinner; this is the "true family harmony" that Keiko strove to build.

Karma is taken to be a strong determinant of human events. Fatalistic predispositions to some undesirable end, if unaltered, can effect the death of an individual and the destruction of an ie. For the most part, little is heard about "good karma"; its results are overwhelmingly bad. After all, everyone has among his ancestors at least one "bad apple," who will have initiated a chain of bad karma which will be visited upon all descendants. However, spiritual training can "resolve" karma, and halt the hereditary transmission of undesirable effects. Karma is resolved in three ways. First, there is the strong, pervasive emphasis on apology and repentence; this is zange metsuzai in action. It is evidently a sine qua non on which all else depends. Second, there is inevitably a reorientation of a domestic (usually husband–wife) relationship and an affirmation of its hierarchical character. Third, there is an idealization of husband and wife undertaking spiritual training together. They are the natural unit for Reiyukai ancestral ritual. These three strands point to sources of human power which can be tapped for the purpose of transcending fate.

Part 4: Healing

Healing is the most complex theme appearing in testimonies, and discussion of it requires a sensitivity to social factors surrounding the relation of religion to medicine. There is no stigma placed on simultaneous reliance upon medical aid and Reiyukai curative measures, though there is a pervasively negative perception of the medical profession as a whole. There are no professional healers in Reiyukai. No drugs or curative substances are prescribed; there are no rituals the sole purpose of which is healing; the patient is not necessarily involved in his own cure; there is no mythology connected with healing; and no explicit etiologies of illness are made at the time of healing. There is much rhetoric to the effect that Reiyukai is not a healing religion. Some group of Reiyukai members performs Reiyukai activities together, and their collective action is considered instrumental to the cure. Sutra recitation and proselytization are thought to be efficacious in healing. Thus, the ancestors and the spirit world are inextricably related to the cure. The domestic group must be united in the care of its own ancestors and concerned for their happiness in the spirit world. The power of ritual is indirect in its influence, going via the spirit world and then "reflected" to the human world. Thus, the notion of a realignment of microcosm and macrocosm is fundamental. This notion is usually inseparable from a value placed on the solidarity of the domestic group, as can be seen in the following text, presented by a fifty-eight year-old mushroom farmer residing in a provincial city with his wife, son, son's wife, and grandchild.

Text 6, 1:55–56

"You call that religion?! Proselytizing people?! Going around with your head in the clouds about something that doesn't bring in a dime! And when your wage is so low, and we're so poor anyhow!" my wife shrieked. I had a short temper, and I'd failed over and over again, any number of times up to then. I'd joined this religion to cure myself of that. I'd held myself in time after time, but this time I exploded instantly.

I punched my wife and kicked her. Then I threw whatever I could get my hands on at her, and rampaged around, destroying everything in reach.

The result was that I was severely chewed out by my senior member in Reiyukai. He said, "You're supposed to be doing spiritual training to try to purify your short-tempered heart, so apologize to your wife by clasping your hands before her."

I felt so wretched I was helpless. I just kept my mouth shut and turned away. Then he spoke again, "Mr. Kawajima, your ancestors are grieving!" Then at last I woke up. I clasped my hands before my wife and repented and apologized to her from the bottom of my heart.

Then without warning my eldest daughter came down with a high fever. I didn't have any money, so I couldn't take her to the hospital, and when I finally had her examined by a doctor a week later, he grumbled expressionlessly, "It's infantile paralysis. Come back when the fever goes down."

I trembled with a feeling of loss as if blood were being drawn from beneath my toenails. Then the doctor said, "If the fever goes down, we can do something for her, so anyhow, bring her back when it goes down."

When I carried my sick child on my back and got on the train to go home, who should be sitting right across from me but five of my senior members from the branch? "What's wrong?" they asked me. When I told them my story, they all spoke at once. "Don't you worry, Mr. Kawajima! We're not going to let this child die. Let her be deformed? Absolutely not!"

Their powerful words violently struck me in my disappointment. My eyes and head were filled with a piercing heat. My seniors earnestly recited the sutra for me. They told me things would definitely be all right if my wife and I would make converts and pray wholeheartedly to the spirit world. At that, my wife, who had so strongly opposed my religion, suddenly burst out crying.

"Truly—there's no excuse I can make. From now on, I'll do it too." As we made our vow before the altar, my daughter took us by surprise when she murmured weakly from the midst of her torn bedding, "Mama, I'm hungry...."

My seniors ran out and came back with some rice balls they'd made for her. Looking at my daughter that way, I was overcome with the thought of how little self-respect as a parent I'd had, and I wept.

I went out immediately to make converts, and the husband of the household I visited was also short-tempered. At the end of one of his fights with his wife, he'd bashed her over the head with a thick table top until it broke in two. I told him my experience and was able to convert him. Now all my children, including my eldest daughter, are active in the Youth Group.

We may state the theme of this testimony by saying that the cure depends on the domestic group uniting itself around Reiyukai. In this text husband and wife are bitterly divided, and the husband's membership in Reiyukai has become the focal point of their differences. The wife objects to her husband spending time with the group instead of pursuing some activity which will be financially rewarding, as they are in great need. The husband becomes enraged and beats the wife. When they take their case to the husband's senior in Reiyukai, Kawajima is made to apologize to his wife for his behavior. The implication is that Kawajima cannot expect his wife to cease opposing Reiyukai until he reforms himself and his short temper. The ancestors grieve at the spectacle of his poor behavior, and it is only inevitable that their grief in the spirit world will be "reflected" back upon the human world in future misfortune for Kawajima and his family. In fact, it is forthcoming shortly. The eldest daughter is stricken with a high fever. For lack of money they must wait a full week to enlist medical help for her, and even when they are able to consult a physician, his insensitivity and lack of compassion are all too apparent as he announces his grim diagnosis: infantile paralysis. It seems to be a matter of indifference to him whether the child's condition improves enough for her to receive treatment. Kawajima is utterly downcast. Still divided from his wife, it seems there is little he can do but leave it to fate. However, he happens upon some of his Reiyukai colleagues in the train. Their attitude is in great contrast to that of the doctor. They express sincere concern for his plight, cancel their own plans, and join together with Kawajima single-mindedly in the hope of curing his child. They recite the sutra for him and urge him to unite with his wife in proselytization, promising the child's recovery if they will do so. In tears, the wife agrees, and she and her husband make a vow before the altar. As soon as they do so, the daughter speaks, asking for food. Spurred by her improvement, the group Kawajima met on the train rushes to procure food for her. Kawajima is overcome with gratitude and with regret for his own past actions. He weeps. He converts a violent man like himself and repays his obligations to Reiyukai by continuing religious activity with his family. The daughter's cure becomes complete upon mending the social rifts in the domestic group through Reiyukai.

Many elements are involved in healing, and in testimonials a healing episode is often combined with other themes we have examined, particularly apology and repentence, and the high value placed on the solidarity of the domestic group.

Healing in Reiyukai is a ritual affirmation of principles of the world view and of group solidarity. The emphasis on group solidarity presupposes the healing of social bonds that have been breached as well. Repairing social bonds requires an expiation of moral guilt for past behavior; thus, repentence is often involved. The group surrounding the sick person, including his family and fellow members of Reiyukai, advise the sick one, and Reiyukai members may advise members of the family of the sick one, and

devote themselves to his recovery. They perform ritual and proselytize together in the belief that sincere, devoted effort will not go
unrewarded; the spirit world must make some response.

We have seen that sutra recitation is performed in healing , and
here there is an implied etiology of illness. If illness were not linked
to the ancestors and the spirit world, there would be no reason to
suppose that ancestor worship would be of any use in its treatment. If ritual is not performed, the ancestors' dissatisfaction will
be reflected upon the human world, perhaps in the form of sickness or accidents. The etiology of illness implied in the ritual is
always the same: human suffering originates in ancestral suffering.
The cure for suffering is to end the ancestors' suffering by giving
them the ritual that provides their sustenance. In so doing the
individual or domestic group is restored to the right kind of
relationship with the spirit world in an affirmation of their basic
solidarity and mutual dependence.

However, we should not imagine that members reason in this
overly abstract manner. When illness strikes, action must be taken
immediately, and we find in the texts no abstract theorizing about
the cause of sickness or the philosophical basis of a cure. They
recite the sutra. If they face any ideological choice at that time, it is
more likely to be one between the explanations of the medical
profession and Reiyukai ideas. What sort of choice is the individual called upon to make in such a case?

Let us imagine a case involving a contagious disease. A doctor,
in consulting with the patient's relatives, will probably introduce
the notion of contagion—the sick person contacted, quite by
chance, the germs of someone having the disease, probably on the
train or some other crowded place. The role of pure chance and
unpredictability is paramount in explaining how the person came
to be afflicted. In Reiyukai, however, we find a persistent drive to
assign a social or emotional cause to every misfortune. That
something called "chance" could cause someone to sicken and die
is utterly unacceptable within this framework.

Further, a satisfactory explanation must link the disease and
moral guilt on the part of all those affected by the disease, not only
the patient but other members of the domestic group. Healing
involves an expiation—via ritual and proselytization—of that

guilt, and anyone who fails to participate may have to bear an even heavier burden of guilt if the patient fails to recover. Not only must horizontal social ties be strengthened, but ties to the spirit world must also be reaffirmed, and the patient's devotion to his ancestors' well-being must be proved. This has the function at the same time of binding the individual more firmly to Reiyukai as well. His obligation becomes all the heavier if the patient is cured. The cure is ideally a group effort, maximizing participation for everyone concerned. The patient is made to feel that he is significant, not a number or a monetary fee, and that his condition is a matter of concern to a large number of people. A network of emotional support, which will be sustained after the immediate crisis, is created. Contrast this with a situation in which the patient is confined, perhaps in isolation, told to ingest strange medicines, and attended at intervals by paid professionals who offer a measured dose of attention, retiring shortly to let him heal or worsen as fate will have it. In this context the ancestors are much more satisfactory as comprehensible explanatory agents, and the accompanying treatment is more satisfying emotionally as well. This is so not because one is more or less true than the other, but because the ancestors are already connected in a world view that is real and intelligible to the individual in a way that germs and germ theory are not.

In considering the question of what kind of efficacy healing has in Reiyukai, we should note that the problem of attributing a cure to one factor or another is difficult even in a purely medical context. Factors on which a patient's recovery may depend include pharmaceutical drugs, rest, withdrawal from a stressful situation, the psychological comfort given, and the placebo effect. Also, illness is universally associated with moral guilt, and healing with expiation of the guilt. Thus, in many cases the social relations of the patient may play an important role in his illness and its treatment.[7]

In some respects illness is similar to the problems of choosing a lifetime employment situation or a spouse for Reiyukai members:

[7] René Dubos, "Determinants of Health and Disease," reprinted in *Culture, Disease, and Healing, Studies in Medical Anthropology*, ed. David Landy (New York: Macmillan Publishing, 1977), pp. 32–40.

that is, the individual feels that none of these situations should be encountered alone. For one thing, one may make choices one may later regret if the advice of elders and those more experienced is not sought and heeded. But more importantly, people around one are implicated in these situations. In the case of marriage, members envision a situation in which the couple will live at some time, perhaps from the wedding ceremony on, with the parents of one of the spouses, usually the husband's. If they are all going to live together, the compatibility of the spouse with the affines is at least as important as his/her compatibility with the partner. This is especially true if they all will be involved in some common economic enterprise, which is inevitable if one includes the common household budgeting, running the household, including such matters as child care or nursing any sick member, not to mention the case of a family business, in which the mutual economic involvement of all members is obvious. The latter point is particularly relevant to Reiyukai, in which a large percentage of members are in fact involved in family-run business.

In addition to the economic aspects of illness, there is also the psychological dimension. Faced by illness, people become more intimately related to each other emotionally, and the threat of damage to the emotional network poses a different, although equally—or more—traumatic threat to the group than the economic crisis that illness can precipitate. However, the latter is especially serious in the case of workers in small- or medium-sized (or family-based) businesses, where social security measures are far less developed than in the case of the "salary man" working for a large corporation.

There is a drive to find emotional satisfaction in the doctor's treatment, and disappointment arises when this is not forthcoming. Why is there such a need to establish some sort of solidarity with the healer? Why is it not simply a matter of handing the sick one over to the appropriate specialist? The answer lies in the persistent association of illness with moral guilt, that is, the feeling that if only better relations had been maintained, the illness would not have occurred. In the case of Reiyukai members, there is the notion that if only the ancestors had been better cared for, their suffering would not be "reflected" back upon the human world.

Given that illness is understood in moral terms, a healer would be expected to offer a solution in those terms, and clearly this is not forthcoming from a physician. He will probably not be able to give satisfaction on this level even if the physical cure is successful. However, in addition to this sort of reason for the pervasively negative perception of the medical profession there are others as well.

Above all, doctors are a professional class, and they must be treated as such. As Reiyukai members view them, they are persons of high social position who must be addressed as *sensei* 先生. One cannot walk in off the street and expect to receive treatment. If one wishes to be kindly received, one must first acquire and present an introduction from someone with prior connection with the doctor. Patients are expected to use polite language, a trial under any circumstances for people without a high level of education, and more trying still if one is ill. Further, one must adopt a self-effacing, deferential attitude, expressing gratitude for the doctor's attentions, praising his competence, and in general presenting oneself as insignificant and troublesome. If one wants a guarantee of continued care, it is advisable to present the doctor with expensive gifts at the winter and summer gift-giving seasons to insure his continued receptivity to one's needs. Money gifts in excess of the cost of treatment are also considered routine.

There is an alarming lack of emergency care facilities so that it may take hours for an emergency case to locate a hospital providing all-night services (this is done on a rotating basis among the hospitals of a given area). Beyond that, one must trust to luck that the attending doctor will be a specialist in the treatment of one's ailment. If that is not the case, one simply waits until such a doctor arrives, which may not be until late morning, or until Monday if the emergency occurs on the weekend. In many areas anything less serious than a matter of life and death can in effect be cared for only between 9:00 a.m. and 5:00 p.m., Monday through Friday.

Also related to the delivery of emergency care is the problem of ambulances. Reiyukai headquarters officials told me that several times they had been called late at night to take members to the hospital in a private car because members were reluctant to call an ambulance which would come with siren wailing, thus alerting the neighbors to distress in the household. There seems to be on the one hand a reluctance to arouse neighbors in the dead of night (even if it might mean quicker conveyance of the sick to a physician), and on the other a reticence to let it be known that there is any weakness in the household—that it is in a vulnerable position. That these factors should receive priority at the expense of speed of treatment is eloquent testimony to the strength of such attitudes.

A problematic aspect of professional health care of the more obvious sort is the cost. Even if one has coverage under the National Health Insurance plan, which will defray 70 percent of the cost of all drugs and treatment in the case of the policy-holder, a serious illness in a dependent, a chronic illness, or one requiring surgery will necessitate great expense and can cause financial damage which can destroy a household's financial resources in the space of a month. The burden is especially heavy, of course, if it is an illness of the breadwinner. Further, the cost is, from the viewpoint of the average person, utterly unpredictable. One is presented with a bill and is expected to pay with alacrity, promptness, deference, and gratitude, whether or not the patient was saved or benefited.

It is common policy in Japanese hospitals for doctors and nurses to use many English words and expressions, to such an extent that the patient is left in ignorance of his illness and its cure. He is expected to be entirely passive, accepting the doctor's judgment with deference and gratitude, even if the treatment is unsuccessful or wrong. Diagnoses and explanations of illness are delivered in language that members say they have difficulty understanding. It is expected that they will not bother the doctor with questions.

Japanese hospitals often permit the patient to be attended by a relative or a paid professional, the *tsukisoi* 付き添い. However, by no means is this always possible. It is common to restrict hours and days when friends and relatives may visit a patient. Some hospitals permit visiting only one day per week, even in the case of child patients. The patient's family is expected to maintain a passive attitude just like the patient himself. The hospital routine makes no allowances for their presence, which is considered a nuisance and a potential health hazard by the doctors and nursing staff. At such a time, members would like to gather at the patient's bedside and recite the sutra with him, but this is also outside the bounds of behavior regarded proper in the hospital, regardless of the fact that members consider sutra recitation vital to a cure. While the hospital staff's viewpoint is understandable, its effect of relegating the patient's group to the sidelines, expecting them to be passive and stay out of the way, is equally understandably alienating. Their interests in the case are not recognized, and they cannot assert themselves in any way.

Reiyukai's attempts to aid fellow members' healing meet only with frustration from the medical profession. The doctors and nurses are surrounded by arcane trappings of what seems to be a particularly cold and unfeeling version of professionalism, in which the patient's condition is explained to them in a confusing mixture of English and Japanese, which they are expected not to question, regardless of their understanding of what is happening.

Members frequently indicate that they do not feel that doctors are terribly competent individuals as a group, and that they may be more concerned with reenforcing inflated notions of their own prestige than with treatment of the patient. Members are particularly indignant at their routine exclusion from the process of curing the patient. They feel they are being left in the dark and ignored even though they may be vitally interested and may be the principal financial backers. What the patient's group seems to crave is a sense of real participation, which to them is appropriate in view of the threat to the group occasioned by the incapacitation of one of its members. They assert that *their* interests are implicated in the member's illness, as well as the patient's, and on that basis they feel entitled to a role in the cure—not only entitled, but *obligated*, to assume such a role in order to release themselves from the sense of moral guilt and the powerless position they are expected to adopt in relinquishing the patient to a doctor, an outsider to the group—one who will not establish any solidarity with them on an equal basis, who instead deigns to offer only crumbs of information in a condescending manner. The difference in social class is keenly felt.

Though in the end we probably cannot give any conclusive

answer to the question whether or not Reiyukai healing "works" in a medical sense, we can say that if people had no genuine sense of the effectiveness of these healings, the associated practices and behavior would not be so frequently reiterated today, nor would they have continued for more than fifty years. It is not a question of championing medicine versus healing nor vice versa. Reiyukai members recognize that neither Reiyukai nor the medical profession can guarantee a successful cure in all cases, and they do not require members to rely exclusively on group curative measures. Members' claims to genuine benefit must be taken seriously by anyone seeking to understand the group.

It would be a mistake to leave the impression that Reiyukai healing is purely a reaction to inadequacies perceived in the Japanese medical system. The attempt to effect religious healing would not vanish even if all the negative factors of the medical profession were rectified overnight. Members seek a mending of social bonds interpreted in terms of a religious world view linking the human world with the realm of Buddhas and ancestors. They believe that when one is in harmony with the structure of the universe, one may expect to be healthy, and that illness is a sign of the absence of such harmony. Thus, for them, the healing process must be a return to correct relationships—within this world and between the microcosm and macrocosm. Therefore, meaningful healing must occur within the group whose ties have been broken; an outside, professional healer can fit into this framework no better than a priest can fit into the relation between ancestors and descendants. Thus no "purely" medical cure can give satisfaction. For that reason, improvements in medical health delivery are unlikely to cause a disappearance of Reiyukai healing.

In conclusion, let us return to the significance of witnessing for the novice. As a member of an audience hearing and discussing testimonies, a novice is exposed to the themes discussed in this chapter, and that experience becomes his introduction to the "teaching" of Reiyukai. When he himself undergoes religious experience and testifies before others, he presents himself as an "experienced" member. The experience of testimony thus becomes the gateway to his taking a leadership role in the group. If he is, as so many of the characters of the testimonies presented here are, somehow outside the family system (second wives, adopted children, adopted husbands, etc.), he finds through testimony not only a more secure place in Reiyukai, but a more secure position in his family. This "reward of the True Law" is a significant factor in the recruitment and retention of a commited membership.

Chapter Six

The Role of Women in Reiyukai

Previous chapters have shown how and why the traditional family system, its roles and values take on religious significance in Reiyukai. Women's normative confinement to the domestic sphere makes it only natural that they would be more involved in a religion centering on the family than would men, thus partially explaining their higher rate of participation, as seen in Chapter 2. Male leaders spontaneously declare that women are the center of the group and that without them, it could not survive. Although statistics presented earlier show women's numerical strength, further examination of their role in the group is still required. What are the religious ideas and strategies Reiyukai women use to achieve their crucially important role in the group? This is the question that this chapter seeks to answer.

As stressed in Chapter 2, a novice member of Reiyukai does not have the same grasp of group teachings as her senior colleagues, and the process through which a newcomer acquires group values is a subject that deserves careful attention. This process of socialization is treated in the first part of this chapter: "The Acquisition of Conservative Norms and Values in Reiyukai." Examination of that process leads to the heart of Reiyukai's ideas about women: they are regarded simultaneously and paradoxically as bearing many hindrances to salvation and as capable of attaining religious power unattainable by men. This paradox is the subject of Part 2. The third part examines the strategies women adopt on the basis of ideas and values acquired in Reiyukai to manage the domestic group. The final part shows how women use their membership in Reiyukai to create for themselves roles in the public sphere, still normatively attached to the family but actually operating outside its confines.

Part 1: The Acquisition of Conservative Norms and Values in Reiyukai[1]

In this part a testimonial is presented to illustrate the process by which a woman becomes involved in Reiyukai. We can see how a woman progresses from being an outsider, to a novice, to a leader of the group. The process is one of first accepting and appropriating Reiyukai's way of interpreting a particular problem, and in so doing, of accepting generally applicable norms and values regarding the domestic group, and of internalizing underlying ideas about the nature of women and men. At the same time, the newcomer learns to submit to the authority of group leaders. Although the process of socialization will be illustrated by a single text, the steps seen here are typical of members' progression in the group.[2]

Text 38, 1:142–47

Thirteen years ago I got married at the age of nineteen. My husband was three years older and had the reputation of being a very dutiful son,[3] so much so that he didn't know the meaning of having fun.

However, since he had just entered his twenties, his salary wasn't very large, so I opened a small, late-night restaurant to help out. I liked the work, but I felt more than anything else that we wouldn't make it unless both of us were working.

But even so, we were always in the red by the end of the month. I went to my mother just about every month to coax money out of her. I thought it was only natural for parents to do that much for their children, so I asked her help without reservation.

[1] An expanded version of this part was published under the title "Sex Role Norms and Values in Reiyūkai," *Japanese Journal of Religious Studies* 6, No. 3 (September, 1979), 445–59.

[2] This testimony illustrates the stages typically marking the indoctrination of a person who first encounters Reiyukai as an adult. It is of course to be expected that the process differs considerably in the case of one who has been a member since childhood.

[3] "Dutiful": *oyakōkō* 親孝行; literally, "filial," one who has filial piety.

After that, my eldest daughter was born, and later another daughter. I'd been married five years by then and had two children. I was so wrapped up with the children, my housework, and running the restaurant that my husband hardly mattered to me. Life didn't seem a bit more fun, and as I had more children, the cost of raising them increased, and as usual we stayed in the red. All I could think of was money, money, money.

When my husband came home tired from work, I'd leave for the restaurant right away to lay in supplies for the night's business. Providing good service for my customers until late into the night, I'd drag my feet home like lead to find my husband and the children asleep. Conversation between me and my husband stopped completely, and we became like strangers.

Well, you can't expect a situation like that to turn out well. My husband, who had such a fine reputation before we married, had learned somewhere to play pinball[4] and bet on the boat races, and was wasting his time. And that's not all. He became completely addicted to a certain woman and stopped coming home for nights at a time. From my point of view, even though I was working all night to supplement our meager income, he betrayed me by being unfaithful with another woman. I had no intention of forgiving him. We fought time and time again. Then one day he simply disappeared.

I grumbled to myself, "Humph! Off with that woman again...." I started looking into my heart, wondering why I wasn't more upset. The love between us had withered up and crumbled like sand, and what remained was withered and lifeless. Making up my mind to separate from this person for whom I felt neither jealousy nor lingering affection, I didn't cry.

"I've got the restaurant, and that's enough to raise the two children. I'm still young—just twenty-four." Muttering to myself, I filed for divorce, and having resolved to separate, I felt that my heart was clear. However, there was someone who was worried about me; it was the old lady next door. "Divorce? Don't say that. Think it over again. I'm a member of Reiyukai, and we have a branch leader who always gives good advice. Why don't you try going to her for advice? She can give you wisdom."

She strongly urged me to go. I didn't really think there was any chance that our dried-up old love could be revived, so I wasn't inclined to listen to what she said. But I wanted someone to complain to about my husband's infidelity which had tattered my youth and dried up the love between us. So I visited the house of this person called the branch leader, hoping to be comforted as I told my sad story.

Branch Leader Onishi said this to me when she saw my face. "You—you're young and pretty now, but in two or three years, you're going to have a face like a pig! You bring that husband you want to get rid of over

---

[4] "Pinball": *pachinko* パチンコ.

to see me. I've got something to tell him that'll make him understand whether he ought to get rid of the likes of you!" [5]

The blood rushed to my head, and I screamed until my hair stood on end and then flew out of her house. Now why did she say an outrageous thing like that to me? Although I thought that since she was a woman she would understand my wounded feelings, she only tore open the wound again with what she said. Could anyone I'd just met understand my pain?

Feeling that way, I lamented and regretted what had happened until it seemed my heart would break. However, when that night had passed, and I felt more calm, I felt a strange, deep emotion. Why did she say such a thing to me, I began to wonder? Usually you don't tell people the first time you meet them that they have pig faces. I'd gone to her in the first place to hear about this religion, Reiyukai, and things like that. Just going by common sense, you'd think she would have explained, "You'll be happy if you practice this religion," inviting me sweetly with comforting words. So why did she fling those terrible words in my face?

After a while I began to want to talk to her once more, quietly, to find out what she meant. I went to Branch Leader Onishi's house again, and this time she spoke to me seriously. "Mrs. Ono, the face expresses the heart. Actually, the face is the heart. Even if you ornament it beautifully on the outside, when you look on the inside, you'll find the world is full of people of unbelievable ugliness." [6]

It was as if I'd been struck suddenly in the head. I thought I was going to pass out. I knew I couldn't lie to this person who so clearly pointed out the ugliness of my heart.

After that I went to see her again and again, and hearing what she said, I realized that when husband and wife get into this kind of situation, it has such a terrible influence on the children that at least one of my children would end up like me.

It was then that I realized that I was really unfilial. I had no consideration for my mother, cajoling money from her as if it were the natural thing to do, making her worry. And then toward my husband, I'd only made him unhappy, losing all feeling of respect for him, feeling that we couldn't make a living without *my* work. When I realized that this was the cause of our present unhappiness, I resolved to join Reiyukai.

From that day on I prayed that my husband would return. I wondered if my prayer would get through to him. On the tenth day after his disappearance, he suddenly showed up. I'd never been so glad as then.

---

[5] Anta, ima wa wakakute kirei da kedo, ni, san nen mo sureba, hito mo miraren buta gao ni naru yo. Sonna ni hanaretai goshujin nara, koko ni tsurete kinasai. Hanarerubeki ka dō ka, yoku wakaru yō ni hanashite okeru kara.

[6] Ono san, kao to iu mono ni wa kokoro ga arawarerun desu yo. Tsumari, kao wa kokoro nan desu. Uwabebakari utsukushiku kikazatte ite mo, ura kara mitara shūaku kiwamarinai kao ga, ima no yo no naka ni wa michiafurete irun desu.

Although I wanted to jump up to meet him, the strength of my old feelings got the better of me, and I couldn't express my feelings meekly, but raised my eyebrows and shouted at him harshly, "Who's there? Oh! It's you. What can I do for you, now that you're showing your face here?"

He yelled back at me, "I don't have any use for you! I only came back because I'm worried about the children. Even if we separate, *I'm* taking the children!"

Maybe it was women's intuition, but I knew in that instant that he still cared for me.

For three days he stayed with the children. He didn't say a word to me—just glared at me with an ugly feeling. But the children followed him around, and he was kind to them. It looked like they were having fun. On the third day, I finally spoke to him.

"Dear, if you feel like making up, please meet Branch Leader Onishi. Please listen to what she says in order to clear up this ugly feeling between us."

"Unnh ... if you say so ...."

He gave in so much more easily than I had expected that I was thoroughly confused. When the two of us went together to see her, she said, "When a husband and wife are continually fighting, the influence will definitely appear in the children." At that point my husband slumped in his seat as if realizing his mistake. Then the branch leader spoke severely to me.

"The cause of all of this is you, you who are the wife. You were probably angry when your husband was unfaithful and was stolen by another woman, but you have *got* to realize that this is *your* fault, and you must repent! And fixing things up is going to take a lot more cooperation than you've shown up to now!"[7]

It was as if her words had pierced my chest. My husband and I returned home thinking our separate thoughts. After that he started coming around to the restaurant about closing time to talk about one thing or another. "From now on, I don't want to hurt my parents and the children any more, or you either. If this can be patched up, I want to make a new start," he said.

I felt the same way. I realized that it had been a mistake to have a small restaurant like that and to be so busy all the time. For that reason, I vowed to resign myself to closing the restaurant and giving myself over entirely to my husband.[8]

---

[7] Subete no gen'in wa, tsuma de aru anata ni arun desu yo. Goshujin ga uwaki o shita, onna ni otto o nusumareta, to anata wa hara o tateteiru deshō ga, sono gen'in wa jibun ni aru to iu koto o, mōichido, yoku, yoku kangaete, zange shinakereba ikemasen. Sō shite futari ga naka yoku yarinaosu tame ni wa, kore made ijō doryoku ga hitsuyō desu yo.

[8] Desu kara, omoi kitte mise o tebanashi, watashi wa otto no mune no naka ni tobi konde ikō to chikaimashita.

Eight years have passed since then. My eldest daughter is a sixth grader now, and the next daughter is in fourth grade. I also have a three-year-old son. We're caring for a nephew, too, so all together there are six of us in the family, but our ancestors' altar is the center of the household.

My husband and I are very active in proselytization, and we became Vice Branch Leaders in one year. We really feel now that life is splendid. Our bitterest experience of eight years ago seems like a lie now. Looking back over our lifetime together is a wonderful recollection for us.

This testimony illustrates seven stages marking the process of acquiring conservative norms and values. The first is close contact with a leader during a period of distress. Onishi puts Ono in a submissive position by undercutting her perception of herself as the innocent, wounded party in her conflict with her husband. It is significant that Onishi refuses Ono the solace she seeks until Ono acknowledges her authority by returning after having been humiliated. At that point she delivers a verdict on Ono as someone whose heart is ugly, and she speaks with sufficient dogmatism that Ono accepts her conclusion as true. In accepting this evaluation of herself, Ono submits to the leader, acknowledging her authority to redirect her negotiation of the problem. In stage one, the client puts herself in the leader's hands.[9]

A second stage is the allocation of increasing amounts of time to the organization and contact with its leaders. Ono returns again and again, repeating her original submission to the leader. As the individual spends more time surrounded by the personnel, opinions, and values of members, she necessarily spends less time with people of different persuasions, who may hold alternative, conflicting views which contradict or undercut the leader's emerging interpretation and solution of the problem. Thus this tentative *entry* into the group entails a partial *withdrawal* from ordinary society. The negative connotations of the withdrawal are compensated for by rewards of friendship and encouragement within the group.[10]

Third, we see that Ono comes to accept an interpretation of her

---

[9] In rejecting Ono's interpretation of the situation, Onishi refuses to grant Ono the sexual solidarity she originally sought.

[10] This repetition constitutes practice in submission, a strategy Reiyukai women use to manipulate and control men to a certain extent.

problem in terms of religious notions linked to social norms. Onishi makes much of the belief that if Ono continues on her course, at least one of her children will "end up like her." According to Reiyukai, karma inherited from a parent can influence the course of a life in progress; thus, if Ono divorces, her children are also likely to divorce. Once Ono accepts this idea, she starts to seek ways to avoid the fate forecasted by this interpretation.[11]

Onishi says that the children's fate is jeopardized when their parents are not living in harmony. That is, the children are endangered not by any open breach in the karmic bond between them and their mother, but by the worsening relation between their parents. That relationship, too, is expressed in terms of karma. According to Reiyukai, there is a karmic bond between husband and wife, and it is the disturbance of this bond that Onishi designated as the real source of Ono's problems, and those liable to befall her children.[12]

The bond between husband and wife has been breached in a very conspicuous manner by the husband's gambling and infidelity, but Onishi is not concerned about that and is willing to concede Ono no comfort on that score. Instead, Onishi blames the wife, and in fact says she is the sole cause of the family's troubles. This rather incredible analysis of the situation is to be understood in terms of the karmic bond between spouses. A basic norm of that bond, according to Reiyukai, is that the husband be the sole breadwinner. He supports his wife, and not vice versa. Even if the husband is injured or is chronically ill, and the wife perforce becomes the major breadwinner, it is recommended that she apologize to the husband for having usurped his role. Gainful employment, in short, is considered a moral lapse on her part, the repercussions of which will be visited upon future generations. If she does take a paying job, the karmic bond between her and her husband is badly damaged, and the responsibility for repairing it

[11] The idea that parents' conduct influences the karma of children is linked to the idea that parents are "one type of ancestor" in that they continue to transmit karma.

[12] The break between husband and wife thus becomes a problem of karma, and as such it is a question of "resolving karma."

falls on her, no matter what extenuating circumstances might suggest. This assessment of female employment stems from sex role conceptions built on more fundamental ideas of separate spheres of moral responsibility and division of labor.[13]

The branch leader's interpretation of Ono's problem incorporates these norms, and the gloomy prognosis motivates Ono to act in accordance with norms and values as she is being *taught* them by the leader. Needless to say, Ono will also continue to repeat gestures of deference, self-effacement, and submission to the leader's authority.

The fourth step is acceptance of blame for the problem. In testimonies the notion that one must accept blame for whatever is wrong is heard again and again. That goes for poverty, sickness, and domestic discord. Thus, Onishi never hints that the husband might accept any blame. In fact, he is vindicated, as if he were well within his rights to gamble and be unfaithful. Onishi speaks of his actions in the passive voice, saying he "was stolen" by another woman, thus further removing him from responsibility for his actions. The message to take the beam out of one's own eye before setting to work on the mote in someone else's is directed in accordance with the status hierarchy of the family: in a mother-in-law versus daughter-in-law situation, it is nearly always the daughter-in-law who is told to yield; in the case of a husband-wife conflict, always the wife; and in general a woman is always supposed to yield to a man.

Acceptance of blame is accompanied by feelings of guilt. A direct concomitant of guilt is the feeling that one has incurred a debt (*on*) which must be recompensed at the individual's own expense: he feels he ought to suffer. The debt is incurred not only toward the injured party of the problem at hand (Ono's husband, by this interpretation), but also to the leader for having alerted the person to her error and shown the way to a solution. Furthermore, the notion that one has incurred a debt toward Reiyukai as a whole for its role in bringing one back to the straight and narrow is typically expressed.

[13] The idea that married women should apologize for gainful employment is linked to their concern for the husband's ego, which is regarded as fragile and liable to injury if a wife is employed.

A fifth stage is repentence and apology. Ono repents and re-
solves to assume a position of complete economic dependence
upon her husband by relinquishing her source of support, the
restaurant. The repentence motif represents Reiyukai's inheritance and transformation of the zange metsuzai theme discussed
in earlier chapters.[14]

Sixth is cessation of activity inconsistent with the norms one will
have accepted in stage three. Ono carries out her vow and closes
the restaurant. The rest of the story is very abbreviated, but it
seems that Ono and her husband became very active in Reiyukai,
proselytizing two hundred people in a single year and thus becoming Vice Branch Leaders. Here the individual demonstrates his
acquisition of approved norms and values.[15]

A final step comes when Ono assumes a leadership role, still
under Onishi's supervision. Ono will typically tell her testimony
over and over again, being rewarded by the group for her success
many times with approval, friendship, and rank. This cannot help
but motivate her to internalize these norms and values thoroughly,
and to do her best to persuade others to do the same.[16]

The norms and values surrounding sex roles seen in this text are
based on the assumption of a clear division of labor and moral
responsibility by sex. Women are responsible for everything that
affects the domestic sphere, while men provide financial support.
This division is supported by ideas about karma which hold that
there is a karmic bond between husband and wife which we may
speak of as horizontal. There are also karmic bonds between
parent and child, symbolized in reciprocal relations between ancestor and descendant in rites of ancestor worship, and we can call
these vertical. A breach in the horizontal bond endangers the

---

[14] Ono apologizes for having operated the restaurant instead of having been
totally dependent upon her husband.

[15] By this stage Ono has brought virtually all her activities within the range of
supervision by the Reiyukai leader. Her life has come to revolve largely around
group membership.

[16] When Ono becomes accomplished in proselytization, she steps into a leader's
role. In this capacity she will assume the work of guiding those whom she has
proselytized, and when they bring their problems to her, she will advise them in line
with the norms and values she herself has been taught through the process outlined
here.

vertical bond as well: one being "reflected" in the other. On this reasoning one can say that a child will experience the same sort of breach in the horizontal bonds they form in future married life. On the other hand, correct adherence to the division of labor and moral responsibility brings rewards. In this case, karma transferred to children will be good, and children will have happy, prosperous marriages. In the context of a domestic problem, this scheme of ideas may be applied diagnostically, to interpret it, finding the source in a transgression of the division of labor and moral responsibility based on ideas about karma.

In the realm of values the reciprocal pair, male dominance–female submission is most important. Women are urged to be meek and submissive (*sunao* 素直) and to build up the husband's ego by performing elaborate gestures of deference and respect, simultaneously indicating self-effacement and humility on their part. These gestures are supported by a number of notions about female pollution that have been given Buddhist coloring and terminology, which we will examine in the next section.

Part 2: The Dilemma of Power

The questionnaire introduced in Chapter 2 showed that 76 percent of respondents affirmed the idea that women are *gōshō ga fukai* 業障が深い. Gosho ga fukai is the key phrase members use to differentiate men and women religiously; gosho ga fukai is true of women, but not of men, they say. Although the Buddhist origins of the phrase are unmistakable, in Reiyukai it has other associations as well, which I tried to discover through interviewing. This part will present members' views on the subject as they emerged in those conversations, and then trace historical origins in Buddhism.

Gosho is a Buddhist term meaning "karmic hindrances," and to say of women, gosho ga fukai, "karmic hindrances are deep," is to imply "deeper than men's." Thus the most basic meaning of the phrase is that women face greater obstacles in achieving salvation than men. Another Buddhist term, nearly homonymous with the gosho meaning "karmic hindrances" is one meaning "five hindrances." The five hindrances apply only to women and enumerate the five states on the road to salvation that women are incapable of achieving. It is gosho in the sense of "karmic hindrances," however, with which Reiyukai members are concerned. It was to the following question that 76 percent of questionnaire respondents replied affirmatively: "Some people say about women, gosho ga fukai. Do you think this is so?"[17]

After the questionnaire results were in, I held interviews in April and May, 1978, with twenty-five branch leaders. I asked them the question appearing on the questionnaire and at the same time solicited their reactions to the fact that such a high proportion of respondents affirmed the notion that women must surmount higher obstacles than men to achieve salvation. All of the women branch leaders (five) said they agreed that women's karmic hindrances are greater, while the men unanimously rejected the idea. In effect, it was the position of male interviewees that men's and women's chances for salvation are equal, while the women held that obstacles are greater for women. The interview then turned to member's interpretations of women's gosho.[18]

[17] The questionnaire item reads: Dansei yori, josei no hō ga gōshō ga fukai to iu hito ga imasu ga, anata mo sō omoimasu ka? The "five hindrances" to which women are subject in traditional Buddhist thought refer to the following five states which they are believed incapable of attaining: a king of the Brahma heaven, a Sakra, a Mara king, a cakravartin, and a Buddha. Gosho meaning "karmic hindrances" outside Reiyukai is a term not restricted to either women or men. It refers to the results of karma in a general way with the negative association of "hindrances": *shō* 障. Needless to say, this point became the focus for great debate in Buddhist philosophy of karma, but in Reiyukai it is more a matter of received knowledge than of philosophical speculation. The development of thought about karmic hindrances in Japanese Buddhism is treated in Uemura Shinkei, "Hagōshō no shisō to hokekyō gaku," *IBK* 11, No. 1 (1963), 20–26. The contrasting view that karmic hindrances are actually empty is discussed in Kōchi Michigaku, "Metsuzai sei ni tsuite," *IBK* 17, No. 2 (1969), 540–41. The connection between karmic hindrances and pollution is treated in Sōba Nakashi, "Kegarekan no dentō to bukkyō," *IBK* 10, No. 2 (1962), 144–47.

[18] Since a significant proportion of male questionnaire respondents affirmed the idea that women are gosho ga fukai, it would seem that the denial of that notion in the interview situation was to some extent conditioned by the circumstances of the interview itself. When I first requested permission to interview branch leaders, Reiyukai officials stipulated a number of conditions. First, they required that I submit a list of questions to be asked of each interviewee, and after I had done so, they took exception to a number of items, largely political or otherwise of a

In the course of the interviews with female branch leaders, four proofs were raised as evidence that women's karmic hindrances are greater than men's. The first dealt with women's comparatively "hard lot" in life compared to men's. A second explained gosho in terms of women's role in the family. A third raised the idea that women are more attached than men to the things of the world, and a fourth dwelt on the pollution of women's bodies.

The theme of women's hard lot as a source or evidence of gosho was introduced by Branch Leader Tomita Yasuko, who works at Shakaden and whose husband is a member of the Japanese Self-Defense Forces.[19]

Tomita: When all is said and done, women are the ones who suffer, no matter what, so it must be because of gosho, don't you think? If men work outside, all the little things, even if it's a question of taking care of children, all that falls to the woman. From that angle and in that sense, you can say about women, gosho ga fukai.

HH: Do you mean that in the course of taking care of children, women build up gosho, from child care itself?

Tomita: Yes, that's right. No matter what, it's always the mother who does everything while the child is small. There are a lot of little things about it that men don't understand. For example, babies cry a lot, right? While they're small, they're always crying. While they're small, everything

sensitive nature. They stipulated that those questions not be asked. Furthermore, they required that an official be present at all interviews, and that the interviews be held at the headquarters. In addition, they reserved the prerogative to select the interviewees. I strongly requested that I be allowed to interview an equal number of women and men, but officials were most reluctant to allow me to interview women leaders at all. The stated reason was that women leaders are too busy; however, behind this reason was the more important fact that male officials appear to fear that women leaders are not sufficiently concerned about the group's public image and might reveal damaging information. This attitude was marked, and it was only with difficulty that officials were persuaded to allow the five interviews with female leaders.

With women leaders it proved relatively easy to establish rapport and to go beyond the rather superficial questions approved, to matters of interest to each of the women. The men, by contrast, seemed almost to have been coached on the "right" answers and were obviously at pains not to say anything wrong. The presence of headquarters officials was in their case a considerably constraining factor, while the women characteristically ignored their presence and quickly seemed to respond to questions with less reserve.

[19] Interview with Tomita Yasuko, Shakaden, Tokyo, April 16, 1978.

is left up to the woman. It's all right as long as the husband is just sitting there watching, but when he's fast asleep, the crying is noisy, so it's the woman who gets up, because the child is pitiful, and picks it up and soothes it so it won't cry. If you compare [men and women] from that kind of angle, you've got to admit that women are the ones who pile up gosho. Thinking of it in that way, you're bound to think that women are the ones with greater gosho.

HH: When you say that, do you mean that if in a prior life they had tried harder, they wouldn't have ended up having to put up with so much trouble?

Tomita: That's right. It's because in their past lives as well they were women that they come to be born as women again, isn't it? If that wasn't so, they wouldn't have been born as women. I'm doing everything in my power to be born as a man in my next life. [Laugh.] Women are really foolish [*bakarashii*]—anyway, I think so. Next time, I'm *absolutely* going to be born a man. I'd rather be a man, wouldn't you? Women really should try harder.

Tomita took it for granted that to be male is more desirable than to be female, and she concluded that since it is women who "suffer, no matter what," their fate must be due to deeds of a past life. In other words, if a person is born female, it must be due to not having lived a "proper" life in previous existences. In fact, if a person is born female, it must be the result of having been born female before as well. The reasoning is circular: if women did not accumulate more karmic hindrances than men, they would not have such a hard lot in life; i.e., they would not have been born as women in the first place. Therefore, they must have been women in previous lives as well, and so on.

A second way of explaining the phrase gosho ga fukai treats it as a matter of women's role in the family. In this case the interviewees were Mr. and Mrs. Arahata, a lively couple in their mid-fifties who act as branch leaders together. When I asked them what they thought gosho ga fukai meant, they replied,[20]

Wife: Doesn't that refer to the fact that women must serve others? People our age have been raised to believe that a woman must serve her husband. A woman should walk one pace behind, I guess, but I'm the one

[20] Interview with Mr. and Mrs. Arahata Takeo, Shakaden, Tokyo, April 30, 1978.

who goes right on ahead. [Laugh.] It's always been like that in Japan, hasn't it? Women have to obey their husbands and serve them.

Husband: You might say it's a matter of [Japanese] ethnicity (*minzokusei* 民族性). From ancient times in Japan, a woman who marries into another family obeys all the members of that family. So, she has to obey her mother-in-law, she has to obey her husband, from ancient times until now. But now times have changed. It's because that practice has always existed in Japan.

HH: Does that mean it's mainly a matter of custom?

Husband: Yes, that's how it is.

HH: And yet, the word gosho seems to have some sort of religious meaning as well, doesn't it?

Wife: Yes, that's true. Even if it is a matter of custom. But the idea that women should obey their husbands and obey their mothers-in-law is just the way things are for women, isn't it? When you join Reiyukai, often the branch leader or the person who proselytized you will tell you, when you ask for help with some problem, that you are gosho ga fukai and should repent and treat your husband with due respect.

The Arahatas accept without question that a woman's position is a subordinate one: she is to obey and serve others. Clearly the position is less desirable than one of commanding authority. So why does this servant's lot fall to women? If must be because of karmic hindrances: therefore we can say about women: gosho ga fukai. While the husband tentatively linked the phenomenon to Japanese society exclusively, his wife seemed to consider it universal.

A third explanation of women's karmic hindrances stressed women's supposedly greater tendency to attach themselves unreasonably to things and other people. Even before I could introduce the topic, Fukuzawa Yue, a branch leader in charge of the Children's Division at Shakaden, volunteered her opinion of women in general.[21]

Fukuzawa: Women—no matter how old they are—I don't like them, do you?[22]

HH: Is that so?

Fukuzawa: Honestly, they're greedy, stingy, and covetous, don't you think so? Truly, that's all there is to women, don't you think so?

[21] Interview with Fukuzawa Yue, Shakaden, Tokyo, April 4, 1978.

[22] "I don't like them, do you?" *iya desu ne?*

HH: Really?
Fukuzawa: Yes, that's what I think. Anyhow, that's how I am.
[Then I read her the questionnaire results and asked for her comments.]
   Fukuzawa: Yes, that's true isn't it? As I was saying before, they're covetous and stingy. Don't you think so? On the other hand, men can't refuse a request. They're frank and candid. I'm not saying they all are, but for the most part, they don't refuse, and they aren't attached to things (*shūchaku shinai* 執着しない). But women—why, I wonder—they refuse the slightest thing, isn't that so? There are plenty of women like that. In that sense, they are gosho ga fukai.
   But that word gosho is strange isn't it? I think there's something in my nature that's attached to things. The degree of gosho depends on the degree of attachment (*shūchaku*). The reason we suffer, are sad, and are in pain is that we're attached. If we weren't so attached, we wouldn't suffer or be sad. I think the degree of my attachment has got to the point of gosho. Women—they're all attached.
   Therefore, when you ask, "Are you gosho ga fukai?" [I had not, in fact, asked her that] I answer "Yes!" Because I am; it's not a question of men or women. Then again, in line with this religion [Reiyukai], really . . . what should I say? I say gosho ga fukai because I'm like that. I think men are frank and good, that's why.
   I really hate women (*onna'tte, daikirai, watashi wa*). I have always prayed that in my next life I would be born as a man—absolutely would not be born a woman. But lately, when I think about it, you know, there's still some feeling of attachment, something vague and unclear in my nature that hasn't changed. If I don't set that to rest (*jōbutsu suru*), even if I'm born as a man in my next life, I'll be the effeminate type. [Laugh.]
   Now I'm filled with the feeling that it doesn't matter if I'm born a man or a woman—just that I must set my clinging nature to rest. For that reason, I'm praying to become meek (*sunao*). That's all.

In part, Fukuzawa's understanding of gosho is a very orthodox Buddhist reply. We suffer because of attachment; release from attachment brings release from suffering. That attachment is the most basic factor binding human beings to the round of birth, death, and rebirth is of course a pan-Buddhist idea. In Fukuzawa's interpretation, however, attachment is a general proposition about women in particular; it applies less to men, in her view. The orthodox view would be that no sex has a monopoly on attachment, but other sources inform Fukuzawa's opinion.
   In addition to its Buddhist associations, the notion of women's greater attachment is the stuff of soap operas and other forms of popular culture. The pitiful spinster who clings to the man she

loves, unable to face the fact that he has lost interest and desires nothing so much as a quick escape from her sticky clutches; the shrewish housewife who cannot forget a minor slight and nurses a grudge against her husband for months; the older woman whose life is enlivened only by petty domestic wrangles with a daughter-in-law—all these are images of female attachment with which the public is bombarded constantly by screenwriters, authors, and songwriters. Men, by contrast, are idealized as too involved in more positive engagement with the world to become mired in emotional trivia; they have a healthy resistance to becoming morbidly obsessed with such things. For Fukuzawa, women's attachment and gosho are linked. The more attachment, the greater the karmic hindrances to salvation. The only solution is to be reborn a man.[23]

In another interview, I spoke with two women branch leaders together. They stated that the dirt of housework becomes gosho. All the boring, unpleasant, repetitive tasks performed by women build up gosho. Then, by gesture and oblique reference they indicated menstruation, sexual intercourse, pregnancy, and child-birth as other sources of karmic hindrances, as well as the dirty trash and effluvia produced. They repeatedly asserted that men are fundamentally different by reason of lacking female sexuality and by being free of housework and child care. Women, on the other hand, deal daily with all kinds of dirt, and they must secure the tolerance and cooperation of their husbands and neighbors in housework, child care, and sexual matters. In return they must treat their husbands respectfully and even worship (*ogamu* 拝む) them. Thus for these two leaders gosho is a question of pollution. Women are polluted by their sexuality, and karmic hindrances arise from this uncleanliness and from the constant contact with dirt that is inherent in housework and child care.[24]

All these interviewees affirmed the notion that women face greater karmic hindrances than men, and they seemed to say, in effect, "Yes, it must be so, or they wouldn't be women in the first place." They all pointed to a different factor which seemed to demonstrate

[23] Images of women in popular culture are treated at length in Muramatsu Yasuko, *Terebi dorama no joseigaku* (Tokyo: Sōtakusha, 1979).

[24] Interview at Shakaden, Tokyo, April 20, 1978.

that women face greater hindrances than men: Tomita, because of women's hard lot, especially in child care; the Arahatas, because of women's subordinate role in the family; Fukuzawa, because of their "attachment"; and the final couple, because of the pollution of housework, child care, and female sexuality. All of these elements were taken as "givens," defining characteristics of women, and as their statements show, the notion gosho ga fukai also approaches the status of a "given" about women. Thus, the interviewees seemed to assert that "Women's karmic hindrances are worse than men's because they are women, and therefore they have greater karmic hindrances, and therefore they are women, because . . ." and so on, indefinitely.

When tracing the origins of Reiyukai's belief that women face greater karmic hindrances to salvation than men, it must be pointed out that there are many cultural motifs about women that may enter members' thought and influence the explanations of gosho presented here. It would be misleading to paint too clear a picture of the sources of their thought. However, one idea—that the solution to women's predicament is to be reborn a man—clearly stands out in interview and other contact with female members. This Buddhist theme, henjo nanshi, first discussed in Chapter 2, offers an important key to Reiyukai notions about women.

In the interviews presented above, two women declared their urgent hope to be reborn as men and made it clear that this was quite a serious aspiration. This idea also arises frequently in conversation with ordinary women members. The Dragon-Girl episode in the Lotus Sutra, discussed in Chapter 2, does not appear in the group's abridged version of the sutra, but the unabridged version is owned by and well-known to active members, and thus the henjo nanshi theme, the notion of changing into a man as a prerequisite for salvation, has become a major element of their thought. This doctrine clearly identifies the major obstacles to female salvation with pollution attributed to the female body.

Much of Japanese religious thought is devoted to pollution and to rituals to mark the passage from a polluted state to one of purity. Besides death, the greatest source of pollution (*kegare* 穢), the other types are connected with women. Themes of female pollution can be seen in the traditional prohibitions barring them from temples, shrines, and sacred mountains. The ban was accompanied by many cautionary tales and legends.[25] In the Kamakura period (1192–1333) there arose a new interpretation, holding that precisely because a woman is naturally disadvantaged, she is more worthy of salvation than men. This theme, structurally similar to the *akunin shōki* 悪人正機 doctrine of Shinran, was developed by Nichiren and resembles the positive claims of the paradox of power and pollution for Reiyukai women.

It was only with the advent of the Kamakura period that serious thought in Japanese Buddhism on the question of women's salvation arose. Prior to that time women were understood principally as symbols of hindrances to male salvation: as representing the problem of desire as it affected men. It was Nichiren whose conclusions were most far-reaching. Nichiren proclaimed that, whereas other sutras denied the possibility of salvation to women, the wicked, and ordinary people, the Lotus Sutra alone could save them. Moreover, in the latter days of the Dharma, he said, it is precisely those people who will achieve salvation, while the rich and powerful are cast into hell. While never firmly denying the traditional notion of the pollution of the female body, Nichiren went a good deal further than his contemporaries and predecessors in this direction. He pointed to the Dragon-Girl episode as offering to all women the promise of salvation, *nyonin jōbutsu* 女人成仏.[26]

Reiyukai's thinking closely resembles the nyonin jobutsu theme as developed by Nichiren. In both cases the restrictions enjoined upon menstruating women as regards ritual performance are extremely limited. In Reiyukai, the only restriction is upon worship of the rising sun during the Shichimenzan pilgrimage.

Members accept that women face greater obstacles to salvation than men, and they use the phrase gosho ga fukai to sum up the

[25] Such cautionary tales are treated in Miyata Noboru, *Kami no minzokushi* (Tokyo: Iwanami shoten, 1979), pp. 60ff.

[26] The history of Japanese Buddhist thought on the question of women's salvation is the subject of Kasahara Kazuo's *Nyonin ōjō shisō no keifu* (Tokyo: Yoshikawa kōbunkan, 1975). Nichiren's thought on the question is treated on pp. 197–220.

stumbling blocks. Yet the implications are not entirely negative. The paradox Reiyukai poses about women is this: women face much greater odds in the struggle to achieve salvation, but if they can overcome these obstacles, they can achieve a degree of spiritual power absolutely unattainable by men. It is to the positive side of the paradox that we turn next.

There are two Reiyukai practices in which women exhibit their spiritual powers. *Okuji* 御九字, though not limited to women, is one of the spiritual powers in which women are thought to excell. The branch leaders receive periodic training in okuji, which is principally, though not exclusively, used in healing. I observed the exercise of okuji at Mirokusan, when a young woman complained of stomach cramps. She and her sister were taken aside, to a quiet corner of the large sleeping room by a female branch leader. The ailing woman kneeled on a cushion, and the branch leader kneeled on the floor facing her. Holding a rosary, the branch leader began to recite the daimoku at a moderate pace. After perhaps three minutes, she turned the other woman's cushion around so that her back was facing the leader. She then began to rub the young woman's back with the rosary in long, elliptical strokes, while the pace of her chanting increased markedly. This continued for perhaps three minutes more. Her voice became louder, and her breathing violent. Continuing to chant, the branch leader moved her arms up and down with hands clasped together over the rosary from the height of her waist to her chest, as her chanting became louder and faster. Then without warning she spun the young woman's cushion around to the original position, facing her, and pointing her joined hands and the rosary at the woman's stomach, made three sharp, thrusting motions, accompanied by a sharp yell each time. That terminated the okuji. She explained later that okuji accomplishes healing by driving out demons that cause sickness (*akuma* 悪魔, *byōma* 病魔).[27]

Okuji is an exorcistic practice derived from Shugendo and folk Buddhist practice. It is conspicuous in the Nichiren school, where

[27] I have made a more detailed study of the historical origins of Reiyukai's healing practices, including okuji and kage no junjo, in "The Transformation of Healing in the Japanese New Religions," *The Journal of the History of Religions* 20, No. 3 (May, 1982), 305–320.

the daimoku is recited to mobilize the magical power of the words themselves. At Nichiren temples, especially those in the mountains, it is not uncommon to see groups of women reciting the daimoku at a fast pace and in altered voices, dressed in the white garb of ascetics.[28]

A second spiritual power, that of communicating with spirits in the spirit world, is entirely limited to women. The ability to act as a medium is called *kage no junjo* 陰の順序, "the method of miracles." It may be linked with healing, as in the following case. A female branch leader was suffering from a fever of unknown origin. She entirely lost her appetite and was confined to bed. She had a vision of her closest ancestors' deaths in the explosion of the atomic bomb over Hiroshima. She witnessed their deaths in a sea of fire and saw how they suffered from a raging thirst. Struggling to sit up in prayer, she asked what they most wanted. The reply was that they wanted water, and upon setting a large glass of water in the ancestral altar, her fever disappeared. This communication with ancestral spirits is kage no junjo.

In other cases two women are involved in kage no junjo, one as a medium who receives messages from the spirits, and another who interprets her utterances to a client who comes seeking advice about some problem. For example, a member whose daughter was retarded came to a branch leader asking the leader to find out the cause of her daughter's condition. The leader entered a trance by reciting the daimoku and began to speak. A third woman interpreted what she said to the client, and the cause of the daughter's retardation was reported due to the suffering of ancestral spirits in the spirit world.

[28] Related practices have been described by Carmen Blacker in *The Catalpa Bow, A Study of Shamanistic Practices in Japan* (London: George Allen and Unwin, 1975), *passim*. Specific practices of the Nichiren school resembling okuji are described in the following works: Sakamoto Kaname "Daimoku kō— nembutsu kō oyobi ko-ankō" in *Nichirenshū no shomondai*, ed. Nakao Takashi (Tokyo: Yūzankaku, 1975), pp. 227–306; and in the same volume, Yasunaka Satoshi, "Taishō ki ni okeru chihō shojiin to kaji–kitō," pp. 185–200. The role of women in the Nichiren school as faith healers is treated in the same volume: "Nichirenshū no josei kitōshi," pp. 339–52. Daimoku recitation used to exorcise the spirits of animals is discussed in Arai Kōjirō, "Kitsune tsuki to daimoku gyōja," *IBK* 19, No. 2 (1971), 652–57.

We have seen in this section that Reiyukai women face a paradox of power and pollution. Both its negative and positive sides have deep roots in Buddhist history and practice, and are intimately linked to women's position in the contemporary family as well. However, it would be misleading to leave the impression that Reiyukai women passively resign themselves to a predetermined fate. They certainly do no such thing. In fact, they have created important strategies for managing their heavy responsibilities in the family. These duties in their understanding are at the heart of the road to salvation since members believe that salvation will come as a result of having fulfilled their duties as wives, mothers, and daughters-in-law.[29]

Part 3: Strategies of Weakness

This section deals with the strategies Reiyukai women adopt to fulfill their roles in the family. Successfully exercised, these often overturn the normative status hierarchy, giving the woman a secure status and a good deal of power in the family even while she appears to remain passive and subject to the will of others.

Behavior toward the husband includes many displays of deference, not radically different from those widely expected of Japanese women, but expressed in much stronger degree. The conventional greeting of a wife to a husband returning from work is *okaerinasai* お帰りなさい, "welcome back." However, Reiyukai leaders instruct their followers to wait for the husband at the door, kneel in the doorway, placing one hand over the other (because to set the hands one beside the other is "like an animal"), bow to the floor, and say *okaeri ni natte irasshaimase* お帰りになつていらつしやいませ, an untranslatable, exag-

---

[29] Many societies regard women simultaneously as polluted and as bearers of great religious power, each with various explanations of the sources of women's power and pollution, and of the differences between their powers and those attributed to men. Recent anthropological research has attempted to explain why notions of power and pollution should be so paradoxically intertwined with each other. Michelle Z. Rosaldo, "Women, Culture, and Society: A Theoretical Overview," in *Women, Culture, and Society*, ed. M. Z. Rosaldo and Louise Lamphere (Stanford: Stanford University Press, 1974), p. 38.

geratedly formal and deferential version of the usual expression. Although this may seem a rather obscure point, women are instructed to perform conventional greetings in an exaggerated manner as a mark of their submission, deference, and acceptance of subordinate status. This status is decreed in some sense because of their supposedly greater karmic hindrances. The following incident from the life of the founder Kotani illustrates this point. She had managed to accumulate a little money and suggested to her husband that it be saved for possible medical expenses in the future. Her husband angrily responded,

"You can't pursue spiritual training as long as you're concerned about things like sickness! Only a person who has allowed the devils of sickness (*byoma*) to enter him gets sick during spiritual training. That's not real spiritual training! Since sickness comes from the entry of the devils of sickness, avoiding those devils is a problem of the heart in the end.

The Buddha said of women, gosho ga fukai, so their karmic hindrances are greater than men's. For fifty-one days you must prostrate yourself [before me] and say 'Good morning.'"

[Kotani Kimi continues] At first, the first time or two, I couldn't get out of it, so I came before my husband and said, "Good morning" as I was told. I said to myself, "The idea—making a fool of myself like this for my own husband—can I really go through with this?" My heart was flooded with tears and nausea. That's how stubborn I was.

At the same time, I was fasting, eating only buckwheat flour. I wasn't allowed even to season it with salt, only to boil it in water. At the end I lost my strength. I'd been told that above everything else I was stubborn, and I resolved to cure myself of it somehow.

Gradually I lost the strength to recite the daimoku. I lost the strength to preach sermons. During those fifty-one days I was told many things by Professor Kubo. I heard many sermons, and I repented. I realized that truly I had been wrong.[30]

In this episode Kotani's husband explicitly cited women's karmic hindrances as the justification for deferential behavior and subordinate status. He ordered his wife to prostrate herself by kneeling on bare ground to deliver the morning greeting. Fifty-one days of this eventually convinced Kotani that she was "wrong"

[30] Kotani Kimi, *Watakushi no shugyō seikatsu, sanjūgo nen* (Tokyo: Reiyukai, 1958), pp. 31–36.

and led her to repent, presumably for her "stubbornness." Here we see clearly that the notion of women's greater karmic hindrances is used to justify and legitimate the relegation of women to a subordinate status. Treating deferential behavior as a kind of spiritual exercise emphasizes the point that in Reiyukai women's low status is underwritten by the notion concerning women, gosho ga fukai.

Low status precludes direct exercise of authority in management of the domestic sphere; thus, other strategies must be employed. In order to manage the domestic group's interpersonal relations successfully, women are required to deal with people whose status is higher than their own. Reiyukai provides them with numerous examples of such strategies and how to execute them. These are communicated in testimonies and in consultation with group leaders. In some cases women are able to secure so much power within the domestic group by these means that their initial inferiority of status is overridden.[31]

One of the most important strategies available to Reiyukai women is to raise their children as members of Reiyukai so that mother and children form an indivisible group that can stand against opposition from other family members. Ancestral rites twice a day in the home plus the numerous activities of the Reiyukai Children's Division afford ample opportunities to involve children in Reiyukai from an early age. If a woman is successful in interesting her children in the group, it becomes difficult for other family members to refuse to participate without becoming outsiders, the odd men out. A case from Osaka may serve to illustrate this point.

Mrs. Takao was married to an oculist who owned his small shop. She had three young children and joined Reiyukai while all three were still quite young. When she informed her husband that she had become a member, he became enraged, destroyed her religious articles, and forbade her to have anything to do with Reiyukai. Dismayed, Mrs. Takao consulted her branch leader, who told her to entrust the guidance of the members she had proselytized to someone else, to go home, and obey her husband,

---

[31] Even while Reiyukai women proclaim an ideology of weakness and dependence upon men, they impress the observer as quite strong individuals.

"because Reiyukai is not a home-wrecking religion." She also told Mrs. Takao, however, to continue reciting the sutra, while her husband was at the public bath. Being fond of a special bath with a small electric current shot through it, he was absent at the bath each evening longer than a trip usually requires. When he left, the mother would assemble her three children, and the four of them would take their religious articles out of their hiding place in the closet, and recite the sutra together. All the children became active in the Youth Group although this also had to be concealed from their irascible father. Meanwhile, his opposition continued, and the wife repented repeatedly for having "forgotten to be grateful," or "henpecking" the husband. Self-criticism before the altar in the children's presence expressed to them their mother's willingness to assume a subordinate position and tacitly underlined the husband's recalcitrance.

Mrs. Takao persevered in this regime until the children were adults. By that time, the eldest son, who had been expected to succeed his father in the family business, had become the head of the Eighth Branch Youth Group and was working at the Eighth Branch office. Subsequently he married within the group and was sent to become the director of the newly-opened branch of the organization in Mexico. Since his wife's parents had no sons, the couple plans to have their first son take her maiden name to perpetuate the family name. Although the eldest son does not criticize his father, it is clear that he has made his life apart from the father and his business.

The second son previously worked in the father's business and studied to succeed him. However, after his elder brother moved to Mexico, he also went to work at the Eighth Branch, leaving his father to carry on alone. The third child, a daughter, is also active in the Youth Group and participates in all of its activities. She acts as a guide for tour groups of overseas members and spends much of her summers so engaged.

The influence of the mother through Reiyukai over these children is unmistakable. It is clear that the price of failure to participate in Reiyukai ritual and activities has for the father been the virtually complete estrangement of his children, the loss of his first grandson as an heir, and the loss of both possible successors to his business. If he requires financial assistance in his old age, it will probably come from his sons' employment in Reiyukai, surely a bitter pill to swallow for one who has opposed the group so completely for some twenty years. We can see from this case that women's use of Reiyukai affiliation in the socialization of their children is a powerful tool for binding them closely to her, to the point of alienating them from those with equally weighty claims on their allegiance. Through this strategy they achieve a heightened prestige in their children's eyes which makes comparison of them to other members of the domestic group who are not involved in Reiyukai highly unflattering to the latter. In this case the mother's heightened prestige and ability to influence her children derive from her use of Reiyukai ideas, rituals, and activities in their training. She can exert this influence without reference to her status, which is normatively lower than her husband's.

Reiyukai women must above all be able to manage their husbands. Economically dependent upon the husband for the most part and holding subordinate status in the family, for them this is no easy task. However, Reiyukai women frequently are able to use their membership in the group in a way that allows them to strengthen their position. Furthermore, they discuss their experiences with fellow members and receive advice from leaders so that their techniques for successfully resolving problems with husbands are well known.

The following testimonial text, presented by a forty-five-year-old chemical salesman, illustrates a man's reaction to a Reiyukai woman's techniques of "husband management" and shows the extent to which his position in a household can be changed.

Text 116, 2:72–75

I hated my father. He was always terribly strict about the least little thing, and I had no memory of his ever having been kind to me. For that reason, I opposed him in everything. Whenever anything was said, we were instantly locked in an awful quarrel.

In our family, relations between fathers and their first sons had been bad for three generations. I got married in 1959, and although it's usual for a first son like me to live with his mother and father, and to think that he should look after them, I said that was ridiculous and moved out, setting up a new place for just my wife and me.

My wife joined Reiyukai after we were married and kept urging me to join too. But I wouldn't do it. My feeling was, "Filial piety? Sutra recitation? The hell with that!" I thought it was fine if my wife wanted to just clean up the ancestral altar and recite some sutra, but I had no inclination to bow before it, and it made me mad when she'd go out to the branch office or the headquarters, leaving the house empty. When at times I was obliged to go and participate in some headquarters festival out of a duty to a senior member and couldn't get out of it, I'd say after hearing testimonies or speeches of a branch leader, "No matter who it is, they all say the same thing. It's nothing but a lot of propaganda. Do you really have to listen to that stuff?"

I was wearing a shield against religion, and when my wife would talk to me about my father, I'd get blue in the face and shout at her. Naturally, our life together wasn't very cheerful. We had two sons, and on the surface we probably seemed to be free of cares, but when we'd been married about ten years, I took a lover and gave myself over to her entirely, unknown to my wife.

But my wife soon found out. At that point I was prepared for defeat. It's usual for the wife's blood to rush to her head, to scream that she'll kill you, divorce you, and take you for every cent you're worth in alimony, making a terrible scene. I was prepared for the worst, but what should happen but my wife said not a word in complaint or hatred. She recited the sutra with all her heart and proselytized. However, within a few days her flesh became so emaciated that it seemed to have been pared off. That was when I first began to think, "There's something to this religion."

Needless to say, there was no doubt that violent rage and sorrow were eddying like a whirlpool in my wife's breast. In my eyes, the sight of my wife enduring it, earnestly repenting, was a wonderfully precious thing. I was nonplussed, and I surrendered. I left my lover, bowed before the altar, and felt like reciting the sutra. But unfortunately, the human heart is not the kind of thing that changes so easily. I piled up days in which I only went through the motions in a half-baked way.

Then in March of 1974 my mother got a hernia and could no longer get out of bed. There was no one to take care of her, so we had to move back in with her and my father. My wife was delighted to help, but I couldn't help feeling suffocated whenever I set eyes on my hateful father, and there were even times when I raised my hand to him. Home life became more and more gloomy until even the children were depressed about it, and started being cold and indifferent.

My wife said I should repent, but I was ashamed to have my children see me like that. Nevertheless, I decided to undertake spiritual training in order to make myself meek. I began to pray with all my heart and resolved that if I couldn't do it this time, I'd give up on Reiyukai.

Then two months later we started holding meetings in our house. The day of our first Reiyukai meeting was a day of great joy and celebration for us as a family, but my father alone had not joined Reiyukai. My father's very existence was an eyesore to me, so I sought advice from my wife and senior member. I said, "Since the old man won't join in our religion, I'd like to send him away somewhere. I feel he's in the way."

"What are you saying?" my wife and senior member exclaimed in surprise. While I was away from home, my senior member came and explained about Reiyukai very kindly to my father. My father said he would like to join, too. After that, we were able to hold meetings and recite the sutra as a family.

From that day's experience, I realized that rather than trying to understand the teaching in your head, the most important thing is to put your senior member's teachings into practice. My senior member said that proselytization is important, so from that time on I began to make converts among my brothers and acquaintances. My brother and his wife, who knew that I didn't get along with my father, were surprised by the change in me and immediately agreed to join.

As I made converts, I realized how many people in the world are unfilial. And at the same time, as I looked back on how unfilial I myself had been up until that time, the feeling that I must repent grew stronger with each passing day.

Then my branch leader told me, "I expect you are repenting by reciting the sutra, but have you actually clasped your hands together before your father and repented? If you don't clasp your hands together now and receive your father's forgiveness, this karma that you are bearing will be passed on to your children." That was on a summer's day in 1975. I reflected on myself. I resolved to apologize to my father that very day, and went home prepared to do it.

When I walked into the house, my father came out and quite un-expectedly kneeled before me. Before I could say a word, he fixed me with a stare and spoke. "When I was reciting the sutra, I realized that I've just been complaining continually, and I apologize. I'm ashamed of myself for quarreling with you all the time, and I can see that I've been small-minded and petty. I apologize with all my heart. I'll never fight with you again. Please forgive me...."

I felt a hot lump rise in my chest, and I couldn't speak. The face of my seventy-year-old father was trembling and flushed. From my eyes tears rushed like a dam bursting, and before I knew it I was prostrate before my father, sobbing my apology for the sin of having been unfilial.

When in your heart you truly become meek, and really make a change in your life, the people around you will also begin to change. It is amazing how, once I realized the sin I had committed and resolved to repent, my father also felt the desire to apologize. I experienced this unmistakably in my own life, and I could hardly fail to throw myself in gratitude at the feet of this invisible, precious thing.

My wife, mother, and children were all overjoyed. For the first time our family was flooded with light. I received a certificate for promoting the realization of the World of the Buddhas and Ancestors (*hotoke no sekai*

仏 の 世界), and began a life of true purpose. I want to tell many people what a precious thing is this way of life in which I am bound to my parents, and my children in turn are bound to me.

In the episode concerning the speaker's extramarital affair, we see that he was influenced to terminate the relationship by his wife's conduct. She neither reproached him nor indicated in any way that he was at fault. Instead, the fact that she responded by repenting seems to imply that she believed she was in the wrong. Although we have no account of her reaction to the situation, she was probably operating on the premise that if a wife is sufficiently fulfilling her duties, the husband will not stray. Conversely, if he does, that is an indication that she is somehow lacking. This notion is widespread among Reiyukai women.

The husband realized that his wife's reaction to his affair was unusual, and he attributed it to her faith in Reiyukai. He seems to have been gratified by her patient endurance, calling the sight of her repenting "a wonderfully precious thing." Yet, at the same time, he was "nonplussed" and separated from his lover.

The wife refrained from asserting her will and apparently did not overtly accuse her husband in any way. She seems to have taken a self-accusing attitude, and it was this that appealed to the husband. Thus, he is freed from the burden of responsibility and can graciously set his wife's distress to rest from a position of noblesse oblige once his wife has reaffirmed her dependence upon him and her inferior status by repentence. His position in the household seems to have been enhanced rather than shaken by the episode.

The wife presents a vivid spectacle of silent suffering as she prays, repents, and goes into a physical decline. She seems ready to endure physical collapse rather than utter a word of reproach to her husband, whose infidelity is the cause of her unhappiness. Without verbally suggesting that his position is questionable, she demonstrates that her health and happiness are in grave danger because of him. The wife appears to accord him a great deal of power over her, by casting herself upon his mercy. In a sense his position is further elevated by having made her unhappy and jeopardized her health, because it is tacitly demonstrated that he has the power to restore her to health and happiness, from a position of magnanimity, simply by giving up his affair. Assuming that the affair may not originally have been entered into with any resolution to dissolve the marriage, and that it seems not to have been of sufficient attraction to seriously consider dissolving his marriage later on, the husband's concession seems momentary and of comparatively negligible emotional disturbance to him. This is especially so in that he is able to return to his wife and children with his position intact and with no barriers to a reaffirmation, via Reiyukai ritual and other activities, of his solidarity with the group and its claims upon him. Through this passive response to the affair, the wife opens the way to a greater exercise of influence over her husband than she could have gained by the kind of confrontation he anticipated.

How did the wife's response to the husband's infidelity lead him to change? It seems to have caught him off guard when he was expecting either to have to defend himself and assert his rights or to back down and endure shame and humiliation. His position on the question of the other woman was not secure, and he knew it. He anticipated loss of the affections of his wife and financial loss, and he faced possible estrangement of the children should the matter have ended in divorce. Instead he finds his wife renewing her submission. Seeing the power he has over her, he may initially have been a bit awed, and then gratified, especially as he knows that within commonly-held ethical perceptions of the situation his behavior has not deserved such consideration.

Thus he is both ashamed of himself and grateful to her, inflated and humbled at the same time. He wants to affirm her submissive behavior so that she will not revert to the accusatory stance he knows is justified, and so that she will display more such behavior, which affords him this gratification. Thus he becomes willing to make significant concessions.

Here, clearly the first order of business is termination of the affair. It is obvious that this is what the wife urgently desires. If she responds with further displays of deference, he becomes more strongly motivated to affirm her behavior by further acceding to her wishes. Once the desire to affirm and the willingness to concede have been created by her unexpected submissiveness, the wife can channel them toward ends that suit her purposes.

We may assume that continued exchanges of concession and deference occur as the husband begins to participate actively in Reiyukai ritual and other activities. This participation will be positively reenforced by other Reiyukai personnel as well as the wife.

The more the couple repeats such exchanges, the more time the husband allocates to Reiyukai activities, and the more he necessarily withdraws from external sources of emotional support (viz., the lover) and, concomitantly the more he will come to depend on that provided by his wife and Reiyukai. She creates in him a dependence upon her which escalates in exchanges of concession and deference until their normative inequality of status becomes completely irrelevant to the real facts of the balance of power in the relationship.

As he retreats further and further from outside standards of validation and sources of support, he becomes increasingly dependent upon those that remain, namely, the wife's marks of approval and those of people whom she will introduce as bearers of legitimate authority: the leadership hierarchy of Reiyukai. She creates an emotional power over him far more deeply rooted than that which he holds over her, and she shares that power out among group leaders.

The husband breaks with the lover, and he subsequently begins a relationship as a subordinate of an unnamed senior member in Reiyukai, who takes over and redirects his relations with his father. He seeks his wife's advice on this matter. He strengthens his bond with her in their joint activities in the home revolving around Reiyukai. Eventually he seems to circumscribe his sphere of activity considerably, bringing more and more of it within the range of his wife's full knowledge and approval. The previous gap in relative power between them is greatly reduced.

In the episode concerning the speaker's relations with his father, we can see the strong influence of his wife's Reiyukai affiliation in leading him to a realization that his conduct since childhood has been entirely wrong, and that he must make fundamental changes in his attitude if he wishes to avoid passing on the karmic results of his mistakes to his children.

Let us recapitulate the timing of these events. The speaker married in 1959, had the affair in 1969, and moved in with his aged parents in 1974. Although in 1969 the wife did not feel able to reproach him for his infidelity, by 1974 she was telling him to repent to his father, and although she was unable to persuade him to kneel before his father at that time, he was convinced that he must undergo spiritual training in humility. The prospect of this man resolving to change himself in this way at his wife's behest is a far cry from the secure stance from which he initiated and carried on his affair five years earlier.

He perseveres and makes enough converts, probably with his wife's help, to hold Reiyukai meetings at his home. He is filled with joy that his mother and children are united with him and his wife around the axis Reiyukai has provided for their household. The only fly in the ointment is his father's obstinate refusal to participate. He seeks advice from his senior member and wife about the problem, whereas five years earlier he was hardly seeking advice about how to conduct relations with his father. At that time he was consumed with hatred and absolutely sure of the rectitude of his position. Now, however, he tentatively proposes ejecting his father from the household and meets with immediate and firm repudiation, which he appears to have received meekly. His previous discussions with his wife on this subject had always included displays of anger. Now he is in no position to assert himself in such a manner.

Furthermore, the senior member takes advantage of an occasion when the man is absent and performs the job of enrolling the father in Reiyukai. Here the senior undercuts the man's position in his own house by entering during an absence and as an outsider performing swiftly the job that was obviously the man's responsibility: proselytizing a close relative, the father. The man not only does not challenge the senior member's actions on this occasion, but also renews his submission to the senior's authority in his resolve to place obedience to the senior's authority before his own rational grasp of the group's teachings. This reaction is unthinkable for the person this man was five years earlier.

Participation in Reiyukai activity and contact with its leaders draw the man inexorably toward the final demonstration of submission and humility: repentence on his knees before his father. He accepts the branch leader's orders to kneel before the father and apologize, and only the father's beating him to it delays his compliance. He rejoices in the cathartic experience of reconciliation, which also spells the reintegration of himself in the domestic hierarchy, beneath his father. He exalts in the language of binding and tying to describe the new relationship between himself and his father on the one hand and between himself and his children on the other. While the wife remains discreetly peripheral to this scene, the positive implications for her are clear.

Her husband has become much more tractable, dependable, and manageable than the truculent, assertive man he was when she married him. His affair presented to the wife and children the prospect of complete estrangement and loss of financial support, but the wife's Reiyukai affiliation not only overcame that crisis but was instrumental in making fundamental changes in the husband's role in their household. While he begins as the undisputed head of a nuclear family, he ends as an obedient son in his father's house and a less authoritarian husband or father.

Meanwhile, his wife experiences pain and humiliation in the early years of marriage through her husband's infidelity, which occurred when she was living apart from anyone who might have lent her support in the home at that time. At the end of the story, she is holding Reiyukai meetings in her home, thus indicating that she has reached a position of leadership and responsibility within the group. When illness prevents the mother-in-law from ordering the household, she assumes this responsibility as well. From the powerless position she occupied at the time of her husband's infidelity, she has risen in power and status considerably, and she has broadened her sphere of influence over her husband in a general way through skillful use of Reiyukai ideas, activities, and personnel. She has solidly unified the domestic group around Reiyukai while seeming to remain passive and powerless. While her husband is allowed the trappings and titles of status and power, clearly it is she who has command of its substance.

The strategies Reiyukai women adopt to manage their families and make their own positions more secure are often highly effective, but in the last analysis they are strategies of weakness. For the most part Reiyukai women are economically dependent upon men. This economic dependence is underwritten by status inequality in the normative realm, and that inequality is closely linked to notions about women's greater karmic hindrances to salvation. However, women are given great responsibility and are expected to manage all the affairs of the domestic group. Lacking the status to do this by direct exercise of authority, they must resort to indirect strategies.

Testimonies and contact with Reiyukai leaders guide women in their households, showing them how to involve their children, how to make Reiyukai affiliation an axis of the family, how to isolate and coerce members who refuse to participate, and how to create an emotional dependence in grown children and husbands upon them. Reiyukai leaders remain available for consultation and will intervene to help a woman negotiate a problem, as we have seen in the last text.

Much of women's interest in Reiyukai derives from its usefulness in managing the family in spite of the handicaps of economic dependence and status inferiority. Yet, while Reiyukai women's interest in such strategies is crucially influenced by economic dependence upon men, we cannot conclude that, minus the economic handicap, their interest would dissolve. In addition to any simple desire for influence, members want to act in a world regulated by proven ethical principles, which connect the human world with the unseen world of the spirits. Raw power by itself would not satisfy the desire to act in harmony with what are believed to be principles universally governing human life in this world and the next. In Reiyukai interpretation the principle, for example, of male dominance is as much a "given" of the cosmos as is the idea of the continued life of ancestors.

Reiyukai women do not carry out these techniques in a calculating way, but step by step, as they witness testimonies and put leaders' advice into practice a bit at a time. It is wrong to think of them as planning the humbling of others. Instead, there are unreasonable expectations made of them which their status inferiority and economic dependence prevent them from fulfilling in direct ways. To the extent that this is true, they must manipulate. That they believe in the ideology of women's inferiority, pollution, and karmic hindrances, and their mirror images of male superiority and legitimate authority is unquestionable. They do not stand outside the system. Their belief in it is greatly strengthened by seeing how it helps them better fulfill their duties as wives, mothers, and daughters-in-law, which they regard as sacred, and they are increasingly motivated to spread their beliefs to others in the conviction that Reiyukai's teaching as a whole is beneficial and true.

Part 4: Into the Public World

Women's strengthened position in the domestic group becomes a bridge to an active role in the public sphere, in the context of Reiyukai as a nationwide organization. Male members state repeatedly and without prompting, "Women run this group. Without them, there is nothing." Observation during the period of field work substantiated such statements and suggested that they are not exaggerated. All the male branch leaders I interviewed were married, and I asked them whether their wives participate in the running of the branch. They were unanimous in saying that it is the wife who actually runs the branch and manages it on a day-to-day basis. Male participation seems to be limited to evenings and weekends. Asked about the administration of monthly hoza meetings, a young male branch leader said, "When it comes to hoza, my wife's the one who participates more earnestly. She's the more serious member." Another said, "She takes care of all the weekday business, since I'm not at home. So it's not my branch, but *ours*. . . . My wife is more important to the members than I am. [Laugh.] But then, husband and wife are one (*ittai* 一体), so it's natural that it should be this way." I asked this same leader what had been the most impressive part of his long membership in Reiyukai, and he replied, "It's that I've been able to have a marriage that is based on our mutual care of our converts. Her strong point is that she is more skillful than I am in caring for them. That is something that makes me happy I joined this religion." These statements show rather poignantly that male leaders recognize and acknowledge with humor and affection the centrality of women in Reiyukai.

Women leaders' role in counseling other women about their problems is the basis of their performance in the public domain as role models for other women. A woman who receives such counsel remembers each step and later emulates her leader's conduct when she advises her own converts. She patterns her own behavior on her branch leader's, as a proven model of success. The authority exercised in this way by women leaders, starting with Kotani Kimi, is powerfully attested to in the testimonies we have examined and in the prayerful reverence with which these women are regarded by their charges, as living Buddhas.

Reiyukai women leaders construct for themselves active roles in the public sphere not only as counselors but in leading pilgrimages, holding meetings, overseeing sutra recitation, keeping records in branch administration, and in other ways functioning in managerial capacities, in spite of the fact that they would not readily be accorded such responsibility in secular society. The opportunities Reiyukai affords these women to apply their energies and skills in the public realm undoubtedly is one of its strongest appeals to them, the more so since they appear not to deviate from their primary roles as wives and mothers.

One way in which their capacity for leadership is channeled is toward the guidance of youth. They sense a lack of purpose in the postwar generations, and refer to them as "the generations that have not experienced war." Often the opinion is heard that the war and its attendant privations gave the survivors a great strength of character, lacking in the generations made soft by insidious Occupation innovations. Under these conditions, Reiyukai's mission to keep its version of Japanese tradition alive and to imbue young members with its spirit seems imperative to female leaders.

Women leaders derive a special satisfaction from their relations with young members. This is not surprising, given that it represents an extension to the public sphere and to other people's offspring of their role as mothers. The mother role is imbued with sacredness linked to the goal of world peace, which they expect to accomplish through young members. Here their attempts to fulfill a primary role take on cosmic significance which immensely increases their sense of satisfaction in leadership.

The role of women in Reiyukai is built of multiple paradoxes. Not least is that in which women leaders stand firmly behind the rhetoric of "woman's place is in the home" while demonstrably, obviously, conspicuously making their leadership responsibilities the occasion for creating independent roles in the public sphere. They devote considerable energy to building up the egos of people with normatively higher status even as they manipulate and control them from behind the scenes. While seeming to be (and telling other women they should be) weak and passive, they become active and strong. As they pass through trials and are made to humble themselves in repentance before men in the home and leaders in the group, they create for themselves a position of strength in the domestic group and of respect among group members. But at the same time they strengthen their positions in the family, they entrench themselves ever more deeply in the ethic of economic dependence upon men and in the ideology of female subordination and inferiority. One wonders what price is paid in accepting the notion, in all its ramifications, that women are gosho ga fukai, and what price is exacted from the women born as daughters to someone who can look another woman in the face and say, "I really hate women, don't you?"

Conclusion

This book has dealt with the problem of the significance of Reiyukai belief and practice in the lives of its members. The assertion that membership in Reiyukai or groups like it has some instrumental effectiveness would not be problematic except for the existence of a tradition of scholarship that has tended to ignore the claims of religious groups in this area as unworthy of serious consideration. Any scholar who has absorbed a functionalist ethos even without finer points of theory is prepared "in principle" to say that membership in a religious group must "of course" yield some instrumental effectiveness. But this theoretical preparedness is much at odds with the treatments of the Japanese new religions that have been advanced so far. An exception to this general trend is the study by Winston Davis, *Dojo, Magic and Exorcism in a Japanese Cult.*

The work of H. Neil McFarland and H. Thomsen speaks repeatedly of the members of the new religions as lacking discernment, unable to appreciate the complexity of their own problems sufficiently to reach the "right" conclusion: that religion is not the appropriate solution to poverty, sickness, and domestic discord. Their approach assumes that religious organizations came into being to absorb such persons, mainly after World War II, when Japan faced social, political, and ethical "crisis." On this view religious organizations either became havens for the nondiscerning or actively went in search of them, in an almost predatory manner.

Sociologically this view is indefensible because it postulates a passive attitude on the part of the members which is not borne out by observation. Historically it is indefensible because it over-emphasizes the role of crisis in the founding of religious movements, a point considered at length in Chapter 1. It also over-emphasizes the power of leaders' personal charisma and tends to conceptualize the "organization" as entirely separate from the membership. Particularly in the early stages of a new religion's history, there is no iron-clad organization separate from the membership. Instead, the bureaucracy of the organization grows out of a small circle of the leader's closest disciples. In Reiyukai these are the people who later founded the group's major branches.

The historical process by which that bureaucracy comes into being is one of members actively guiding the leader/founder and shaping her/his decisions so as to form a group whose character corresponds to consensus on their collective mission. The persons who are able to get close enough to the leader to do that are those who have taken up the founder's ideas and made them work in their own lives. They are, for example, people who have experienced a healing and then used that experience as the starting point of a reorganization of the structure of power relations in their families, as I have documented in Chapter 5. They are people who, subsequent to such an experience, go on to teach those ideas and techniques to other people. In this process they assimilate Buddhist ideas and form an active commitment to *their* organization and its goals. In this they are not passive. They are not neutral, undiscerning pawns of the organization—they *are* the organization.

When McFarland says, however, that, "The causes of crisis, they suppose, must be knowable and susceptible to some kind of direct counteraction," he is more right than he knows. The members of Reiyukai and of the new religions generally suppose precisely that. They are too discerning to suppose that passive resignation is their only realistic course of action. They devote immense intellectual labor to discerning the causes of crisis, as Kubo and Kotani did in Taisho Japan, and to formulating the problem in religious terms. No formulation of the problem that fails to point to a solution is acceptable to them. Furthermore, this activist stance is a hallmark of the new religions generally, and in this respect Reiyukai is typical.

Although the view of the new religions as collections of or

cynical predators upon the weak and undiscerning is particularly
explicit in the works singled out here, it is by no means restricted to
them. It is prevalent in Japanese scholarship on the new religions
up until very recent times, owing to the difficulties Japanese
scholars face in conducting field research on these groups. Opportunities for field research among the new religions have been
very limited. Hence Japanese scholarship has tended to absorb
the attitudes of the popular media toward the new religions, which
have almost without exception adopted a facile scientism and the
assumption that "of course" the claims of real-life effectiveness
so characteristic of the new religions are not to be taken seriously.
This is not to say that whereas scholars have been unable to
undertake field research, the media *has* been able to do so. Far
from it. In fact, the character of the lives of members of the new
religions has simply been left unexplored. This book has attempted to redress that situation by examining in detail those
claims of the new religions which have been dismissed by the media
and previous research—the claims of 1) healing, 2) upward
mobility, and 3) providing solutions to perceived crises in Japanese
society.

It is my position that if those problems—precisely the ones that
occasion members' joining these groups in the first place—were
not meaningfully, *effectively*, addressed by membership in these
groups, the groups would not continue to attract a following. In
fact their collective following consists of perhaps 20 to 30 percent
of the population of Japan, measured by membership statistics,
and moreover their influence in society extends far beyond those
numbers. According to government statistics compiled in 1981,
over forty-three million Japanese are members of the new religions.[1] Even allowing a substantial margin for numerical inflation, these figures suggest that the new religions command the
loyalties of a significant proportion of the society. When we bear
in mind the fact that members are well-schooled in obedience to
the group and can be counted on to vote as a block, we can readily
appreciate that their influence is potentially immense.

---

[1] Ministry of Education, *Shūkyō nenkan*, 1981.

The new religions typically emphasize the attainment of blessings in this life, and members expect such things as healing, solution of domestic problems, and improvement of material circumstances as proof of the truth of the religion's teaching. We can understand how and why members believe that they have received these "rewards of the True Law" by examining the context in which they are won. That context is one in which a member in a particular set of social circumstances struggles, with the aid of Reiyukai leaders, to apply to his situation religious ideas which themselves have a long history. The individual gives life to those ideas by wringing from them a means to change his own circumstances. That the quest for such benefits cannot be dismissed as crass opportunism has been shown in these pages. Furthermore, if members did not believe that their situation is genuinely improved through membership in the new religions, they would not remain affiliated with them.

Seen in historical perspective, Reiyukai is one of a number of Buddhist laymen's groups which have been arising since the beginning of the nineteenth century, starting with Nyoraikyō (如来教) (founded 1802) and Butsuryuko, (founded 1857). Nineteenth- and twentieth-century Japanese religious history has followed a "Protestant" impulse to validate the authority of lay religious experience, to make holy writ available to devotees, and to create religious organizations that directly address the problems of society. These trends are clearly visible whether one examines Buddhist-, Shinto-, or Shugendo-derived religions of the nineteenth and twentieth centuries. In Reiyukai we find a complete rejection of the Buddhist clergy and its formal structures of ordination, the possession and daily recitation by all members of an abridgment of the Lotus Sutra, and a constant, pervasive attempt to address problems of the individual and society in religious terms. In this their lay Buddhist practice is exceedingly vigorous and attuned to contemporary Japanese society. Epitomizing this "Protestant" impulse, Reiyukai members are representative of the membership of the new religions in general.

Reiyukai adopts a traditionalist position centered on a familistic ethic interpreted in Buddhist terms. Members value duty to the family and proper performance of traditional roles therein.

Duty to the family is closely linked to the rites of ancestor worship, and the ancestors become quasi-universal deities. A bilateral character is introduced to their cult, which is paradoxically in contrast to members' stated aim of restoring the traditional patrilateral ie. Ancestor worship becomes the focus of a voluntary association, quite an anomaly in the history of religions. In fact, it was the role of the priesthood in the cult of ancestors that up until the development of Reiyukai guaranteed the necessity of the Buddhist priesthood and greatly hindered the development of lay groups. In having developed a ritual and an organization that obviate priestly intervention, Reiyukai has created an epochal innovation in Japanese religious history. It is no wonder that the sixteen groups which have split off from it have retained Reiyukai's doctrinal and liturgical core of lay ancestor worship through use of the Lotus Sutra. Reiyukai clearly stands at the head of a strong trend of laicization of ancestor worship that is likely to have an enduring appeal in Japan.

In Reiyukai as in virtually all the Japanese new religions, healing is a central practice. Healing practices are combined with reliance upon the medical profession—the phenomenon of "dual use." Healing takes place in a social context of the patient, his family, and Reiyukai leaders confronting the professional practitioners of the medical institution. The two are opposed in their orientation toward the cure, which Reiyukai believers hold must come about through an adjustment of social relations and a religious realigning of macrocosm and microcosm. The links between these spheres are the ancestors and shared, inherited karma. Only when the ancestors are properly served by their descendants' full commitment to the ie, expressed in shared Reiyukai ritual, can the healing occur. Thus healing constitutes a reaffirmation of the world view and of group solidarity.

Healing is frequently the occasion on which a person joins Reiyukai, and obligation to the group incurred through healing becomes part of a strengthened link between the novice and Reiyukai. After a healing the individual typically testifies to the experience and proselytizes others as a partial repayment of the obligation to Reiyukai. As one who experiences a healing converts others, he may soon find himself in a position of leadership in which he must guide converts through the healing process. Healing thus creates social networks in which members are rewarded with rank in Reiyukai and the recognition of other members. The possibility of rising in rank through these networks creates a continuing incentive to perpetuate healing. Gaining rank and prestige through networks of healing, witnessing, and proselytizing is not merely a question of self-aggrandizement, because healing is believed to have the soteriological function of saving the ancestors. Thus the motivation to participate in networks of healing is a powerful one indeed.[2] Seen in this light the question of healing in the new religions is best understood as a religious and social phenomenon, not a mechanistic problem of whether healing "works" when transposed to a medical framework. For the historian of religions the most important thing is members' overwhelming affirmation of healing and our need to understand that affirmation.

The claim by Reiyukai members that they have experienced an improvement of their material circumstances as a result of membership must be taken seriously. We saw that in its early history Reiyukai began with a core membership of urban proletariat in an area where the poorest class concentrated. Gradually it was able to establish headquarters in a more affluent neighborhood and to attract a following from among the self-employed and owners of small businesses. Furthermore, members regularly report in testimonies how they and their families have come to enjoy greater prosperity thanks to Reiyukai. These claims are not simply extravagent rhetoric. Reiyukai's familistic ethic dictates that the good of the family be the first priority in economic life. Frugality and a high premium on savings are important group values helping members attain economic stability and a higher standard of life. Channels of mutual aid within the group are another powerful means toward that end.

However, these achievements are not without cost. A price is paid in a progressively deeper entrenchment in a narrow, familistic ethic which has little appreciation of novelty, spontaneity, crea-

[2] Helen Hardacre, "The Transformation of Healing in the Japanese New Religions," *The Journal of the History of Religions* 20 No. 3 (May, 1982): 305–320.

tivity, or genius. At least in the minds of older members, that ethic is linked to a chauvanistic nationalism of the past. The familistic ethic underwrites a social system in which women and other nonelite groups pay a tremendous price in lost opportunities for Japan's economic successes. Alternative visions of life outside the family system or the religious organization of Reiyukai itself are, in the case of women, ruled out of consideration from the outset. Yet it is also true that Reiyukai's elaborate techniques of helping women restructure power relations in the family do enable them to improve their position in the family, to achieve a position in which they can take pride. That achievement can come, in the group's view, only through a humiliation in which they are taught Buddhist ideas of karma and repentence as interpreted by Reiyukai. This paradox we see in Reiyukai is one that may be found quite generally in the history of religions: religion's dual potential for both liberation and bondage.

The claims of Reiyukai members about the instrumental effectiveness of membership are shown to be borne out. This conclusion can be stated so bluntly only by making the assumption that the reader will bear in mind the qualifications introduced to it in the course of this study. This conclusion differs significantly from those of former studies of the new religions.

The new religions represent the most vital and vigorous sector of contemporary Japanese religious life. Their members are in constant dialogue with religious ideas bequeathed to them by previous Japanese religious history and by the history of Buddhist thought. A full understanding of their thought and behavior must begin with a personal encounter; listening, creating an atmosphere in which they can articulate most fully what they want to say about society and what they take to be most important in life. Their beliefs and practices must be interpreted in light of the double context of religious ideas on the one hand and members' actual position in society on the other. This conceptualization of the "context" of Reiyukai's thought and behavior allows us to understand the group's place in the history of religions. The intense effort members devote to the task of making religious ideas function in contemporary society is a testament to their determination to transform themselves and their society to fit more nearly their ideas of the good society and the good life.

Appendix

Questionnaire Results

This appendix presents the results of a questionnaire designed for and administered to 2,000 members of Reiyukai over the period March, 1977 to January, 1978. This questionnaire was intended to complement the fieldwork carried out mainly in Osaka from July, 1976 to March, 1977, in which I became acquainted with many members on an individual basis, lived with members, and shared the daily routine of those working at the Eighth Branch. During my stay in Osaka, I realized that there exist significant features peculiar to each of the major branches, and that in order to obtain an overall view of the group and a thorough understanding of the social attitudes of the members, it would be necessary to carry out research on a wider scale than was possible in the method of participant observation. It was for these reasons that I decided to carry out the questionnaire.

Three purposes guided the design of the questionnaire. The first purpose was to gather basic sociological information on members and information concerning their participation in various Reiyukai activities. To accomplish this goal, I prepared questions on such matters as age, occupation, frequency of sutra recitation, and so on, items included in Parts 1 and 2 of the questionnaire. The second purpose was to determine the extent to which social attitudes prevailing among Eighth Branch members were held among members nationwide. In contact with Eighth Branch members, a number of social attitudes on such questions as the legal equality of the sexes and the reinstitution of "morality education" seemed quite prevalent, and I wanted to determine if these attitudes also characterized members in other areas. These matters are included in Part 3 of the questionnaire. The third purpose was to gather information on members' social attitudes in such a way that they could be compared as a group with those of the rest of Japanese society. It was hoped that the general place and significance of Reiyukai in Japanese society would be illuminated by this means.

The design of the questionnaire was not a matter that could be undertaken entirely independently; it was necessary to gain the approval and cooperation of Reiyukai headquarters to execute a project affecting the whole group. Having moved to Tokyo and become a research student in the Department of Religious Studies at the University of Tokyo, I sought the aid of department chairman Wakimoto Tsuneya. Professor Wakimoto arranged a formal introduction to the president of Reiyukai, Kubo Tsugunari. When I explained the project I hoped to carry out, President Kubo very kindly agreed to allow members to be surveyed and to help in the design and administration of the questionnaire. He assigned two officials of the Overseas Missions Bureau, Mr. Torii and Mr. Kawabata, to work with me. I began meeting with the two of them to discuss the project regularly, and at the same time I continued to consult with members of the Religious Studies Department at the university. During that time, I received invaluable aid from Professors Wakimoto, Inoue Nobutaka, and Nakamura Kyōko, and from a number of students in the department.

Consultations on the design of the questionnaire required the better part of the spring, summer, and fall of 1977. It became apparent that a number of questions I had hoped to include concerning political attitudes (especially regarding the imperial system) or certain religious practices (kage no junjo) could not be included because the Reiyukai leadership felt they were too sensitive. In the end a number of questions had to be dropped due to this refusal to allow their inclusion. For this reason, the questionnaire as it finally emerged is not as comprehensive as it should be, and it is regrettable that the project could not proceed unhindered. However, one must recall that Reiyukai is quite exceptional in permitting this kind of research at all, and that it had allocated significant time and energy to cooperation with a project from which it had no prospects of any return. At the time of its execution, no similar project had been undertaken on such a scale by either Japanese or foreign researchers, and that it could carried out at all is a tribute to the openness of Reiyukai.

There were numerous problems to be confronted in the execution of the questionnaire. Lacking the funds and time to administer the instrument directly, it was decided to send the questionnaire by mail, with an introductory letter, instructions, and return envelope. Reiyukai would not permit me access to membership files in order to ensure a correct sampling of equal numbers of various leadership categories, and it was necessary in the end to compromise significantly in the area of sampling. Officials divided the 2,000 questionnaire packets among the group's branches in proportion to the representation of each branch in the group's total membership. The leader of each branch then divided the branch's questionnaire's among subleaders, who distributed them to members in their charge. Given that it was impossible to control all aspects of the distribution, there is reason to suspect that those who finally received the questionnaire were those regarded by leaders as "good members" who could be counted upon to give "right answers" to the questions. Also, the proportion of leaders among the questionnaire respondents is far higher than their presence in the group as a whole. Nevertheless, if one thinks of the results of Part 3 as representing largely "approved" views, and bears that caveat in mind, significant data can still be gained. Finally, it should be noted that Reiyukai did not want me to release the text of the questionnaire to a commercial printer and so offered to print it at cost on its own press. When complete, it ran to sixteen pages.

The questionnaire was distributed in December, 1977 and returned by early February, 1978. Of the 2,000 sent out, 667 were returned, giving a response rate of 33 percent, rather higher than anticipated or usually achieved in mailed samples. When basic statistical information had been tabulated, I provided Reiyukai with a copy of the results.

In the following presentation, each question will be given in English translation, followed by the Japanese original, and then in some cases a reference to other surveys which have employed the same question. I relied on Yasuda Saburō, *Shakai chōsa no hando-bukku* (Tokyo: Yūzankaku, 1969) in order to assure that results of this questionnaire could be directly compared to previous work of a similar nature and where possible, duplicated exact wordings of previous surveys. Following these data are presented tabulations of response and significant cross-correlations.

Part 1: General Questions 第一部：一般的質問

1. Sex 性別 N = 657
   a. Male 男   292   44%
   b. Female 女   365   56%

2. Age 年令 N = 660

a. under 15:	0		d. 41–50:	134	20.3%
b. 16–30:	75	11.4%	e. 51–60:	165	25.0%
c. 31–40:	113	17.1%	f. over 60:	173	26.2%

3. Are you living in a rural or an urban area? あなたの住んでいるところはどういう所ですか。 N = 656
   a. Urban 都市部   459   70%
   b. Rural 農漁村部   197   30%

4. Were you born in an urban or a rural area? どんな所で生れましたか。 N = 655
   a. Urban   278   42.4%
   b. Rural   377   57.6%

5. Occupation 職業 N = 655
   Instructions: 注意:
   I. In case you are not employed, please indicate the occupation of the head of the household. 無職の方、世帯主の職業を記して下さい。
   II. In case you have more than one job, please indicate the job from which you earn the greater income. 二つ以上の仕事をもっている場合、収入が多い仕事を記して下さい。
   III. The listings below, small, medium, and large enterprises, indicate respectively, small: under 29 employees; medium: 30 to 999 employees; large: over 1,000 employees. 以下の「小・中・大」企業は小企業：29人以下、中企業：30—999人、大企業：千人以上、それぞれのことです。
      1) Small enterprise owner-operator
         小企業経営者   88   13.4%

2) Small enterprise management
小企業管理者   23   3.4%

3) Small enterprise professional worker
小企業専門職   22   3.3%

4) Small enterprise clerical, sales, service
小企業事務, 販売, サービス   40   6.1%

5) Small enterprise titled worker
小企業役付労務者   8   1.2%

6) Small enterprise ordinary worker
小企業一般労務者   29   4.4%

Total workers in small enterprises   210   31.8%

7) Medium enterprise owner-operator
中企業 [as above]   13   2.0%

8) Medium enterprise management   21   3.2%

9) Medium enterprise professional worker   18   2.7%

10) Medium enterprise clerical, sales, service   35   5.3%

11) Medium enterprise titled worker   4   0.6%

12) Medium enterprise ordinary worker   29   4.4%

Total workers in medium enterprises   120   18.2%

13) Large enterprise owner-operator
大企業 [as above]   2   0.3%

14) Large enterprise management   9   1.4%

15) Large enterprise professional worker   10   1.5%

16) Large enterprise clerical, sales, service   26   4.0%

17) Large enterprise titled worker   9   1.4%

18) Large enterprise ordinary worker   11   1.7%

Total workers in large enterprises   67   10.3%

19) Small-medium enterprise worker in
fishing, forestry, agriculture
小・中企業農・林・漁労働者   16   2.4%

20) Large enterprise worker in fishing,
forestry, agriculture 大企業農・
林・漁労働者   0

21) Owner of fishing, farming, forestry
business 農・林・漁業主   22   3.3%

22) Family worker in farming, fishing,
forestry 農・林・漁家族従業者   8   1.2%

23) Self-employed 自営業   45   7.0%

24) Day laborer 日雇労務者   7   1.1%

25) Police, security 官公保安   2   0.3%

26) Civil Service 公務員	64	9.7%
27) Retired 隠居	33	5.0%
28) Unemployed 失業	12	1.8%
29) Other その他	29	4.4%

6.a. Household composition 同居している家族の構成: [The following are the choices indicated on the questionnaire.]

a. Husband 夫
b. Wife 妻
c. Father/Father-in-law 父 / 義父
d. Mother/Mother-in-law 母 / 義母
e. Grandfather 祖父

f. Grandmother 祖母
g. Elder brother 兄
h. Elder sister 姉
i. Child 子
j. Younger brother 弟
k. Younger sister 妹
l. Other その他

6.b. Total number of persons in your household 合計

a. 1 person	20	3.2%	e. 5 persons	126	20.2%
b. 2 persons	82	13.1%	f. 6 persons	88	14.1%
c. 3 persons	92	14.7%	g. 7 persons		
d. 4 persons	126	20.2%	or more	90	14.5%

Average size of household, assuming a maximum of seven persons per household, is 4.4 persons.

7. What is the highest level of schooling you completed? あなたの最終学歴は次のどれに当りますか。 N = 655

a. Less than primary school 小学校以下	6	1.0%
b. Primary school 小学校	160	24.4%
c. Middle-school (prewar system) 旧制中学校	146	22.3%
d. High school (prewar system) 旧制高等学校	83	12.7%
e. Middle school 新制中学校	61	9.3%
f. High school 新制高等学校	104	15.8%
g. Junior college 短期大学	9	1.4%
h. Technical school 専門学校	40	6.1%
i. University 大学	44	6.7%
j. Graduate school 大学院	2	0.3%

8. What is your marital status? あなたは今、次のどれに当りますか。 N = 557

a. Unmarried 未婚	38	6.8%
b. Married 既婚	385	69.1%
c. Have ever divorced 離婚経験あり	28	5.0%
d. Separated 別居中	4	0.7%
e. Remarried 再婚	29	5.2%
f. Widower/widow 配偶者と死別	73	13.2%

9. If you have ever been married, was your marriage arranged or a "love match"? 結婚経験がある場合、あなたは   N = 593
   a. Arranged 見合   407   68.6%
   b. "Love match" 恋愛   186   31.4%

10. How many children do you have?   子供は何人いますか。
    N = 624

a. No children	67	10.7%		e. 4 children	79	12.7%
b. 1 child	72	11.5%		f. 5 children	41	6.6%
c. 2 children	195	31.3%		g. 6 or more		
d. 3 children	138	22.1%		children	32	5.1%

    The average number of children, assuming a maximum of 6 per household, is 2.8 children per household.

11. In your family, which parent attends to the discipline and education of the children? If you do not have children of your own, please answer according to the situation in the household where you were brought up. あなたの家庭では子供のしつけや教育に当る親は父と母のどちらですか。あなたが自分の子供を持っていない場合、自分の家の状態を考えて答えてください。 N = 605

a. Father	45	7.5%	c. Both	287	47.4%
b. Mother	261	43.1%	d. Other	12	2.0%

12. Who handles the finances in your household? あなたの家庭では誰が家計の管理をしていますか。 N = 540

a. Husband	60	11.1%	c. Husband		
b. Wife	301	55.8%	and wife	127	23.5%
			d. Other	52	9.6%

    [Koyama Ryū, *Gendai kazoku no kenkyū* (Tokyo: Kōbundō, 1960).]

13. At what age do you plan to retire? 職場やその他の義務的な業務から身を引くとすれば何才ぐらいですか。 N = 613

a. Under 55	41	6.7%	d. Over 66 years	97	15.8%
b. 55–60 years	183	29.8%	e. Don't plan		
c. 61–65 years	153	25.0%	to retire	115	18.8%
			f. Other	24	3.9%

14. With whom do you want to live in your old age? 老後、誰と一緒に暮したいのですか。 N = 702

a. Alone	12	1.7%	d. With relatives	4	0.6%
b. With my			e. In old-age		
children	357	50.9%	home	1	0.1%
c. With spouse	312	44.4%	f. Other	16	2.3%

    [Koyama Ryū, *Gendai kazoku no kenkyū* (Tokyo: Kōbundo, 1960).]

15. In your family, has the wife worked after marriage? 結婚の後、
妻が仕事（内職を含めて）をもったことがありますか。 N = 579
   a. Yes   370   64%
   b. No   209   36%

16.a. How much is your monthly income? あなたの1カ月の収入
は副収入を含めていくらぐらいですか。 N = 599
   a. Less than ¥100,000
      149   24.9%
   b. ¥100,000–150,000
      137   22.9%
   c. ¥160,000–200,000
      122   20.4%
   d. ¥210,000–250,000
      75   12.5%
   e. ¥260,000–300,000
      46   7.7%
   f. ¥310,000–400,000
      33   5.5%
   g. ¥410,000–500,000
      20   3.3%
   h. Over ¥500,000
      17   2.8%

16.b. How much is your annual income (including bonuses)? あなたの
1年の収入は、ボーナスや臨時収入を含めて、大体いくらぐら
いですか。 N = 566
   a. Less than ¥500,000
      74   13.1%
   b. ¥500,000–600,000
      18   3.2%
   c. ¥610,000–700,000
      8   1.4%
   d. ¥710,000–1,000,000
      32   5.7%
   e. ¥1,010,000–1,500,000
      68   12.0%
   f. ¥1,510,000–2,000,000
      93   16.4%
   g. ¥2,010,000–3,000,000
      136   24.0%
   h. Over ¥3,000,000
      137   24.2%

16.c. What is the yearly income of your household, including the income
of all family members? あなたのほかに同居している家族で収
入のある方がいる場合、同居している家族全体の収入は、あな
たを含めて、年収入いくらになりますか。 N = 467
   a. Less than ¥500,000
      14   3.0%
   b. ¥500,000–600,000
      4   0.9%
   c. ¥610,000–700,000
      3   0.6%
   d. ¥710,000–1,000,000
      9   1.9%
   e. ¥1,010,000–1,500,000
      28   6.0%
   f. ¥1,510,000–2,000,000
      53   11.4%
   g. 2,010,000–3,000,000
      113   24.2%
   h. Over ¥3,000,000
      243   52.0%

16.d. What proportion does the wife's income make up of your family
income? 現在、妻の収入は家庭の収入の約何％ですか。
N = 461

a. 0%	240	52.1%	d. 21–30%	42	9.1%
b. 1–10%	83	18.0%	e. 31–50%	41	8.9%
c. 11–20%	36	7.8%	f. Over 50%	19	4.1%

16.e. If there are children in your family, whether living in the household or apart, what proportion of the household income do they contribute? あなたの家族に収入のある子供がいる場合（同居とか別居）、その子供の仕事による収入は家庭の収入の約何％ですか。 N = 340

a. 0%	145	42.7%	d. 21–30%	43	12.7%
b. 1–10%	36	10.6%	e. 31–50%	37	10.8%
c. 11–20%	26	7.6%	f. Over 50%	53	15.6%

Part 2: On Religious Practice 第二部：信仰参加について

1. At what age did you join Reiyukai? 何才の時に霊友会に入会しましたか。 N = 650

a. Since childhood/parents are also members	79	12.2%	d. 31–40 years	195	30.0%
b. 10–20 years	78	12.0%	e. 41–50 years	88	13.5%
c. 21–30 years	193	29.7%	f. Over 50 years	17	2.6%

2. What was the relation to you of the person who proselytized you? 導きの親とあなたとの入会以前の関係は。 N = 655

a. Relative	117	17.9%	g. Parent	163	24.9%
b. Friend	88	13.4%	h. Co-worker	9	1.4%
c. Neighbor	134	20.4%	i. Employer	3	0.5%
d. Spouse	36	5.5%	j. Teacher	2	0.3%
e. Child	5	0.8%	k. Other	31	4.7%
f. Unrelated evangelist	67	10.2%			

3. If you keep a Book of the Past, how many posthumous names have you recorded in it? あなたが過去帳を持っている場合、その過去帳には何人の方の名前が記録されていますか。 N = 638

a. Don't have a kakochō	23	3.6%	d. 51–100 names	88	13.8%
b. 1–10 names	14	2.2%	e. Over 100 names	447	70.1%
c. 11–50 names	66	10.3%			

4. How many times per month do you recite the Blue Sutra? 月に青経巻を何巻読誦していますか。 N = 653

Age at Entrance by Sex and Rank

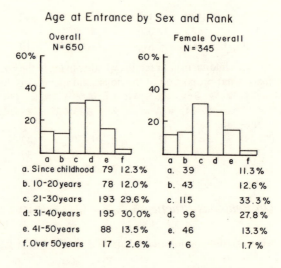

Overall
N = 650

a. Since childhood	79 12.3%
b. 10-20 years	78 12.0%
c. 21-30 years	193 29.6%
d. 31-40 years	195 30.0%
e. 41-50 years	88 13.5%
f. Over 50 years	17 2.6%

Female Overall
N = 345

a.	39 11.3%
b.	43 12.6%
c.	115 33.3%
d.	96 27.8%
e.	46 13.3%
f.	6 1.7%

Male Overall
N = 294

a.	32 10.9%
b.	56 19.0%
c.	68 23.1%
d.	91 30.9%
e.	38 13.0%
f.	9 3.1%

Female Shibuchō
N = 101

a.	2 2.0%
b.	9 9.0%
c.	41 40.6%
d.	32 31.7%
e.	16 15.8%
f.	1 0.9%

Fig. 13

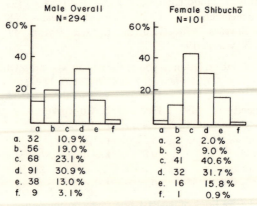

a. Don't recite it	3	0.3%	e. 31–40 times	161	24.6%
b. 1–10 times	32	5.0%	f. 41–50 times	64	9.8%
c. 11–20 times	29	4.4%	g. 51–60 times	103	15.8%
d. 21–30 times	99	15.3%	h. Over 60 times	162	24.8%

5. How many times per month do you recite the Miroku sutra?
弥勒経は月に何巻読誦していますか。 N = 645

(continued)

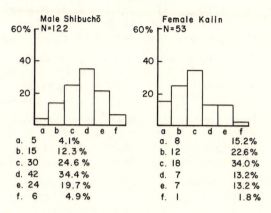

Male Shibuchō
N=122

a.	5	4.1%
b.	15	12.3%
c.	30	24.6%
d.	42	34.4%
e.	24	19.7%
f.	6	4.9%

Female Kaiin
N=53

a.	8	15.2%
b.	12	22.6%
c.	18	34.0%
d.	7	13.2%
e.	7	13.2%
f.	1	1.8%

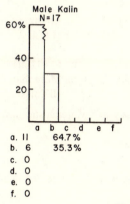

Male Kaiin
N=17

a.	11	64.7%
b.	6	35.3%
c.	0	
d.	0	
e.	0	
f.	0	

Fig.13

a.	Don't recite it	53	8.1%	e.	31–40 times	138	21.4%
b.	1–10 times	154	23.9%	f.	41–50 times	16	2.5%
c.	11–20 times	94	14.6%	g.	51–60 times	16	2.5%
d.	21–30 times	142	22.0%	h.	More than 60 times	32	5.0%

6. How many times per month do you recite the Gōhō sutra? 行法経
は月に何巻読誦していますか。 N = 626

a. Don't recite it 95   15.2%   e. 31–40 times   60   9.6%
b. 1–10 times   198   31.6%   f. 41–50 times   6   1.0%
c. 11–20 times   108   17.2%   g. 51–60 times   7   1.1%
d. 21–30 times   134   21.4%   h. Over 60 times 18   2.9%

7.   How many times have you gone to Mirokusan? 弥勒山へ行った
     ことは何回ありますか。 N = 658
     a. 0 times   8   1.2%   c. 6–10 times   60   9.1%
     b. 1–5 times   74   11.3%   d. Over 10 times 516   78.4%

8.   How many times have you gone to Shakaden? 釈迦殿へ行ったこ
     とは何回ありますか。 N = 650
     a. 0 times   11   1.7%   c. 6–10 times   50   7.7%
     b. 1–5 times   226   34.8%   d. Over 10 times 363   55.8%

9.   Have you participated in the training in Shichimenzan? 七面山修
     行に参加したことがありますか。 N = 645
     a. Yes   552   85.6%
     b. No   93   14.4%

10. Have you presented a testimony? If so, how many times? 霊友会に
     入会してから「体験」を発表したことは何回ありますか。
     N = 644
     a. 0 times   100   15.5%   c. 6–10 times   42   6.5%
     b. 1–5 times   262   40.7%   d. More than
                                          10 times   240   37.3%

11. Did you participate in this year's winter austerities? 今年の寒行を
     しましたか。 N = 632
     a. Yes   221   35.0%
     b. No   411   65.0%

12. What is your rank in Reiyukai? 霊友会でのあなたの資格は何で
     すか。 N = 657
     a. Seeker   12   1.8%   d. Junshibuchō 105   16.0%
     b. Junhōzashu   75   11.4%   e. Shibuchō   231   35.1%
     c. Hōza shu   161   24.5%   f. Kaiin   73   11.2%

13. How often do you go to the branch for meetings or other activities
     per month? 集いとか他の事で月に何度位支部に行きますか。
     N = 634
     a. 0 times   24   3.8%   c. 6–10 times   77   12.1%
     b. 1–5 times   431   68.0%   d. Over 10 times 102   16.1%

14.a. Have you ever been a member of a religious group other than

Distribution of Leadership Ranks

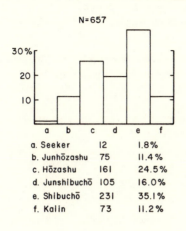

a. Seeker	12	1.8%
b. Junhōzashu	75	11.4%
c. Hōzashu	161	24.5%
d. Junshibuchō	105	16.0%
e. Shibuchō	231	35.1%
f. Kaiin	73	11.2%

Fig. 14

Reiyukai? 霊友会以外に他の宗教団体に入ったことがあります
か。 N = 645
a. Yes   87   13.5%
b. No   558   86.5%

14.b. If so, of what group were you a member? (「はい」と答えた人)何
の団体ですか。

Christian	10	Daijōkyō	1
Shingon sect	1	Ikegami honmonji	1
Seichō no Ie	4	Nihonzan	1
Sōka gakkai	5	Daishi kō	1
Tenrikyō	5	Rosutata	1
Nihon kyō	1	Shigisankō	1
Nichiren sect	1	Busshōgonenkai	1
Jōdo sect	1	Konkōkyō	1

14.c. Where do you conduct memorial services? あなたの場合はどこ
で法事を行いますか。 N = 677

a. Don't hold   c. At my home 422   62.3%
   them   31   4.6%   d. At the temple 134 19.8%
b. At the honke 71   10.5%   e. Other   19   2.8%

15.a. Have you ever consulted a branch leader about a personal problem at his/her house? 個人的な問題で支部長のお宅を訪問して相談をしたことがありますか。 N = 615
    a. Yes   389   63.3%
    b. No   226   36.7%

15.b. (For those who answered "yes") What sort of problem did you ask advice about? List two typical problems. (「はい」と答えた人)その相談内容はどんなものですか。代表的なもの2つを下に記して下さい。
643 persons listed at least one personal problem in the blanks provided for this purpose.

16.   Do you have the power to perform kuji? おくじを頂いていますか。 N = 643
    a. Yes   509   79.2%
    b. No   134   20.8%

17.a. Have you ever apologized to another person as part of your Reiyukai training? 霊友会の教えを行うことにより自分が悪かったと気付き自分以外の人に心から謝るということがありましたか。 N = 632
    a. Yes   549   86.8%
    b. No   83   13.2%

17.b. If so, to whom did you apologize? (「はい」と答えた人)誰に対して謝りましたか。

a. Mother	209	e.	Michibiki no oya	122
b. Father	143	f.	Friend	80
c. Child	99	g.	Employer	11
d. Branch leader	183	h.	Other	125

Part 3: Questions on Social Attitudes 第三部：社会的意識について

1.   In your opinion, what are the three biggest problems facing Japan today? 今日、日本が直面する3つの大きな問題は次のうちのどれだと思いますか。

a. Energy	168	g.	Increase of people who don't "know *on*"	275
b. Inflation	185	h.	Crime	150
c. Problems of the aged	123	i.	Need to control strikes and demonstrations	13
d. Education	322			
e. Divorce	22			
f. Social welfare	96			

j. Need to reform the
   Constitution   24
k. Pollution   217
l. 200-mile limit on offshore
   fishing   43

m. Limited fishing resources
                         190
n. Population   42
o. Other   14

2. There are many people these days who feel that there is such a gap between the generations that it is impossible to achieve mutual understanding. Do you agree? 現在戦前と戦後の世代に大きな隔りがあって、お互いの橋わたしが不可能とまではいかなくとも困難だと考えている人がいますが、あなたはどう考えていますか。 N = 637

   a. Agree   224   35.2%
   b. Not concerned 238   37.4%
   c. Disagree   175   27.4%

   [Tsuchiya Shimizu et al., *Nihon no howaito karaa—chōsa ni arawareta seikatsu ishiki* (Tokyo: Daiamondo, 1963).]

3. Do you think the Japanese form a single family? 日本人のすべてが一家族だとあなたは思いますか。 N = 622

   a. Yes   427   68.6%
   b. No   195   31.4%

4. Recently the number of aged people in Japan who are discontented is increasing. Are you personally concerned about this problem? 最近日本では悩みを持った老人が増えてきていますが、こういった問題に関心がありますか。 N = 630

   a. Extremely concerned   317   50.3%
   b. Fairly concerned   236   37.5%
   c. Not very concerned   77   12.2%

5. Do you think there should be a law established to assign to one of a couple's children the duty of supporting the parents in old age? 子供の中から特定の子が、その親の老後の面倒をみるように法律で定めるべきだと思いますか。 N = 635

   a. Yes   274   43.1%
   b. No   361   56.9%

   ["Sōzokusei no kenkyū," *Kokusai kirisuto daigaku nōson kōsei kiyō* (1960), vol. 2.]

6. Under the present law the former family system has been abolished. Do you approve or disapprove of its abolition? 現在の民法では昔の家族制度は廃止されていますが、この家族制度の廃止はよいことだと思いますか、又はよくないことだと思いますか。 N = 609

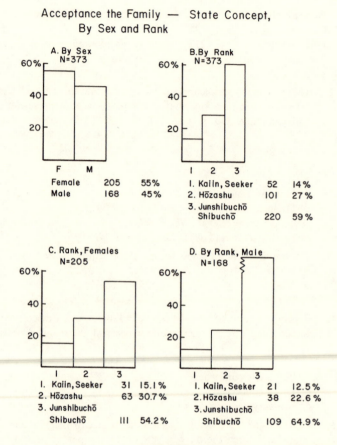

Acceptance the Family — State Concept, By Sex and Rank

A. By Sex N=373

Female	205	55%
Male	168	45%

B. By Rank N=373

1. Kaiin, Seeker	52	14%
2. Hōzashu	101	27%
3. Junshibuchō Shibuchō	220	59%

C. Rank, Females N=205

1. Kaiin, Seeker	31	15.1%
2. Hōzashu	63	30.7%
3. Junshibuchō Shibuchō	111	54.2%

D. By Rank, Male N=168

1. Kaiin, Seeker	21	12.5%
2. Hōzashu	38	22.6%
3. Junshibuchō Shibuchō	109	64.9%

Fig. 15

a. Approve	179	29.4%
b. Disapprove	430	70.6%

[See references, Chapter 3.]

7. Do you think that the ie, inherited from the ancestors, should be
    perpetuated, and that it is important to train children likewise to
    perpetuate it? 先祖から伝わった家というものを存続させ、子供
    にも同じように存続させることを教えるという事は重要だと思
    いますか。 N = 667

a. Yes	650	97.5%
b. No	17	2.5%

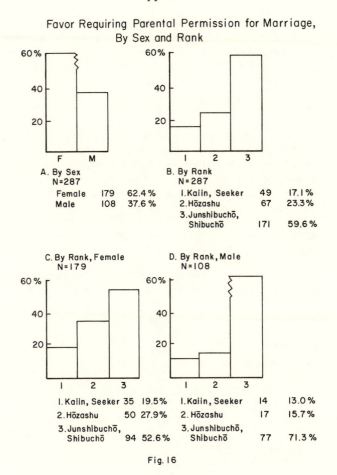

Fig. 16

8. Under the present law, all children inherit their parents' property equally. Do you approve of this system? 現在の民法では、全ての子供が両親の財産を平等に相続することとされていますが、この制度に賛成しますか。 N = 606

   a. Approve   347   57.3%
   b. Disapprove   259   42.7%

[See references in Chapter 3.]

9. Under the present law, a man or woman who has reached the age of twenty may marry without parental consent, but under the old law parental permission was required. Which do you think is better, the

present or the former system? 現在の法律では20才に達した男女は両親の許可なしに結婚することができますが、昔の法律では両親の許可が必要でした。あなたは現在の制度がよいと思いますか、それとも昔の制度がよいと思いますか。 N = 629

a. The present system   292   46.4%
b. The former system   337   53.6%

[See references, Chapter 3 and Fig. 16.]

10. Generally speaking, do you think it is best for a parent to choose a husband or wife for the children, or do you think it is best if the child finds his/her own husband or wife? 一般的に子供の結婚の相手は親がみつけてやるべきだと思いますか、あるいは本人自身がみつけるべきだと思いますか。 N = 652

a. Parent should choose   111   17.0%
b. Child should choose   402   61.6%
c. Other   139   21.4%

[See references, Chapter 3.]

11. If a couple has no children, do you think they should adopt a child? もし夫婦に子供がない場合養子をもらうべきだと思いますか。 N = 638

a. Yes   452   71.0%
b. No   75   12.0%
c. Other   111   17.0%

[See references, Chapter 3.]

12. Do you think that a wife owes *on* to her husband? 妻は夫に恩義があるとあなたは思いますか。 N = 629

a. Yes   104   16.5%
b. No   27   4.3%
c. Husband and wife have
    on to each other   498   79.2%

13. Recently the divorce rate is increasing in Japan. Are you concerned about this? 最近日本の離婚の割合は増加しています。あなたはこれに関心がありますか。 N = 625

a. Extremely concerned   246   39.4%
b. Fairly concerned   286   45.8%
c. Unconcerned   93   14.8%

14. Which of the following means would you favor to decrease the rate of divorce? 離婚率を小さくしていくには次のどんな解決策がよいと思いますか、よいと思うもの全てを○で囲んでください。

a. Abolish "love marriage" 7   d. Strengthen divorce laws
b. Abolish coeducation   13   149
c. Reinstitute morality   e. Other   91
   education   512

15. When a husband and wife divorce, do you think the ex-husband should be required to pay for the support of the wife and the education of the children? 離婚した妻とその子供がいる場合、夫は別れた妻と子供に生活費と養育費を負担しなければならないと思いますか。N = 567

a. Yes   483   85.2%
b. No   84   14.8%

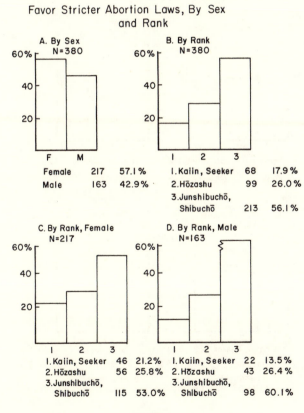

Favor Stricter Abortion Laws, By Sex and Rank

A. By Sex N=380

Female   217   57.1%
Male   163   42.9%

B. By Rank N=380

1. Kaiin, Seeker   68   17.9%
2. Hōzashu   99   26.0%
3. Junshibuchō,
   Shibuchō   213   56.1%

C. By Rank, Female N=217

1. Kaiin, Seeker   46   21.2%
2. Hōzashu   56   25.8%
3. Junshibuchō,
   Shibuchō   115   53.0%

D. By Rank, Male N=163

1. Kaiin, Seeker   22   13.5%
2. Hōzashu   43   26.4%
3. Junshibuchō,
   Shibuchō   98   60.1%

Fig. 17

16. Do you think that laws concerning abortion should be made more strict? 人工妊娠中絶の法的条件をきびしくしなければならないとあなたは思いますか。 N = 601

   a. Yes   487   81.0%
   b. No   114   19.0%

[See references, Chapter 3 and Fig. 17.]

17. The equality of the sexes has been established by law; do you approve of this? 現在の法律では男女平等が確立されましたが、これはよいことだと思いますか。 N = 619

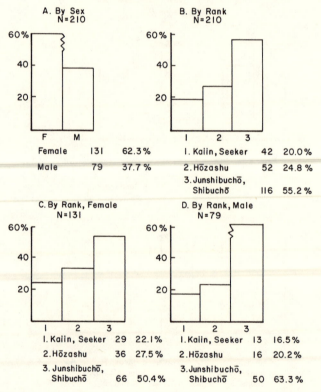

Opposition to Legalized Equality of the Sexes, By Sex and Rank

A. By Sex N=210

Female   131   62.3%
Male   79   37.7%

B. By Rank N=210

1. Kaiin, Seeker   42   20.0%
2. Hōzashu   52   24.8%
3. Junshibuchō, Shibuchō 116   55.2%

C. By Rank, Female N=131

1. Kaiin, Seeker   29   22.1%
2. Hōzashu   36   27.5%
3. Junshibuchō, Shibuchō 66   50.4%

D. By Rank, Male N=79

1. Kaiin, Seeker   13   16.5%
2. Hōzashu   16   20.2%
3. Junshibuchō, Shibuchō 50   63.3%

Fig. 18

a. Approve   443   71.6%
b. Disapprove   176   28.4%
[See references, Chapter 3 and Fig. 18.]

18.   There are some people who say of women, *gōshō ga fukai*; do you
      agree? 男性より、女性の方が業障が深いという人がいますが、
      あなたもそう思いますか。　N = 613
      a. Yes   466   76.0%
      b. No   147   24.0%
      [See discussion, Chapter 6 and Fig. 19.]

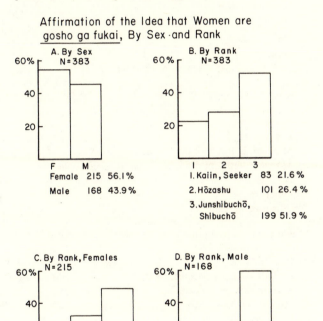

Affirmation of the Idea that Women are
gosho ga fukai, By Sex and Rank

A. By Sex N=383
Female 215 56.1%
Male   168 43.9%

B. By Rank N=383
1. Kaiin, Seeker 83 21.6%
2. Hōzashu   101 26.4%
3. Junshibuchō,
   Shibuchō   199 51.9%

C. By Rank, Females N=215
1. Kaiin, Seeker 51 21.7%
2. Hōzashu   64 29.8%
3. Junshibuchō,
   Shibuchō   100 46.5%

D. By Rank, Male N=168
1. Kaiin, Seeker 32 19.0%
2. Hōzashu   37 22.0%
3. Junshibuchō,
   Shibuchō   99 59.0%

Fig. 19

19. Do you think that filial piety should be legally required of children? 子供が親孝行をすることが法で制定されるべきだと思いますか。 N = 606
    a. Yes   244   40.3%
    b. No   362   59.7%
    [See references, Chapter 3.]

20. Do you think it is necessary to establish as a regular part of the school curriculum a course of "morality education" suitable to the present day? 今の時代に合った道徳(修身)教育を正式の科目として、学校で教えることは必要だと思いますか。 N = 635
    a. Yes   602   94.8%
    b. No   22   3.5%
    c. Other   11   1.7%
    [See references and discussion, Chapter 3.]

21. Which of the following do you think is the best way to live? あなたにとって次のどれが一番よい生き方だと思いますか。 N = 640
    a. Unmarried   3   0.5%
    b. Married, living with parents and children   547   85.5%
    c. Married, with children, but separate from own
       parents   63   9.8%
    d. Other   27   4.2%
    [See discussion, Chapter 3.]

22. Which political party do you support? あなたはどの党を支持しますか。 N = 607
    a. Jimintō (LDP)   494   81.4%
    b. Shakaitō (Japan Socialist Party)   38   6.3%
    c. Kyōsantō (Communist Party)   3   0.5%
    d. Minshatō (Democratic Socialist Party)   44   7.2%
    e. Kōmeitō   1   0.2%
    f. Shinjiyū kurabu (New Liberal Club)   27   4.4%

23. If Japanese society were divided into five strata, where do you think you would fit in? 日本の社会全体を五つの層に分けたとすれば、あなた自身は、この水準のどれに入ると思いますか。 N = 587
    a. Upper 上   28   4.8%
    b. Upper-middle 中の上   90   15.3%
    c. Middle 中   337   57.4%
    d. Lower-middle 中の下   113   19.3%
    e. Lower 下   19   3.2%
    [See references, Chapter 3.]

Acceptance of the Employer/Parent Analogy, by
Sex and Rank

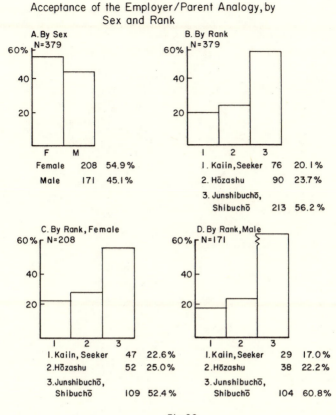

A. By Sex
N=379

F	M	
Female	208	54.9%
Male	171	45.1%

B. By Rank
N=379

1. Kaiin, Seeker	76	20.1%
2. Hōzashu	90	23.7%
3. Junshibuchō, Shibuchō	213	56.2%

C. By Rank, Female
N=208

1. Kaiin, Seeker	47	22.6%
2. Hōzashu	52	25.0%
3. Junshibuchō, Shibuchō	109	52.4%

D. By Rank, Male
N=171

1. Kaiin, Seeker	29	17.0%
2. Hōzashu	38	22.2%
3. Junshibuchō, Shibuchō	104	60.8%

Fig. 20

24.　Some people think that the relation between employer and employee is just like that between parent and child, and that if the employee works hard, the company will take a parental attitude and look after him. Do you agree with this attitude? 会社と従業員との関係はちょうど親子のようなものでああり、従業員が会社のためによくつくせば会社も親身になって従業員の面倒をみてくれるという意見がありますが、あなたはそう思いますか。

N = 622

a. Yes　　　　　　　447　　71.9%
b. No　　　　　　　175　　28.1%

[See discussion, Chapter 3 and Kojima Kazuo, *NHK Hōsō bunka kenkyū nenpō*, vol. 10 (1965).]

Bibliography

Abe Masatarō. "Senzo sūhai to sono shakaiteki kitei." *Nenpō shakaigaku kenkyū* 1 (1944): 134–61.

Anesaki Masaharu. *The Religious Life of the Japanese People.* Tokyo: Kokusai Bunka Shinkōkai, 1970.

Aoi Kazuo, "Fūfu kankei." In *Gendai kazoku no kenkyū*, edited by T. Koyama. Tokyo: Yoshikawa kōbunkan, 1960.

――― and Masuda Kōkichi, eds. *Kazoku hendō no shakaigaku.* Tokyo: Baifūkan, 1973.

Arai Kōjirō. "Kitsune tsuki to daimoku gyōja." *Indogaku bukkyōgaku kenkyū* (hereafter *IBK*) 19, No. 2 (1971): 652–57.

Arichi Tōro. *Kindai nihon no kazokukan.* Tokyo: Kōbundō, 1977.

Aruga Kizaemon. "Hotoke to iu kotoba ni tsuite." *Kokoro* 27, No. 10 (1974): 10–13.

―――. "Ie seido to shakai fukushi." *Shakai jigyō* 38, No. 9 (1955): 3–10.

―――. "Nihon ni okeru senzo no kannen." In *Aruga Kizaemon chosakushū* 11 vols. Tokyo: Miraisha, 1966–1971. Vol. 7, pp. 325–56.

Ashita. Reiyukai regional magazine.

Blacker, Carmen. *The Catalpa Bow, A Study of Shamanistic Practices in Japan.* London: George Allen and Unwin, 1975.

Bukkyō shisō kenkyūkai, ed. *On.* Bukkyo Shisō vol. 4. 4 vols. Kyoto: Heirakuji Shoten, 1978.

De Visser, M. W. *Ancient Buddhism in Japan.* 2 vols. Paris: Librairie Orientaliste, Paul Guenther, 1928.

―――. *The Dragon in China and Japan.* 1931. Reprint. Wiesbaden: Martin Sandig, 1969.

Dubos, René. "Determinants of Health and Disease." Reprinted in *Culture, Disease, and Healing, Studies in Medical Anthropology*, edited by David Landy. New York: Macmillan Publishing, 1977.

Dutt, N. *Early Buddhist Monachism.* London: Kegan, Paul, Trench, Trubner & Co., 1924.

Fortes, Meyer. *Oedipus and Job in West African Religion.* Cambridge: Cambridge University Press, 1959.

————. "Pietas in Ancestor Worship." *Journal of the Royal Anthropological Institute*, No. 91 (1960): 177–87.
————. "Some Reflections on Ancestor Worship in Africa." In *African Systems of Thought*. Oxford: Oxford University Press, 1965.
Fujii Masao. *Bukkyō girei jiten*. Tokyo: Tokyodō shuppansha, 1977.
————. "Gense riyaku." In *Girei no kōzō*, edited by Tamaru Noriyoshi, pp. 179–238. Tokyo: Kōsei shuppan, 1972.
Fujin mondai tantō shitsu. *Fujin mondai ni kansuru yūshikisha chōsa*. Tokyo: Prime Minister's Office, 1978.
Fujin ni kansuru shomondai chōsa kaigi. *Fujin ni kansuru shomondai no sōgō chōsa hōkokusho*. Tokyo: Ministry of Finance, 1974.
————. *Gendai nihon josei no ishiki to kōdō*. Tokyo: Ministry of Finance, 1974.
Fukumoto Hiroshi. "Kazoku hendō to sono ijō." In *Kazoku hendō no shakaigaku*, edited by Aoi Kazuo and Masuda Kōkichi. Tokyo: Baifūkan, 1973.
Fukushima Tadao, ed. *Kazoku: seisaku to hō*. 7 vols. Tokyo: Tokyo daigaku shuppan kai, 1975–1977.
Fukutake Ichirō. *Nihon kazoku seido shi gaisetsu*. Tokyo: Yoshikawa kōbunkan, 1972.
Fuse Akiko. "Chingin rōdōsha no rōdō." *Shakaigaku hyōron* 27, No. 1 (1976): 18–55.
————. "Fujin o meguru henka." In *Kazoku hendō no shakaigaku*, edited by Aoi Kazuo et al. Tokyo: Baifūkan, 1973.
————. "Gendai nihon ni okeru shufu no shūrō." In *Kokusai josei gakkai hōkokusho*. Tokyo: published privately, 1978.
————. "Kazoku to shokugyō." In *Kazoku shakaigaku*, edited by Fukutake Takeshi, 3: 182–204. 18 vols. Tokyo: Tokyo daigaku shuppankai, 1976.
Gotō Yasushi. "Meiji no tennōsei to minshū." In *Tennōsei to minshū*, edited by Gotō Yasushi. Tokyo: Tokyo daigaku shuppankai, 1976.
Hall, Robert K. *Shūshin, the Ethics of a Defeated Nation*. New York: Bureau of Publications, Teachers' College, Columbia University, 1949.
Hardacre, Helen. "Sex Role Norms and Values in Reiyukai." *Japanese Journal of Religious Studies* 6, No. 3 (September, 1979): 445–59.
————. "The Transformation of Healing in the Japanese New Religions." *The Journal of the History of Religions* 20, No. 3 (May, 1982): 305–320.
Hasegawa Kazuo. "Shisetsu no rōjin no shinri." In *Rōjin no seishin igaku to shinrigaku*, edited by Kaneko Jirō et al. *Kōza nihon no rōjin*. 4 vols. Tokyo: Kakiuchi shuppansha, 1972.
Herold, Renate. "Nihon to ōbei ni okeru fujin rōdō no mondai." In *Kokusai josei gakkai hōkokusho*. Tokyo: published privately, 1978.
Holt, John. "Merit for the 'Departed': The Living and the Dead in Early Buddhist Tradition." Paper presented at the 1980 meeting of the

International Academy of the History of Religions, Toronto, August 1980.
Holtom, David C. *Modern Japan and Shinto Nationalism.* Chicago: University of Chicago Press, 1947.
———. *Shinto, National Faith of Japan.* London: Kegan, Paul, Trench, Trubner, 1938.
Hsu, Francis L. K. "Variations in Ancestor Worship Beliefs and Their Relation to Kinship." *Southwest Journal of Anthropology* 25 (1971): 153–72.
Ide Fumiko and Esashi Akiko. *Taishō demokurashii to josei.* Tokyo: Gōdo shuppan, 1977.
Ikeda Eishun. "Meiji bukkyō no hito tokushitsu: jūzen dōtoku no mondai o megutte." *IBK* 17, No. 2 (1968): 711–14.
———. *Meiji no bukkyō—sono kōdo to shisō.* Nihonjin no kōdō to shisō, vol. 31. Tokyo: Hyōronsha, 1976.
Ishii Ryōsuke. *Japanese Legislation in the Meiji Era.* Translated by W. J. Chambliss. Tokyo: Kosai Publishing Co., 1968.
Iwamoto Yutaka. *Mokuren densetsu to urabon,* vol. 3. *Bukkyō setsuwa kenkyū.* 5 vols. Kyoto: Hōzōkan, 1968.
Jiyūtō kenpō chōsakai. "Nihon koku kenpō kaiseian yōkō." In *Nihon fujin mondai shiryō shūsei,* edited by Ichikawa Fusae. 10 vols. Tokyo: Domesu shuppan, 1978–1980. Vol. 5, pp. 537–49.
Kageyama Gyōo. *Nichirenshū fukyō no kenkyū.* Kyoto: Heirakuji shoten, 1975.
Kano Masanao. "Meiji kōki ni okeru kokumin soshikika no katei." *Shirin* 69 (March, 1964): 18–46.
———. *Shihon shugi keiseiki no chitsujo ishiki.* Tokyo: Chikuma shobō, 1969.
Kasahara Kazuo. *Nihon shūkyōshi.* 2 vols. Tokyo: Yamakawa shuppansha, 1977.
———. *Nyonin ōjō shisō no keifu.* Tokyo: Yoshikawa kōbunkan, 1975.
———. *Tsumi to batsu.* Kyōikusha rekishi shinsho, Nihonshi 80. Tokyo: Kyōikusha, 1980.
Kawashima Takashi. "Kazoku seido no fukkatsu." In *Nihon fujin mondai shiryō shūsei,* edited by Ichikawa Fusae, 5: 568–79. 10 vols. Tokyo: Domesu shuppan, 1978–1980.
Kawashima Takeyoshi. *Nihon shakai no kazokuteki kōsei.* Tokyo: Nihon Hyōronsha, 1965.
Kawamura Kōshō. "Zaishō shōmetsu ni tsuite." *Seishin* (Minobusan), No. 29 (1953): 154–56.
Kawasaki Enshō. "Toshi ni okeru ie no shūkyō no henyō." *Ryūkoku daigaku bukkyō bunka kenkyūjo kiyō,* No. 13 (June, 1974): 70–84.
Kazoku kenkyūbukai. "Sengo ni okeru kazoku no jittai." *Shakaigaku hyōron* 7, Nos. 27 and 28 (1957): 114–45.
Keizai kikaku-chō, ed. *Shōwa gojū-roku nenpan kokumin seikatsu ha-*

kusho. Tokyo: Ōkurashō insatsu kyoku, 1981.

Keizai kikaku-chō kokumin seikatsu chōsa-ka, ed. *Kokumin no seikatsu to ishiki no dōkō.* Tokyo: Ōkurashō insatsu kyoku, 1976.

Kino Seiichi. "Ie o meguru ideorogii no kako to genzai." *Kagaku no shisō* 7 (January, 1973): 47–55.

Kishimoto Hideo. *Japanese Religion in the Meiji Era.* Translated by John Howes. Vol. 2: *Japanese Culture in the Meiji Era.* Tokyo: Ōbunsha, 1956.

Kiyonari Tadao. "Toshi jieigyō no saiseisan." In *Gendai no kazoku* (special issue of *Jurist*), Spring, 1977.

Kiyota Nuhiko. "Katei seikatsu to fujin." *Reiyūkaihō,* No. 160 (June 12, 1943), p. 2.

Kōchi Michigaku. "Metsuzai sei ni tsuite." *IBK* 17, No. 2 (1969): 540–41.

Köhler, Werner. *Die Lotus-Lehre und die modernen Religionen in Japan.* Zurich: Atlantis Verlag, 1962.

Kokumin seikatsu kenkyūjo, *Nihonjin no seikatsu ishiki.* Tokyo: Chibundō, 1970.

Kōmoto Mitsugu. "Minshū no naka no senzokan no ichisokumen." In *Nihon no shūkyō no fukugōteki kōzō,* edited by Sakurai Tokutarō. Tokyo: Kōbundō, 1978.

———. "Toshikazoku ni okeru senzo saishikan." In *Gendai shūkyō e no shikaku,* edited by Shūkyō shakaigaku kenkyūkai. Tokyo: Yūzankaku, 1978.

Kōseishō ōkura kanbō tōkei jōhōbu. *Kokumin seikatsu jittai chōsa hōkokusho.* Tokyo: Kōsei tōkei kyōkai, 1980.

Kōsei tōkei kyōkai. "Hoken to nenkin no dōkō." *Kōsei to shihyō,* special issue (October, 1978).

Kotani Kimi. *Ten no ongaku.* Tokyo: Reiyukai, 1972.

———. *Watakushi no shugyō seikatsu, sanjūgo nen.* Tokyo: Reiyukai, 1958.

———and Ishihara Shintarō. *Ningen no genten.* Tokyo: Sankei shimbun, 1969.

———and Kubo Tsugunari. *Aokyōkan, Namu myōhō renge kyō, asa-ban no otsutome.* Tokyo: Ishiyama Kyōshindō, 1978.

Koyama Takashi. "Ie no ishiki." In *Gendai kazoku no kenkyū,* edited by Koyama. Tokyo: Yoshikawa Kobundō, 1960.

———. "Tokyo kinkōson no kazoku." *Sonraku shakai kenkyū nenpō* 10 (1960): 1–23.

"Kubo Tsugunari." *Gendai,* No. 13 (December, 1978): 7.

Kusada Isaburō. *Konjō o naose.* Taiken bukkyō, vol. 6. Tokyo: Hotoke no sekaisha, 1974.

Lee, Edwin B. "Nichiren and Nationalism: The Religious Patriotism of Tanaka Chigaku." *Monumenta Nipponica* 30, No. 1 Spring (1975): 19–35.

McFarland, H. Neill. *The Rush Hour of the Gods.* New York: Harper

Colophon Books, 1967.
Maeda Takashi. "Nihon sonraku ni okeru sosen sūhai to sōzoku no jittai." *Shakaigaku hyōron* 10, No. 2 (1960): 87–105.
Mainichi Shimbun. "Atarashii minpō kakuan no shōten." *Mainichi shimbun,* March 25, 1947.
————, ed. *Shūkyō o gendai ni tou.* 5 vols. Tokyo: Mainichi shimbunsha, 1976.
Maruyama Masao. *Thought and Behavior in Modern Japanese Politics.* Expanded ed. London: Oxford University Press, 1969.
Matsudaira Yasuo. *Arakawa-ku no rekishi.* Tokyo furusato bunko, vol. 19. Tokyo: Meichō shuppan, 1979.
Matsumura Jūgon. "Nichirenshū 'Rinshū mandara' no seiritsu to tenkai." In *Nichiren kyōgaku no shomondai,* edited by Miyazaki Eishū. Kyoto: Heirakuji shoten, 1974.
Miki Takako. "Fujin no tachiba." *Reiyukaihō,* No. 159, (May 12, 1943), p. 4.
Minami Hiroshi. *Taishō bunka.* Tokyo: Kyōsō shobō, 1965.
Ministry of Education. *Shūkyō nenkan.* 1947, 1981.
Miyata Noboru. *Kami no minzokushi.* Tokyo: Iwanami shoten, 1979.
————. "Nihonjin no shūkyō seikatsu to gense riyaku." *Nihon bukkyō,* No. 34 (1972): 43–57.
Mizuno Kōsen. "Gō setsu ni tsuite." *IBK* 2, No. 2 (1954): 110–20.
Mochizuki Kankō. "Debadattahon ni okeru nyonin jōbutsu ni tsuite." *Seishin* (Minobusan), No. 37 (1963): 44–57; pt. 2, No. 38, 26–28; pt. 3, No. 39, 23–42.
————. "Nyonin jōbutsu—henjo nanshi ni tsuite." *Seishin* (Minobusan), No. 36 (1962): 68–78.
Mochizuki Taka. "Onna ni totte no kekkon." In *Onna ga kangaete iru koto,* edited by Nihonjin kenkyūkai. Tokyo: Muroseidō, 1975.
Morioka Kiyomi. *Gendai shakai no minshū to shūkyō.* Nihonjin no kōdō to shisō, vol. 49. Tokyo: Hyōronsha, 1973.
————. *Ie to gendai kazoku,* Tokyo: Baifūkan, 1976.
————. "Kakukazoku no gendai teki ishiki." *Gendai no kazoku* (special issue of *Jurist*), Spring, 1977, pp. 60–66.
Murakami Shigeyoshi. *Butsuryū kaidō Nagamatsu Nissen.* Tokyo: Kōdansha, 1976.
————. *Kindai minshū shūkyō no kenkyū,* Tokyo: Hōzōkan, 1972.
————. *Kokka shintō.* Tokyo: Iwanami shoten, 1970.
————. *Nihon hyakunen no shūkyō.* Tokyo: Kōdansha, 1968.
————. *Nihon shūkyō jiten.* Tokyo: Kōdansha, 1978.
Muramatsu Yasuko. *Terebi dorama no joseigaku.* Tokyo: Sōtakusha, 1979.
Naganuma Masao. "Keishin sūso to bukkyō." *Reiyukaihō,* No. 134 (April 12, 1941), p. 1.
Naikaku sōridaijin kanbōgishitsu. *Kazoku seido ni tsuite no seron chōsa.*

Tokyo: Prime Minister's Office, 1957.
Naikaku sōridaijin kanbō kōhōshitsu. *Danjo byōdō ni kansuru seron chōsa.* Tokyo: Prime Minister's Office, 1975.
———. *Kazoku hō ni kansuru seron chōsa.* Tokyo: Prime Minister's Office, 1969.
———. *Kazoku ni kansuru seron chōsa.* Tokyo: Prime Minister's Office, 1969.
Nakajima Yōichirō. *Kantō daishinsai.* Tokyo: Yūzankaku, 1973.
Nakamura Masanori. "Keizai kōsei undō to nōmin tōgō." In *Shōwa kyōkō,* edited by Tokyo daigaku shakai kagaku kenkyūjo. Tokyo: Tokyo daigaku shakai kagaku kenkyūsho, 1978.
———. "Toshi kasō shakai." In *Kindai Nihon no kiso chishiki.* Tokyo: Yūzankaku, 1972.
Nakane Chie. "Bunka ni okeru oyako kankei no sōi." In *Kōza oya to ko.* Tokyo: Tokyo daigaku shuppankai, 1973.
Nakano Michiko and Ikenokami Masako. " Setai no raifu saikuru." *Jinkō mondai kenkyū,* No. 133 (January, 1975): 30–42.
Nakano Tadashi. "Ie no kōzō to ishiki oyobi henyō." In *Shōka dōzokudan no kenkyū,* edited by Nakano Tadashi. Tokyo: Miraisha, 1974.
———. "Kazoku to shinzoku." In *Kōza shakaigaku,* edited by Fukutake Tadashi, 4: 209–33. 10 vols. Tokyo: Tokyo daigaku shuppankai, 1957.
Nakao Takashi. *Nakayama Hokekyōji shiryō.* Tokyo: Yoshikawa Kōbunkan, 1968.
———, ed. *Nichirenshū no shomondai.* Tokyo: Yūzankaku, 1975.
Naoi Michiko and Sodei Takako. "Rishibetsu josei no seikatsu to rōgo." In *Kokusai josei gakkai hōkokusho.* Tokyo: published privately, 1978.
Nase City. "Sumiyoi machizukuri no tame no shimin ishiki chōsa." Nase City, October, 1977.
Nawata Sanae. "Reiyukai." In *Reiyukai, Risshōkōseikai, Sōkagakkai.* Vol. 2, *Shinshūkyō no sekai,* pp. 6–81. 5 vols. Tokyo: Daizōkan, 1979.
Nihon bukkyō kenkyūkai, ed. *Nihon shūkyō no gense riyaku.* Tokyo: Daizō shuppan, 1970.
Nihon chiiki kaihatsu sentā, ed. *Nihonjin no kachikan.* Tokyo: Chibundō, 1970.
Nihon fujin dantai rengōkai, ed. *Fujin hakusho.* Tokyo: Sōdō bunka, 1977.
Nihon ginkō. *Chochiku ni kansuru seron chōsa.* Tokyo: Bank of Japan, 1977.
Nihon hōsō kyōkai. *Nihonjin no ishiki—NHK seron chōsa.* Tokyo: Chibundō, 1975.
———. *Oyaji: chichi naki jidai no kazoku.* Tokyo: NHK, 1974.
Nihon hōsō kyōkai seron chōsa jo. *Shōwa yonjū nendo kokumin seikatsu jikan chōsa.* Tokyo: Nihon hōsō shuppan kyōkai, 1966, 1971.
Nishida Tenkō. *Zange no seikatsu.* Tokyo: Shumbunsha, 1967.
Nishino Nichien. "Nagamatsu Seifū to Honmon butsuryūkō." *Asoka,*

special issue 2: Kindai shūkyō, 1968.

Norbeck, Edward. *Religion and Society in Modern Japan*. Houston: Tourmaline Press, 1970.

Oguri Junko. *Nihon no kindai shakai to Tenrikyō*. Nihonjin no kōdō to shisō, vol. 7. Tokyo: Hyōronsha, 1976.

Ōhara Kenjirō. "Rōjin no jisatsu." In *Rōjin no seishin igaku to shinrigaku*, vol. 4 of *Kōza Nihon no rōjin*, edited by Kaneko Jirō et al. 4 vols. Tokyo: Kakiuchi shuppansha, 1972.

Ōhara Takashi. "Fukuda Hideko ni miru fujin kaihō shisō no hatten; *Sekai Fujin* o chūshin ni." In *Kindai Nihon shisōshi no kiso chishiki*. Tokyo: Yūzankaku, 1975.

Ōhashi Ryūken. *Nihon no kaikyū kōsei*. Tokyo: Iwanami shoten, 1977.

Okabayashi Shigeo. "Rōjin no kazoku kankei to kyojū keitai." *Shakai fukushi ronshū* 15 (December, 1971): 1–16.

Okazaki Toshimasa, ed. *Shakaden kara no shuppatsu*. 2 vols. Tokyo: Hotoke no sekaisha, 1976.

Ōkubo Sawako. "Fujin no rōgo hoshō—dokushin fujin o chūshin ni." *Gekkan fukushi* 51, No. 11 (November, 1974): 16–23.

Pharr, Susan J. "The Japanese Woman: Evolving Views of Life and Role." In *Japan: The Paradox of Progress*, edited by Lewis Austin. New Haven: Yale University Press, 1976.

The Reiyukai, Its Aims and Practice. Tokyo: Reiyukai, n.d.

Reiyukaihō, Fortnightly journal of Reiyukai.

Risshō daigaku Nichiren kyōgaku kenkyūjo, ed. *Shōwa teihon Nichiren shōnin ibun*. 4 vols. Minobu: Sōhonzan Minobu Kuonji, 1965.

Rōdōshō Fujin-shōnen kyoku, ed. *Fujin rōdō no jitsujō*. Tokyo: Ministry of Finance, 1978.

"Rōgo no seikatsu o yutaka ni suru tame." *Gekkan fukushi* 51, No. 9 (September, 1968): 10–34.

"Rōjin to sumai." *Kenchiku to shakai* 50, No. 4 (April, 1969): 39–60.

Rosaldo, Michelle Z. "Women, Culture, and Society: A Theoretical Overview." In *Women, Culture, and Society*, edited by M. Z. Rosaldo and Louise Lamphere. Stanford: Stanford University Press, 1974.

Saitō Masao. "Toshi no rōjin mondai: kazoku to rōjin no mondai o chūshin to shite." *Toshi mondai* 49, No. 3 (1958): 61–71.

———— and Satō Mamoru. "Tōhoku nōson mibōjin kazoku no jittai." *Shakaigaku kenkyū* 7 (1953): 41–55.

Sakamoto Kaname. "Daimoku Kō—nembutsu kō oyobi ko-ankō." In *Nichirenshū no shomondai*, edited by Nakao Takashi. Tokyo: Yūzankaku, 1975.

Saki Akio. *Godai kyōso no jitsuzō*. Tokyo: Yagumo shoin, 1970.

————. *Kyōso—shomin no kamigami*. Tokyo: Aoki shoten, 1955.

Sakurabe Hajime. "Kudoku o kaisen suru to iu kangaekata." In *Gō shisō no kenkyū*, edited by Ōtani daigaku bukkyō gakkai. Kyoto: Bun'ei dō shoten, 1975.

Sakurai Tokutarō. "Minkan shinkō." In *Shūyōgaku jiten*, edited by Hori Ichirō and Oguchi Eiichi. Tokyo: Tokyo daigaku shuppankai, 1973.

———. *Nihon minkan shinkōron*. Tokyo: Kōbundō, 1973.

Sangharakshita, Bhikkhu. *A Survey of Buddhism*. Boulder: Shambala, 1980.

Sasaki Ryūji. "Nihon gunkoku shugi no shakaiteki kiban no keisei." *Nihonshi kenkyū*, No. 68 (September, 1963): 1–30.

Satomi Saion. "Shichimen shinkō no keifu to tenkai." In *Kindai nihon no hokke bukkyō*, edited by Mochizuki Kankō. Kyoto: Heirakuji shoten, 1968.

Shakusha Kōki. "Zange metsuzai ni tsuite." *Bukkyōgaku kenkyū* 30 (1973): 22–42.

Shimamura Atsuki. "Daitoshi ni okeru kenryoku to minshū no dōkō." In *Taishōki no kenryoku to minshū*, edited by Koyama Hitoshi. Tokyo: Hōritsu bunkasha, 1980.

Smethurst, Richard. *A Social Basis for Prewar Japanese Militarism*. Berkeley: University of California Press, 1974.

Smith, Robert J. *Ancestor Worship in Contemporary Japan*. Stanford: Stanford University Press, 1974.

Sōba Nakashi. "Kegarekan no dentō to bukkyō." *IBK* 10, No. 2 (1962): 142–47.

Sōrifu. *Fujin ni kansuru shomondai chōsa kaigi*. Tokyo: Prime Minister's Office, 1968.

———. *Fujin no genjō to shisaku*. Tokyo: Prime Minister's Office, 1967, 1968.

Sōrifu rōjin taisaku shitsu. *Rōgo seikatsu e no tenbō ni kansuru chōsa*. Tokyo: Prime Minister's Office, 1977.

Sōrifu seishōnen taisakuhombu. *Sekai seinen ishiki chōsa*. Tokyo: Prime Minister's Office, 1977.

Suzuki Masayuki. "Nichiro sensō no nōson mondai no tenkai." *Rekishi gaku kenkyū* 1974 special issue: 150–61.

Taeuber, Irene. "Family, Migration, and Industrialization in Japan." *American Sociological Review* 16 (1951): 149–57.

Takagi Hirō. *Nihon no shinkō shūkyō*. Tokyo: Iwanami shoten, 1959.

Takeda Chōshū. *Nihonjin no ie to shūkyō*. Tokyo: Hyōronsha, 1976.

———. *Sosen sūhai*. Kyoto: Heirakuji shoten, 1957.

Takenaga Chikao. "Gendai kazoku ni okeru rōrei jisatsu no ichikōsatsu." *Tōhoku fukushi daigaku ronsō* 8 (March, 1969): 133–52.

———. "Rōjin hōmu ni okeru oyako kankei no bunseki." *Tōhoku fukushi daigaku ronsō* 13 (March, 1974): 249–66.

Takiuchi Daizō. "Saikin no oyako shinjū tō shite mita nihonjin no kodomokan tsuite," *Kyōiku* 23, No. 6 (June, 1973): 26–37.

Tanabe Keiko. "Fukkatsu imi suru mono." *Sekai* 3 (1955): 21–69.

Tanaka Kōhō. *Tanaka Chigaku*. Tokyo: Shinsekaisha, 1977.

Tanaka Tadako. "Rōgo o kangaeru fujintachi no katsudō." *Gekkan shakai kyōiku* 16, No. 11 (November, 1972): 70–75.

Thomsen, Harry. *The New Religions of Japan*. Tokyo: Charles E. Tuttle Co. Publishers, 1963.

Togawa Isamu. *Gendai no shinkō shūkyō*. Tokyo: Taiyō, 1976.

Tokoro Shigemoto. *Kindai shakai to Nichirenshugi*. Nihonjin no kōdō to shisō, vol. 18. Tokyo: Hyōronsha, 1972.

————. *Nichiren no shisō to Kamakura bukkyō*. Tokyo: Fuzanbō, 1965.

Tokyoshi Arakawa-ku yakusho. *Arakawa-ku shi.* 2 vols. Tokyo: Kawaguchi insatsujo, 1936.

Tomomatsu Entai. "Zaike bukkyō no katsudō." In *Kōza kindai bukkyō*, edited by Hōzōkan henshūbu, 2: 217–19. 6 vols. Kyoto: Hōzōkan, 1961–1963.

"Toshi to rōjin." *Toshi mondai kenkyū* 17, No. 6 (June, 1965): 3–98.

Uemura Shinkei. "Ha-gōshō no shisō to hokekyōgaku." *IBK* 11, No. 1 (1963): 20–26.

Usui Jishō. "Rōjin no shūkyō." In *Rōjin no seishin igaku to shinrigaku*. vol. 4 of *Kōza nihon no rōjin*, edited by Kaneko Jirō et al. 4 vols. Tokyo: Kakiuchi shuppansha, 1972.

Vogel, Susanne. "Sengyō shufu." In *Kokusai josei gakkai hōkokusho*. Tokyo: published privately, 1978.

Wagatsuma Hiroshi. "Kenpō dai nijūyon an wa kaisei subeki ka?" In *Nihon fujin mondai shiryōshūsei*, edited by Ichikawa Fusae, 5: 579–92, 10 vols. Tokyo: Domesu shuppan, 1978–1980.

————. "Some Aspects of the Contemporary Japanese Family: Once Confucian, Now Fatherless." *Daedalus* 106, No. 2 (Spring, 1977): 181–210.

Watanabe Hōyō. "Tanaka Chigaku no shūkyō undō ni tsuite." In *Kindai nihon no hokke bukkyō*, edited by Mochizuki Kankō. Kyoto: Heirakuji shoten, 1968.

Watanabe Umeo. *Gendai nihon no shūkyō*. Tokyo: Daitō shuppansha, 1950.

Wilkinson, Thomas O. "Family Structure and Industrialization in Japan." *American Sociological Review* 27 (1962): 678–82.

Yamamuro Kōhei. "Kaku kazokuron hihan ni taisuru gimon ni kotaete." *Shakaigaku hyōron* 16, No. 3 (1966): 121–29.

————. "Oyako kankei." In *Gendai kazoku no kenkyū*, ed. Koyama Takashi. Tokyo: Yoshikawa Kōbundō, 1960.

Yamate Shigeru. "Mai hōmu shugi." *Gendai no kazoku* (special issue of *Jurist*), Spring, 1977, pp. 136–42.

Yanagida Kunio. *About Our Ancestors*. Translated by Fanny H. Mayer and Ishiwara Yasuyo. Kyoto: UNESCO, 1970.

Yasuda Saburō. *Gendai nihon no kaikyū ishiki*. Tokyo: Yūhikaku, 1973.

Yasumaru Yoshio. *Deguchi Nao*. Tokyo: Asahi shimbunsha, 1977.

————. *Nihon nashionarizumu no zen'ya*. Vol. 94; Asahi sensho (Tokyo: Asahi shimbunsha, 1977).

————. *Nihon no kindaika to minshū shisō.* Tokyo: Aoki shoten, 1974.

————. "Tennōsei no minshū to shūkyō." In *Nihon nashionarizumu no zen'ya.* Asahi sensho, No. 94, pp. 39–81. Tokyo: Asahi shimbunsha, 1977.

Yuzawa Yasuhiko. "Kazoku mondai no sengoshi." In *Gendai no kazoku* (special issue of *Jurist*), Spring, 1977, pp. 41–49.

Index

Library of Congress Cataloging in Publication Data
Hardacre, Helen, 1949–
   Lay Buddhism in contemporary Japan.
   Bibliography: p.
   Includes index.
   1. Reiyūkai.   I. Title.
BQ8372.H37 1984   294.3´9   83-43075
ISBN O-691-07284-1 (alk. paper)

Helen Hardacre is Assistant Professor of Religion at Princeton University.
She is author of a related book, *Kurozumikyo and the New Religions of
Japan* (Princeton, forthcoming).